THE LUCKIEST GUY

IN

a memoir by

James A. Lockhart

This book is dedicated to:

My mother, Ruby V. Lockhart
Without whom none of this would be possible

And

My wife, Suzanne M. Lockhart
For her unfailing encouragement and support

THE LUCKIEST GUY IN VIETNAM

ISBN (Print Edition): 978-1-54392-812-9
ISBN (eBook Edition): 978-1-54392-813-6

TABLE OF CONTENTS

PART FOUR: INTERBELLUM

PART FIVE: VIETNAM ACT 2

PART SIX: POSTBELUM

FIGURES

INTRODUCTION

★ ★ ★

I have been lucky. I have been very, very lucky. During my two-and-one-half years in Vietnam I never earned the Purple Heart Medal. I never got a scratch—at least not one delivered by the enemy. I don't have nightmares or flashbacks, although sometimes I thoughtfully review my actions from that period. I have been very lucky.

As well as I am aware of my luck, I also know of the indescribable suffering and losses incurred from that war by many of the participants, as well as the pain that some still endure. The families and loved ones of those killed, wounded and scarred in other ways do not have their suffering carved on a black granite wall: it is indelibly marked on their souls. I don't rejoice at my own good fortune without experiencing an enduring consciousness and sadness for all casualties, direct and indirect.

I am sharing my wartime experiences and observations because, despite the intense media coverage of the war and the massive subsequent analyses, misconceptions still abound in the public mind. Often certain images and second-hand accounts form a person's understanding and opinions about what happened there.

Sometimes generalizations are taken as specifics and specifics are generalized.

In this account, I will present a different view of Infantrymen in combat than what many readers may have taken for granted. This view is from my perspective as an Infantry leader during a 12-month period in Vietnam. I believe that readers will be surprised at what they did not know about soldiers living under pressure in the field, day after day.

I am equally convinced that the story of a Special Forces unit wrestling to accomplish a secret mission will be new to most readers. For those who have read about this unit, they will find an account of the early stages that has not been previously published as well as anecdotes unknown to previous writers.

I don't intend to state how luck specifically impacted every episode in this book. Each reader can make judgments about particular events and the extent that luck—good or bad—influenced them.

In addition, I will not try to propose a definition of luck; however, I am presenting here a few examples of good luck:

> When your enemy is careless or decides to stay home that day.
>
> When your commander doesn't give stupid, certain death orders.
>
> When your commander allows you freedom to make your own decisions in the field.
>
> When the men under your command are competent, reliable and motivated.

When your support (artillery and helicopters) are available and proficient.

When you make a minor mistake, you get a pass.

I have organized this book into a chronological sequence with a before, during and after Vietnam time line. The "during" portion is divided into first tour, interval and second tour. In keeping with a focus on my experiences in Vietnam, I am not including my full personal history except for the one-and-one-half year period that describes my only prior leadership experience before Vietnam, including the events that pulled me into the war. A section on post-Vietnam is included to show the war's lingering but significant impact on me and others.

This is not intended to be a military book only for military-oriented people. With that in mind, I intend to take care not to drift off into the cryptic realm of abbreviations, acronyms, jargon and obscure military terminology. Therefore, I hope the reader will bear with me as I try to maintain a balance between an interesting pace and explaining important but not-well-known terms. With some of the more difficult-to-remember and recurring terms, I will reiterate their meaning in the quest for clarity.

When referring to ranks, I'll spell the title completely in its first appearance (Lieutenant Colonel) and subsequently use the abbreviation (LTC). The same will be done for the names and numbers of military units of which only a few will appear.

Some of the other challenges in this area are the various units of measure used in military weapons. For example, the calibers of some weapons are specified in inches (4.2 inch mortar) and some in millimeters (81 millimeter mortar). When there is a potential area of confusion, I'll present the Army standard measurement first and follow with the more familiar one if necessary.

Another possible area of confusion is the measures of distance in which the military uses meters and kilometers. At relatively short distances, a meter (39.37 inches) is very close to a yard (36 inches). One hundred meters is just over nine yards longer than 100 yards—the playing length of a football field—so this distance is fairly easy to visualize. However, one kilometer (1,000 meters) is five-eights of a mile, a much more abstract concept to most Americans. So while I'll use meters and kilometers to conform with military usage, anything over 100 meters will be followed by the English equivalent measure in parentheses.

Keeping it simple, all times will be in the am/pm format; e.g. 7pm instead of 1900 hours.

Vietnamese words and place names will be represented without the normal diacritical marks followed by their phonetic pronunciation unless the pronunciation is self evident. In the field we never used the Vietnamese names of localities except as a general reference because of the difficulty in pronunciation and the similarities of many names. Therefore I will use only a few here. We always used map grid coordinates instead of place names and this technique will be described later.

Without a doubt, my greatest regret is not having maintained a diary during my time in Vietnam. Because of this, the names of many comrades whom I have described in this account are lost to me. At that time, everything we owned was carried with us in the field. I felt that any accurate diary which listed our successes, if I had been captured, would have worked to my disadvantage. So most of the men who were so important during this period in my life can't be included by name.

I am including brief accounts of genuine heroes with whom I have crossed paths and their impact on my life.

I will explain later how I was able to reconstruct some events during that period from official documents. Most, however, are retrieved from indelible memories.

After each major section covering one tour, a chapter titled "Reflections" will be presented. These comments will address background issues that didn't arise naturally during the narrative. I will also use them to discuss some topics in more detail than was appropriate earlier.

All photos and maps follow the end of the text as figures.

Looking back, I feel that, except for the first few months of each tour, I was able to perform my duties "my way." This means that I was given an amazing amount of freedom by my commanders and that freedom was the greatest luck of all. By presenting my handling of that independence, some readers may see boastfulness or arrogance in this account. However, I have done my very best to record events accurately. It will be clear that my failures have been reported with the same veracity as successes.

And so, in a final statement of my good fortune, I have had the privilege of reliving two of the most eventful, important and satisfying periods of my life in the preparation of this memoir. Using play backs—not flashbacks--I have been able to remember and record events that can never occur again. I am sharing most of them with pride and some with guilt. I hope that all readers can experience this renewal of the best achievements of their lives at some time.

PART ONE

ANTEBELLUM

CHAPTER 1

Japan

★ ★ ★

In May 1966, I was a U.S. Army sergeant stationed at Camp Drake, in Saitama Prefecture, Japan, on the western outskirts of Tokyo. Life was good. One dollar would buy 400 yen; by contrast, fifty years later a dollar yielded only 110 yen. A large bottle of Kirin beer on the economy cost 100 yen or 25 cents. This was important to a soldier earning $300 a month.

I lived in a two-storey duplex on Fuji View Avenue in military housing on a former Imperial Japanese Air Force base. Two months after my arrival the clouds cleared and there, framed at the end of the street, was a breathtaking view of Mount Fuji.

The overseas military club system was flourishing with low prices for food, drinks and the live B- or C-level floor shows which we thought were first-class.

It seemed to me then that this pleasant lifestyle would continue into some vague and undefined point in the future.

In the Army, a sergeant is known as a Non-commissioned Officer or NCO. However, no one in the Army ever thought of a sergeant as an officer without a commission. The first four ranks of enlisted people were: Recruit, Private, Private First Class and Specialist Fourth Class. I'm sure that some thoughtful system produced these names. The fifth level of enlisted rank was "Sergeant"... period. The levels above "Sergeant" were Staff Sergeant, Sergeant First Class, Master Sergeant (or First Sergeant, depending on position), and Sergeant Major, which was at the ninth level of rank. All persons at each NCO level could be addressed as "Sergeant" except those in the rank of First Sergeant and Sergeant Major. If anyone ever addressed a Sergeant Major as anything but "Sergeant Major," they would immediately understand their error. A Sergeant Major was sometimes affectionately referred to as "S'madge," but never to his or her face.

To the military purist, there was an NCO rank called "Corporal," which was one level below "Sergeant." In 20 years of military service I have never met or seen a corporal.

Like all enlisted people, and officers as well, I was a member of an Army branch which managed the careers of soldiers according to their jobs in related specialties. I was in the Signal Corps branch and my military occupational specialty was Communications Center Specialist. In the communications center, or comcenter, where I worked in Japan, we received and printed messages from the military network and made them available for the U.S. units in the Tokyo area. We also took their outgoing messages, converted them into teletype format and sent them into the same worldwide network.

As a sergeant, I was assigned as a shift supervisor, usually called a trick chief, in the comcenter with two men under me. It was a 24-hour operation. In order to provide a fairly normal schedule for the comcenter soldiers, three regular shifts were scheduled: days (8am-4pm), eves (4pm-12am) and mids (12am-8am) for five nonconsecutive days each week. A fourth or swing shift covered the irregular gaps that occurred every week.

Serving as a trick chief in the comcenter would be my only practical, day-to-day leadership experience before eventually arriving in Vietnam.

This was post-post-World War II--more than 20 years after the surrender--and Japan was still in a constant state of building: cement trucks were on the roads around the clock. There was still no sign of the prosperity that would emerge in later years. The Japanese seemed to be hardworking and friendly and many were curious about Americans despite the long period of occupation.

Most of the enlisted soldiers working in the comcenter were ardent, frequent and welcome customers of the corner bar near the camp, which was named the Corner Bar for obvious reasons. Sometimes I would accompany them and was treated especially well as the boss of the bar's best patrons.

The Vietnam war was not a major issue in my professional military life then. I knew that if I were to be transferred to Vietnam, as a comcenter specialist I would live in a well-guarded area and work in an air-conditioned building. This was due to the classified nature of the messages we handled and the need to prevent our teletype and cryptographic equipment from overheating. In many ways I envisioned a potential tour in Vietnam as being much like Japan.

Although I had been in the Army for over four years and a sergeant for two, this was my first assignment in which I supervised other soldiers. So I was learning how to lead in a low-pressure, slow-moving environment. It was in this setting that I learned indirectly about the realities of Vietnam.

The comcenter was in a building that included some units to which we provided service. One unit we supported was on the other side of the post: the 249th General Hospital, which treated many of the serious casualties evacuated from Vietnam. We would receive message after message of six pages in length, the maximum possible in the system, listing the wounded soldiers who were being sent to the 249th. These messages included name, rank, unit, service number and nature of wound. The most commonly listed wound was "GSW" or Gun Shot Wound. Nevertheless, Vietnam and its toll still seemed disconnected from us in the comcenter despite the explicit daily reminders that we handled.

The comcenter had one locked entry door and a delivery window beside it, which was shrouded by curtains inside to maintain security of the interior. A buzzer would summon us to unlock the door for fellow comcenter workers or to deliver messages to our customers through the window. Inside were copies of current and filed classified messages, cryptographic devices and sometimes top secret transmissions. A .45 caliber pistol was on hand in case USSR agents would attempt a daring penetration. In charge of the center was a long-time civilian employee with an Army staff sergeant as his deputy. Another civilian, a washed-up alcoholic, performed some services that we didn't understand.

Since our building had other units also operating on a 24-hour basis and Japanese labor was cheap, the snack bar down the hall was always open. Often on an evening or midnight shift, only two of us would be on duty. If one was typing a long message onto paper teletype tape for transmission, the other would go to the snack bar for coffee and return with his hands full carrying a tray.

Despite the seemingly impenetrable physical security features of the comcenter, a soldier, returning from the snack bar laden with a tray of coffee and unwilling to disturb his occupied coworker, could open the door from the outside with a well-placed kick. Naturally, this security flaw was outrageous and therefore kept in strict secrecy from the management by us shift workers.

Unexpectedly but inevitably, on one weekend the alcoholic civilian came in to do some work that had not been completed on time. Then to his amazement the door of the inviolate fortress banged open to reveal a soldier returning from a coffee run. The shocked civilian fled in confusion and the lock was quickly changed by the stunned and incredulous civilian manager.

This security upgrade lead to another situation that taxed my still underdeveloped leadership skills. On a major holiday in 1966, I was assigned to the midnight shift with only one other soldier, Jon, because it would be a slow night. Jon was a very devoted customer of the Corner Bar and that night he had clearly exceeded his limit. He was smashed. I had several options at that time, most of which would be harsh for Jon, but I decided to keep the incident to myself and assign him an unofficial punishment.

In the meantime, I went to the snack bar to get us both much-needed coffee. Since the door lock had been fixed, I had to ring the buzzer when I returned. No response. I rang again. Nothing. I knocked on the door and yelled for Jon. I couldn't be too loud and attract attention from other around-the-clock offices on our floor. I would look really stupid standing in the hall, locked out of my own comcenter.

So I went to the delivery window which was barred and had a sliding wooden shade for security in addition to the interior curtain.

I was able to wedge a spoon under the shade and raise it—another security issue that would have to be addressed. I could see into the comcenter because the security curtain had been pulled aside—yet another issue.

Lying on a table, 20 feet away, was Jon, dead to the world and snoring away. Mindful of too much noise, again I called to him but with no success. It would be about 30 minutes before one of our regular customers would arrive for a scheduled pickup of messages, but sometimes the officer-courier would appear earlier or later. If discovered, this situation would be very bad for Jon and not pleasant for me.

Desperate, I cast about for a solution before the courier arrived. Even worse would have been for a high precedence teletype message to arrive and not be processed.

I thought of throwing something at Jon but the bars were too narrow. Finally, I saw a hand-pump water fire extinguisher mounted in the hallway. I brought it over to the small shelf of the delivery window, aimed the nozzle through the bars and pumped. The water streamed out about 10 feet and died away. Another more vigorous pumping action shot the water more than 15 feet, three-quarters of the way there but still not enough. With desperation and waning strength, I finally caught Jon in the face with an extended burst of very nasty, stagnant water. Sputtering and disoriented he awoke and opened the door.

There were no high precedence messages, the courier had not arrived and no one else in the building was the wiser. Jon mopped up the water but he was so useless that I let him sleep it off for the rest of the night. Later that week, on his day off, I had him come in early and spend the day rearranging a hot, dusty supply closet while

I supervised. He had obviously had another night on the town and was feeling miserable but his record was still clean. I felt no sympathy because it was my day off, too.

Another event was instructive but even less enjoyable. During the evening, weekend and midnight shifts there was little message traffic in or out. Somehow the Great Whist Craze emerged to pass the endless hours before our shifts ended. The card game was so compelling that frequently off-duty comcenter shift workers would join us. We would move several of the message processing tables together and group chairs around them to play that addictive card game and replace everything near the end of the shift.

During these lulls in traffic, our only connected station would send us short messages called channel checks to be sure that our circuits were still working. These came in as hard copy on a teletype printer and in punched tape form. Whist or no, we would immediately take the punched tape and send it back on the same channel for confirmation. The channel checks were given a handling precedence of Operational Immediate or just below the top precedence of Flash. Other messages came in with Operational Immediate precedence for transmission purposes only but our local addressees had a lower effective delivery precedence of Routine, which didn't require a notification or instant processing. Further, we knew when our local customers were going to pick up their Routine precedence messages so we didn't need to process them as they came in…because we were busy playing Whist.

So there we were on one quiet Saturday afternoon when the buzzer rang and our civilian boss was at the door awaiting admittance. We scooped up the cards but couldn't delay opening the door in order to rearranging the telltale tables and chairs.

The boss went over to the teletype machines and looked at the precedence of the six seemingly unprocessed messages: four channel checks and two messages for a customer who wouldn't pick them up for another four hours. Although the precedence for all of them were Operational Immediate, the channel checks had been returned immediately using punched tape and the two messages were really Routine for delivery purposes to our customer. However, the boss only scanned the hard copies of the six Operational Immediate transmissions which appeared to have gone unprocessed while we played cards. He wasn't familiar with the realities of message handling. Nevertheless, he sent a letter describing this transgression to my military superiors at Camp Zama, the Signal Corps headquarters in Japan.

This experience transformed what to me had been an abstract Army dictum into a painful reality: the person in charge—officer or NCO—takes the credit or blame for any action based on its outcome. I had learned this in principle several years before at an NCO academy but now the lesson had a palpable sting as a black mark on my record.

Over time the letter, an administrative procedure, was removed from my file, but there was no more playing Whist in the comcenter.

With the removal of the letter, I became competitive for promotion to Staff Sergeant, a much more difficult hurtle to overcome than attaining my then current rank of Sergeant. Promotions only occurred when vacancies opened and unit allocations arose and these were not frequent. A periodic promotion board was held to establish a list of Sergeants who could be promoted, in order by scores. The promotion board members, all equal or senior in rank to Staff Sergeant and including at least one officer, would evaluate each candidate's personnel file and assign credit for achievements. Then the candidates would appear before the board in person for an oral grilling which featured questions about the chain of command, general orders, technical job problems and obscure military trivia.

I was always good at testing so I knew I had done well in my first appearance before a promotion board. In addition, I was receiving proficiency pay, amounting to $30 each month, which supplemented my $303 in regular pay and allowances. After that first promotion board in May 1966, the results were published and I saw that I was in fourth position. However, I was amazed to see that the top spot on the list had been given to a woman. WHAT!?

She had about the same time in rank as me and she worked at the headquarters location in Camp Zama (where all of the board members were also assigned). Women were being given wider roles in the armed services at that time, especially in job specialties like those in the Signal Corps. This would make filling the ranks of the combat arms such as Infantry and artillery with male draftees easier. But all of that aside, I honestly believed that I was the most qualified for promotion.

Every day on the comcenter bulletin board that damning promotion list proclaimed that I had been beaten out for promotion by a girl. The troops were not openly mocking toward me but my contemporaries, the other trick chiefs, were not so restrained. Beaten out by a girl.

The promotion allocations trickled in and as I came to the top of the list, another board was convened in August, so I would be starting from scratch again. But I now had a good feeling for how the board worked and I had prepared even more diligently for this one.

Also, only one other sergeant who had appeared before the previous board would compete in this one. I was very confident.

When the new list was published I was even more disappointed and humiliated. At the top of the list was—another woman. Even worse, I was in the ninth position. At the rate promotion allocations were coming in, I would never get to the top of the new list and would have to face yet another board.

Writing this today, fifty years later, all this seems petty and chauvinistic but then it was a painful personal reality. At that time, after nearly five years of Army service, I had never worked with a woman, directly or indirectly. The Army was still a very male-oriented organization and no one I knew was anxious to change that, despite overall policy to the contrary.

This episode made me reevaluate my present and future situation in the Army. I felt that if I had been unfairly treated by the promotion board twice, why not next time? I certainly wasn't going to remain a sergeant, hoping for a break someday. That left two choices: leave the Army or find another career path within it.

I knew I liked the Army. After all, it had sent me to a pleasant and rewarding assignment in Korea and now I was in Japan during an exciting time. The Army had also shipped over my 1965 Mustang, a rarity even in nearby Tokyo, which enhanced my macho status considerably. I also knew that the military retirement benefits were worthwhile, although at age 25 they were not primary motivating factors.

And so, if I decided to stay in the Army, what career path would I pursue? The Signal Corps would not easily give up an NCO like me in whom it had invested so much training and who had my job experience to another Army NCO specialty. However, it was obvious from the casualty reports on the teletype that vacancies were occurring daily in Vietnam. If I volunteered for Officers Candidate School (OCS), my unit could not block my application or selection. I could try for a commission in the Signal Corps, which would be natural with my background and which, in any case, was not the Infantry.

So I submitted my application for OCS with three choices of branches: Signal Corps, Adjutant General Corps and Military Intelligence. These seemed to be the career areas to which I would most likely be assigned with my existing qualifications. I appeared before an OCS selection board in late 1966 and very quickly received orders to report to Infantry OCS. Never fearing, I understood that some Infantry OCS graduates could opt for commissions in other branches. This was the thought process that eventually resulted in me becoming an Infantryman.

The unavoidable question was: Did my unit think I would make a good Infantry lieutenant but not an acceptable Signal Corps staff sergeant?

Thus, the first chapter of my leadership preparation, however meager, had ended and I was on the indirect but inexorable road to Vietnam.

I left Japan in January 1967, to start a new phase in my Army career, thanks in large part to the two women I'd never met and who had bested me at those promotion boards.

CHAPTER 2

Officers Candidate School

★ ★ ★

I reported to Officers Candidate School at The Infantry School at Fort Benning, Georgia, on January 15, 1967. OCS was the source of the officers known as 90-day wonders in World War II, except it was now 180 days. Its mission was to produce officers who were proficient in small unit tactics and leadership. An unstated component of the curriculum was to ensure that graduates could perform their duties under stress or, as we knew it, harassment. Since most of the newly minted officers from Infantry OCS would soon be in Vietnam leading rifle platoons, the harassment seemed to be appropriate. Attrition was expected to be high.

Infantry OCS was a crowded and busy place. At the height of the Vietnam War approximately 7,000 Infantry lieutenants were produced each year from that program alone.

The overall curriculum was a balance between Counterinsurgency Operations (Vietnam) and Conventional Warfare (Europe). So we were instructed in moving across German plains in mechanized personnel carriers to defeat Soviet aggressors as well as moving in jungles and rice paddies amid an unfriendly Asian population.

Candidates, as we students were known, came mostly from two groups. There were "prior service"-- sergeants like me--who had two years of college and had been vetted by a selection board as potentially successful officers. The other group consisted of college graduates who had been drafted and then volunteered for the program, wisely avoiding becoming privates in an Infantry company. These were called "college ops."

Upon our arrival, we were informed that we were now under the "New Program." One thing this meant was there absolutely would be no more spit shining of floors, wherein the candidates on hands and knees polished every inch of the barracks floors with wax and soft cloths. In fact we were ordered to use buffers with stiff brushes to scratch the mirrored floors that our predecessors had painstakingly made pristine.

This did not mean that the floors would not be immaculate and shiny: just no more spit shining.

The program was divided into two parts. During the longer, initial phase, every possible measure was taken to heap pressure on each candidate. We double-timed everywhere. We were constantly inspected and found inadequate. Everything we did was wrong. Poorly shined brass and boots were deemed "grody." The second phase began when we "turned blue." This meant that we were seniors and the helmet liners that we wore everywhere were painted pale Infantry blue over the previous black. Things changed as we marched instead of double-timed but occasionally a surprise devastation of our lockers by the cadre reminded us that we were still in OCS.

The support cadre was typical of any Infantry company: supply, administration, cooks, etc. Our immediate concern was the Tactical Officers who were comparable to the Drill Sergeants in Army basic training. They were all recent OCS graduates who seemed anxious to take revenge on us for the misery they had endured during their tenure as candidates.

Another group of officers comprised the Training Committee. Again this was like the basic training model which separated the day-to-day administration, maintenance and harassment by the Tactical Officers from the presentation of the curriculum. Training Committee officers were assigned to The Infantry School and presented classes to all students in Infantry OCS. These officers were very highly qualified, extensively rehearsed and mostly combat veterans.

My orders stated that I had to arrive at my assigned company before 8:30pm. As an NCO with over five years of service, I tried to puzzle out the advantages of an early-versus-late arrival but I was out of my depth and had no one to advise me. I chose to report earlier rather than later.

This choice made me one of the first prior service candidates to arrive. Naturally the tactical officers pounced on me. Why was I wearing those sergeant's stripes if I was an OCS candidate? I corrected that flaw and was quickly presented with several more deficiencies.

I was then notified that I was the Student Company Commander, but there was no further information, guidance or instructions as to what that meant.

The barracks was a three storey, modern brick building. The first floor consisted of administration, supply, command, arms room, etc. The second and third floors had one open 50-man platoon bay, basic training style, at each end with latrines and cadre offices in the center. The cadre assigned newly arriving candidates to one of the four platoons and we trudged up to our assigned spaces with our gear.

Since I had been appointed as student company commander and had no other instructions, I began to assert my authority. During the day as more candidates were arriving, I assigned a runner from each platoon to carry the few edicts I received from the cadre back to their comrades. As the platoons became larger I appointed platoon leaders to take charge of the ever-growing requirements of each group and gave them the authority to appoint subordinate squad leaders. But then I was brought up short. Not so fast; appointing platoon leaders and squad leaders is our prerogative, said the Tactical Officers. Sir, yes, sir.

When all 220 of the assigned candidates had arrived, we were called out to the adjacent parade field for our first attempt at assembling as a unified group.

The full complement of candidates in company formation was an impressive sight. There were the four platoons with 13 men in each of the four ranks. Each platoon was a specific distance from the others in a line. Standing several steps in front of each platoon was the platoon leader.

I was standing alone several steps in front of the platoon leaders facing the formation while the Tactical Officers were yelling at everyone.

Although I got my share of abuse, I wasn't worried because we were about to perform drill and ceremonies, which was simply the organized movement of a group of men in formation from one place to another. I had taught classes on this in Korea and studied the field manual (FM 22-5) to prepare for the promotion boards in Japan.

I was directed to move the company to the other side of the huge parade field, which measured 200 yards by one-half mile. No problem. I began to give my best parade ground command for the company to turn to the right: "Right!" and waited for the platoon leaders to echo: "Right!" But nothing happened; the platoon leaders were not as in tune with drill and ceremonies as me.

Everyone again got reamed by the Tactical Officers. Then we tried again: "Right!" echoed by "Right!" and then I continued with "Face!" and the mass of men turned to the right.

Now instead of four ranks of men we had four files or a column; but four files are ungainly when controlling a marching group so they must be reduced to a column of two files. At this point I knew that the platoon leaders were in serious trouble because they wouldn't be able to follow the next commands, but I had to press on.

"Column of twos from the left!" This should have elicited an echo from the lead platoon leader and a "Stand fast!" from the others. The left two squad leaders of the lead platoon should have turned their heads to command their squad, "Forward!" The right two squad leaders should have commanded, "Stand fast!" When I continued with the sequence by commanding "March!" it was bedlam.

The Tactical Officers stopped the mass confusion, regrouped everyone, allowed a quick lesson on the procedure and we tried again with fits and starts until we finally got moving.

I was trying to follow directions from multiple Tactical Officers while willing the platoon leaders to somehow, miraculously become instant masters of the esoteric intricacies of Army drills and ceremonies. Suddenly a Tactical Officer came up to me and said, "Bang. You're wounded and can't carry on. What are you going to do?" I issued one final command to the company ("Continue the March!")

which I sadly knew that no one understood and then called to the student XO (executive officer, second in command) to take over.

Although this was without question the correct response, it was met with the usual drollery and contempt by the Tactical Officers and the company floundered about the parade field in disarray.

After several days of this, the cadre decided to replace me with a candidate who was a warrant officer and an older man. I felt that as a sergeant who had previously supervised no more than two soldiers, I had performed magnificently. However, the warrant officer proved to be calmer, cooler and inspired more confidence than I did.

One benefit of this experience was that I became well-known to all of the candidates in the company, not just in my own platoon. Also, during this chaotic initial period I had been a lightening rod and deflected some of the Tactical Officers' attention away from many of them.

The non-curricular plan for OCS was to rotate the leadership positions in the company so that each candidate could gain experience and be evaluated. These positions were company commander, platoon leader, platoon sergeant, and squad leader as well as staff positions such as supply officer and mess officer, who had no real authority. I had been company commander and not failed miserably as far as I knew and that would give me a big check mark.

I also now applied an important life lesson that I had learned at Fort Detrick, Maryland, prior to moving to Japan. This was the principle that if someone—anyone--could do what I thought was a high-pressure job, so could I. I took a critical look at the recently commissioned Tactical Officers and thought: "If these guys made it through OCS, so can I." I looked at my fellow candidates and thought: "If any of these guys can graduate, so will I."

After my removal as student company commander, I was assigned as mess officer, with undefined duties related to the mess hall. The mess hall was a large room with enough tables for about one-third of the candidates. The Tactical Officers sat at a long table facing the room with their backs to a partition behind which were the kitchen and serving line. They could observe the candidates at all times except when they were moving through the serving line behind the partition. As part of the "New Program" the square meal had been discontinued. This was the process of eating by bringing the fork vertically from the mess tray to the level of the mouth, moving it horizontally to the mouth and reversing the procedure back to the tray.

Still remaining, however, was the prohibition against "eyeballing," which was a dastardly infraction. Upon entering the mess hall, each candidate would stand at parade rest, wait until the person in front moved a prescribed distance, then come to attention, march several steps forward, stop and resume parade rest. Anyone not keeping their eyes directly to the front was guilty of eyeballing and the penalties were ruthlessly meted out.

For me, however, as the student mess officer, things were different. The other candidates could come in, endure fairly lackluster harassment and leave while others took their places. But the mess officer was there for the duration of the meal and was the favorite target of the Tactical Officers if they could not find any other suitable victims. For them there was something chronically wrong with the meal or the service, both of which I had no control over and for which I was inevitably called to account in front of their table.

One of the Tactical Officers' favorite punishments for these transgressions was for me to run several laps around the mess hall.

But since the mess hall was actually an integral part of the much larger barracks building, they all got a jolly laugh at my expense. I quickly learned that if I didn't get to the mess hall early and eat before the scheduled mess period, there would be no chance of a meal for me.

Since the leadership and staff positions were normally rotated among the candidates every week or 10 days, I was surprised to remain as student mess officer for several months. I had some thoughts as to why, but no facts. Perhaps the Tactical Officers got a certain pleasure out of focusing their wrath on me personally during the three meals each day and my reactions fostered a sense of perverse satisfaction for them. Or, I hoped, they felt that I had done an acceptable job as the first student company commander, performing satisfactorily despite my rank, and in their minds, were letting me slide in a position that would let other less-experienced candidates function in the more meaningful leadership positions. In other words, I thought I was safe for graduation. But who could say?

One final situation arose from the mess officer assignment. When the Tactical Officers would summon me to the front of their table to be rebuked, they would call my name as if it were a parade-ground command, in the manner of atten-SHUN or parade-REST. So I would be cowering in the kitchen trying to finish my meal when one of them would thunder "lock-HART!" Soon the "HART," which in a normal command would sound like a whip crack, was dragged out so it became a very unique "lock-HAAART!" It was not an easy experience to forget.

The interesting result of all this was similar to what happened during my short period as student company commander when I had inadvertently shunted some of the Tactical Officers' attention onto myself to the benefit of my comrades. Thus, in the mess hall their preoccupation with me gave some respite to the inveterate eyeballers.

And so during those initial months at Fort Benning, after lights out and the Tactical Officers had gone home, a call would arise from one of the four platoon bays in a sing-song and be answered and echoed back and forth: "lock-HAAART!" At one point when the company was to select its motto, this call was nominated. I can still hear those calls echoing through the barracks.

I did not know then that my personal Military Occupational Specialty had been changed from Communications Center Specialist to Infantryman at some point during the OCS program. This meant that if I had quit or was washed out of OCS, I would be assigned as an Infantryman to a place that needed Infantrymen instead of returning to the nice, safe Signal Corps.

After a certain point in the program, attrition had thinned the ranks of candidates. Some didn't think the constant psychological and physical pressure was worth the price to obtain a commission. Others didn't want the responsibilities of an officer. And still others had less clear reasons. As one candidate who decided to resign said, "It's just not my cup of tea."

However, at some point equilibrium had to be reached where the tough training standards for commissioning officers met the always steady demand for new lieutenants. This meant that near the end of the program, the harassment was minimized but kept somewhat alive for appearances. In a turnabout, as graduation neared, candidates who were opting to quit were discouraged. The demand was so great for Infantry officers that in the week before we graduated, we were evicted from the barracks in favor of a new class arriving early. We moved into local motels and no one complained.

I left OCS with a sound understanding of the Infantry craft. To be honest, I didn't focus on such conventional concepts such as the number of trucks required to move a given quantity of rations in a specified period of time over a secondary European highway: I knew I could quickly find that information in an Army field manual. If I was ever assigned to Europe, everything there seemed to be done in a rote, by-the-book manner to which I could easily adapt.

Vietnam, however, seemed to require a more nuanced approach. Naturally, the lessons learned by the French and British fighting insurgencies in Asia along with the more recent U.S. combat experiences provided the basic doctrine for operations there. But, since our enemies had also read the same books, occasional departures from rigid and formulistic tactics could keep them off balance. This concept had a very strong appeal to me.

Looking back at the OCS policy of rotating candidates through leadership positions from company commander down through squad leader, I realize that, except for my company commander tenure, I had only one other short assignment and that was as a squad leader. Considering that minimum exposure along with my limited leadership time as an NCO, I graduated from OCS with very little experience as an actual leader.

Throughout my entire OCS experience, one individual stood out and has since grown immensely in my esteem. That was First Lieutenant Rick Rescorla, the cadre executive officer and chief tactical officer for about the first two-thirds of our program. First of all, he was a Brit, born in Cornwall. Numerous tales circulated about his past experiences in counter-insurgency operations with the British Army and Constabulary in Northern Rhodesia. In addition, he was a veteran of the U.S. 1st Air Cavalry Division in Vietnam.

One legend said that Rick had come to a rear area base in Vietnam for R&R after a tough six months in the field, straight out of the bush with all his combat gear on. An administrative officer told him that there was a problem with his R&R and there would be a delay. So, it was said, Rick, from a flat-footed stance, jumped straight up onto the man's desk with his muddy boots, brandished his machete and challenged that decision, which was quickly reversed.

He was tall, wide at the shoulder and narrow at the hip. He looked like an Infantry officer. It was difficult for me, at five feet eight inches in height, to feel equal to this man, especially as we candidates were constantly sleep-deprived and run ragged by the cadre.

Rick had a witty, biting humor that made all of us appreciate his charisma while being eager to keep on his good side. He was the first person I had ever heard, when expressing impatience, use the expression, "Let's get on with it, ladies...while we're still young."

On one early morning we were milling around on the parade field trying to get organized for our first run of the day. When Rick joined us, one candidate with a seeming death wish began to chant, "Mad dog! Mad dog! Bow wow wow!" The rest of us quickly moved away from him so as not to be mistaken for the culprit and the chant quickly fizzled. Other times Rick would lovingly taunt us by summarizing the challenges of OCS into a few words: "Six months! Six loooong months!"

Rick's legend was validated when he was prominently featured in Lieutenant General Hal Moore's account of the 1st Cavalry Division's epic 1965 Battle of the A Shau Valley, "We Were Soldiers Once... and Young." His photo appears on the cover of the book and he is briefly portrayed in Mel Gibson's movie "We were Soldiers."

Rick, before he was reassigned about midway through our course, called me into his office. This was after the mess officer experience and, although I thought I had paid my dues in spades and was probably safe for graduation, I was apprehensive about the meeting.

Using the required form of address, I loudly announced: "Sir, Candidate Lockhart reporting as ordered, sir."

He waved me to a seat and asked, "Who do you think are the five best leaders in your platoon?"

I was surprised by the question and presumed that I might have accrued some measure of credibility by enduring the Tactical Officers' abuse for so long.

I quickly mentioned four individuals who were respected in the platoon and would undoubtedly be popular and effective leaders of enlisted men.

"That's four. Who's the fifth?"

I took a big chance by feigning astonishment and then making a two-handed Gallic gesture toward myself that said unequivocally, "Moi!" It was after that encounter that I was never assigned to a leadership position or bothered with harassment by the cadre. I took that as a positive outcome of my interview.

Rick Rescorla left the Regular Army but remained in the reserves, eventually retiring as a colonel.

In retirement he became a security manager for Morgan Stanley in New York City, a position for which he was eminently qualified. He demanded that the Morgan Stanley employees in the World Trade Center South Tower comply with monthly evacuation drills despite the fact that they detracted from productivity and engendered resentment.

On September 11, 2001, the theory behind his drills became a reality after the first plane hit the North Tower. Implementing the evacuation plan immediately, he shepherded the nearly three thousand Morgan Stanley employees down 44 flights of stairs. As was his wont, he soothed their frayed nerves by singing Cornish songs from his youth as he had done for the soldiers fighting in the A Shau Valley in Vietnam.

His next action was, in my opinion, one-hundred-percent predictable. When everyone seemed safe, he went back up to the offices to check for stragglers. And that's when the South Tower collapsed.

I know of no criteria for the word "hero" that Rick Rescorla did not meet. His life is memorialized by the opera "The Heart of a Soldier" which premiered in San Francisco on September 10, 2011; a documentary called "The Man Who Predicted 9/11" on the History Channel (available on Youtube); a statue at Fort Benning—home of the Infantry; a memorial in his home town in England and other tributes. To get a fuller appreciation of this remarkable man, search online.

CHAPTER 3

Fort Knox and Fort Lewis

★ ★ ★

My class of Infantry OCS graduated on July 3, 1967. Most newly minted second lieutenants were not shipped directly to Vietnam. A decompression period was normally allowed for us to get used to our new rank and mentally prepare for our eventual assignments in southeast Asia. A few OCS graduates were assigned to Europe, which was under-strength due to the demands of the war. Many of my fellow Infantry School graduates and I were assigned first to short-term Army schools and then to an Infantry training center. There was no chance of returning to the Signal Corps.

Five or six of us reported to The Armor School at Fort Knox for the eight-week Organizational Maintenance Officer course. This was an important preparation for an officer involved in any motor pool or tank-related activities. We removed the engine from a 52-ton tank for an oil change, rode in the commander's hatch through the back acres of the fort and repaired the tracks of an armored personnel carrier. However, I never used any of this valuable knowledge in my later career.

On weekends, several of us enjoyed freefall parachuting with the skydiving club on Fort Knox.

My next assignment was to Fort Lewis, Washington, near Seattle, in an Advanced Infantry Training company where soldiers learned Infantry skills after basic training. There were five of us with new lieutenant's gold bars in the unit, in addition to the company commander, who was a captain, and the executive officer, a first lieutenant.

As with every military unit, there were extra duties for officers: I was assigned as Mess Officer, Utilities Officer, Area Fire Marshall, Unit Tax Advisor and Physical Security Officer. My colleagues were assigned such duties as Unit Maintenance Officer, Conservation Officer, Postal Officer, Voting Officer, Education Officer, Safety Officer and on and on until, even with a surplus of lieutenants, each of us had four or five extra duties.

Quickly a problem arose in my area of responsibility as Mess Officer. The company mess section was chronically late in delivering the noon meal to the troops at distant firing ranges, causing disruptions in the training schedule. This would be my first test in problem solving as an officer.

Despite my long tenure during OCS as Mess Officer, I had gained no knowledge about food service because I had had no real authority or control in its operations. Luckily, this present issue seemed to be one of scheduling and transportation instead of cooking.

I immediately met with the Mess Sergeant to discuss the situation. Using my finely honed leadership techniques, we discussed alternatives and agreed on a measurable goal to better accomplish the mission. Taking into account inclement weather (the norm at

Fort Lewis), mechanical failures and personnel issues, we reasoned that the truck carrying the noon meal must depart from the mess hall for the firing ranges earlier than previously scheduled. Therefore, my directive to the Mess Sergeant was: "Starting tomorrow, the chow will be on the road by 11am."

I decided to enlighten one of my colleagues who did not have the benefit of prior service by explaining the problem I had faced and the steps I had taken to solve it. To reinforce the lesson, I invited him to accompany me on the last step of the leadership process--supervision.

On the next day, we arrived within view of the mess hall at 10:45am. An Army stake-bed truck was being feverishly loaded by cooks and overseen by the Mess Sergeant who frequently consulted his watch. Everything seemed fine, although as the deadline approached the activity around the truck seemed more hectic.

Finally, a box-like metal container was loaded onto the rear of the truck. It contained 10 thick aluminum trays of cake which slid into racks; these were a familiar sight to any soldier who had been served a meal during training in the field. But the cooks, obviously in a panic, failed to place the rear gate on the truck bed behind the container of cake. The driver quickly backed the truck onto the company street and—just in time—floored the accelerator in triumph.

As the truck lunged forward, the door of the metal container swung open and the 10 trays of cake flew out onto the company street. The driver, unaware, sped out to the range to feed the hungry troops.

My colleague, clearly impressed with my leadership skills, shook my hand and said, "Well done, lieutenant. Mission accomplished. The chow is on the road by 11am."

Another event stands out in my mind that should be a cautionary tale for any young manager or executive.

The Army was, at that time and as it should have been, trying to preserve it cherished traditions. This was particularly true with regard to new, young officers like me who were not from West Point and who needed those traditions ingrained in them.

So per custom, each month the newly arrived officers in the battalion were invited to the commander's quarters for a formal reception. Most of us would never see him again unless we were in serious trouble but here was a chance for us to practice our social graces. Calling cards were appropriate but we were exempted since most of us were soon to be shipped to Vietnam.

The colonel was a dignified gentlemen and his wife was attractive and younger. The children were trotted in, introduced formally and sent off to bed.

One young lieutenant's wife had apparently heard that it would be valuable for her husband's career to make a lasting impression on the colonel and his lady. From her strong accent she was from the South.

Using a sure-fire strategy, she began to gush about how cute the kids were and mostly about how closely they resembled the colonel. Those of us who had done our homework knew that the kids were from the colonel's lady's previous marriage.

My leadership experiences at Fort Lewis were superficial and mainly consisted as acting as firing range safety officer. However, my preparation for leading American soldiers in combat was complete: next stop—Vietnam.

PART TWO

VIETNAM
ACT 1.0

CHAPTER 4

Adventures with Company B

★ ★ ★

The famous Tet Offensive of 1968 was begun by the North Vietnamese Army (NVA) and Viet Cong (VC) on January 30 and was one of the largest general attacks against South Vietnamese and U.S. forces of the war. Principal cities such as Saigon and Hue, as well as military and administrative centers, were the objectives for the 100,000 well-trained men who sought not only military victory but a general uprising among the people of the South. Eventually, by February 25, the NVA had been defeated or repulsed with heavy casualties and the VC had lost most of its core cadre. I arrived in Vietnam one week later.

Very few low-ranking soldiers, NCOs or officers knew anything about their ultimate assignments upon arrival in Vietnam except that they were nearly always placed in the career fields for which they had been trained. For me, the overwhelming odds pointed to becoming an Infantry platoon leader slogging through the rice paddies, but the quirky machinery in wartime could overturn that outcome without reason or explanation.

I could never have anticipated the unusual series of assignments that awaited me during that year.

Unlike most soldiers who deplaned with me at Ton Son Nhut military airfield near Saigon, I was not carried away by the exotic odors of the Orient. After my initial Army enlisted training, I had been stationed for 19 months in Korea, which had its own powerful combination of spice and fertilizer smells. Japan also had a noticeable background aroma of the Far East.

As for the often-cited blast of withering heat, I welcomed it. During my winter Basic Training at Fort Knox, KY, in 1961, I had contracted a low-level case of pneumonia: no weather could be too hot for me.

Despite my lack of meaningful leadership experience, OCS had done its job and trained me for probable assignments and I felt prepared for whatever awaited. This included a firm grasp of the nature, composition and armament of the enemy.

The NVA soldiers were citizens of North Vietnam and, as such, wore standard green or khaki uniforms and were well-equipped with the AK-47 assault rifle and other modern Infantry weapons. The South Vietnamese citizens of the Viet Cong (VC) were organized in three levels: Main Force, Local Force and guerilla. The Main Force units were full-time South Vietnamese communist soldiers and sometimes were reinforced by NVA. They were also well-equipped. The Local Force units were less-well equipped, had mixed uniforms, if any, and, as their name denotes, were not mobile in the way the Main Forces were. The part-time guerillas were generally local peasant farmers who laid mines and booby traps, acted as snipers and served as replacements for the Local Forces. They also performed logistic functions for the NVA and other VC units.

Statistics have shown that a significant percentage of U.S. Infantry casualties were caused by this third team of black-pajama-wearing guerillas who fit Americans' stereotypical image of VC as daytime farmers and nighttime fighters.

Incoming U.S. personnel were considered replacements at that time since they had not arrived with a unit. We were all taken to a nearby facility to await further assignment. As a second lieutenant with less than nine months of commissioned time, I had about the same priority and influence on my fate as a private. As a Reserve Component officer (the meaning and further significance of which I will explain later), with no connections or achievements to secure a prime assignment in a "good" division, I stoically awaited my orders. They soon came for the 23d Infantry Division, known as the "Americal," based at Chu Lai.

For military control purposes, the Republic of Vietnam (RVN) was divided into four corps areas, or military regions. This was a departure from the classic military corps concept which was a grouping of divisions instead of a geographic area. According to tradition, each corps was designated by a Roman numeral starting in the north. The country's 43 provinces were divided among the corps areas. Chu Lai was located in I Corps, commonly called "Eye Corps." Since I Corps was closest to North Vietnam, it was easiest for the NVA to infiltrate their troops there. See Figure 1. Map of Vietnam.

The Americal Division's area of operation was located south of Da Nang and north of Quang Ngai City, near the border with North Vietnam in what is called the South Central Coast. The terrain is dominated by the massive Annamese Cordillera mountain range that straddles Vietnam's western border with Laos and reaches elevations of over 2,500 meters (8,200 feet). Fingers of jungle-covered ridgelines extend eastward nearly to the beaches of the South China Sea, leaving fertile, narrow coastal strips and large V-shaped valleys between them. For an Infantryman, the jungle, open rice paddies and mountains each presented its own unique challenges.

I trickled down the chain of command from division to brigade to battalion to an Infantry, or rifle, company, landing on March 6 in Company B, 1st Battalion 52d Infantry, 198th Light Infantry Brigade, Americal Division. Company B had been in Vietnam since October 1967, and had had some bad luck in November when six men were accidentally killed, including four drowned. Otherwise its casualties, at the rate of four or five per month, weren't much different from the other three rifle companies in the battalion, familiarly known as 1/52 or First of the Fifty-second.

"Company B" was the official designation of the unit, but it was referred to by many variations of that name: B Company, Bravo Company and Bravo were all used. For consistency, I'll use the standard nomenclature throughout this narrative for all companies and the 1/52 format for all battalions. A rifle company's strength was authorized at 144 men but, in my experience, never exceeded 120 in field strength.

My assignment was as the Weapons Platoon Leader. A standard Army weapons platoon had three 81mm (3.19 inches) mortars and two recoilless rifle anti-tank weapons for a total strength of one officer and 34 enlisted men. Since the enemy, at that time, had no tanks, I was to lead only the men who plotted targets and fired the mortars. My position was not considered critical to the success of the company; in fact it had been vacant for some time prior to my arrival. The mortar platoon was very experienced and proficient in operating without the supervision of an officer. This meant that I was effectively a strap hanger or a fifth wheel but this gave me time to observe the company's operations without any serious responsibility.

The plum assignment for a lieutenant in an Infantry company was rifle platoon leader, but unfortunately all three of those positions in Company B were already filled. The incumbent platoon leaders seemed confident and competent after four months on the job in Vietnam. A rifle platoon was authorized 44 men, but in practice only 20 to 35 men were available for duty.

I was content for the time being to learn the ropes while waiting for a platoon leader vacancy to occur.

Despite its initial non-combat losses, the men of Company B had a positive attitude due to the charismatic leadership of the company commander, Captain Leonard G. Goldman. Their esprit de corps was manifested by the designs on the backs of their body armor vests, or flak jackets: a large Star of David framed by the words "GOLDMAN'S ANGELS."

While the bulk of Company B was conducting combat operations in the field, I was initially sent to occupy myself with 3d Platoon which was securing a bridge over the Song Tra Bong (Tra Bong River) in the southeastern sector of the Americal area of operations. It was normally referred to as the Binh Son bridge due to its proximity to the town of that name. The bridge served Highway 1, a major north-south artery, and any damage to it would have been a significant disruption for civilian and military traffic.

3d Platoon seemed relaxed and secure in their ability to protect the bridge. Occasionally, the platoon leader would order a hand grenade to be thrown into the river to "stir the water." This was a sure method of discouraging enemy frogmen and sappers on rafts from attempting to plant demolitions on the important bridge.

The leader of 3d Platoon had his own method of stimulating morale. He was a big guy with a square head, white-blond hair and small spaces between his even teeth; let's call him "Kranz." He looked like he belonged in the turret of a German panzer tank in a World War II movie. In the spirit of good fun and friendly competition, his platoon adorned their flak jackets with large swastikas and "KRANZ'S KRAUTS." I was personally leery about the blatantly conflicting symbols but no one in Company B seemed to take 3d Platoon's emblems in any way other than an edgy, tasteless joke.

Occasionally, during my time at the bridge, I would accompany a patrol to learn the ropes but never as the leader. On one patrol I was in the file behind a very short Vietnamese soldier assigned to us as an interpreter. Instead of a helmet, he wore a soft bush hat. As we were wading across a fairly deep stream, he suddenly disappeared and his hat was left floating on the surface; he had stepped into a hole and his equipment dragged him to the bottom. I quickly fished him out, sputtering and coughing, and carried him to the far bank. He seemed more embarrassed than grateful.

I also was invited by a nearby unit to participate in a night patrol which sought to surprise the participants in a VC leadership meeting at a nearby village. Again, I was essentially another rifleman tagging along in a follow-the-leader line of men. It was so dark that I couldn't understand how the captain who was leading the patrol could navigate accurately, but indeed he did and we eventually arrived at the objective, which was deserted—no VC. If something had gone wrong, I could not see how the captain could have controlled the men in the dark. I decided that I hated night patrols.

Protecting the bridge was a good example of troops being tied down at a static location, well known to the enemy, and unable to contribute to the search for and engagement of the VC and NVA except for limited local patrols.

Bridge duty continued for 10 more days with only minor enemy incidents and on March 17 Kranz's platoon and I joined the rest of Company B at Landing Zone (LZ) Gator, about five kilometers (3.1 miles) northwest of the bridge. An LZ such as Gator was a semi-permanent base located away from the rear areas. Its purpose was to provide security for an artillery battery (four to six guns) or heavy mortars which supported the rifle companies patrolling in the battalion's area of operation; for that reason it was also referred to as a fire support base or firebase. LZs frequently bore female names such as Ann and Dottie, presumably inspired by wives or girl friends of commanders whose units had constructed them. Naturally, one wondered about LZs with names like Gator and Baldy.

For the relative locations of all LZs mentioned herein, see map at Figure 2.

Anyone assigned to a large, mostly secure headquarters and logistical support base along the South China Sea coast was considered to be "in the rear." If someone was on an LZ, he was considered to be "in the field" relative to those "in the rear." However, to any Infantryman, when he was on an operation in the jungle or rice paddy and not on an LZ, he was truly "in the field." Therefore, "in the field" took on a two-layered definition.

An assignment in the rear area was not a guarantee of safety. The brigade base camp, LZ Bayonet, while named an "LZ," was actually "in the rear" adjacent to the division headquarters at Chu Lai. On July 24, one cook was killed and 13 cooks were wounded along with four motor pool personnel at Bayonet. This was due to a mortar attack and it underscored the fact that no one, in the rear or otherwise, was immune to danger.

Life on the firebases was marginally superior to life in the field in terms of sleep. I had grown up in a small Ohio town which was the intersection of Wabash Railroad lines from Detroit, Toledo, Chicago and St. Louis. The trains from each of these cities arrived at the large switching yard and were disassembled and reassembled to form new trains. This was done on a 24-hour basis. Visiting relatives would complain of lack of sleep due to the constant train whistles from the switching yard. Having been exposed to the noise for our entire lives, we said, "What whistles?"

It was not so easy to become acclimated to the artillery and mortars on the firebases which were in action around the clock. In addition to fire missions in support of Infantry companies in the field, the artillery and/or mortars fired "H&I" missions during the night. These were harassment and interdiction barrages designed to give a nasty surprise to any enemy who might be travelling on a major trail, camping on a hilltop, gathering water at a prominent stream or wandering through some random jungle thicket. No one that I knew of ever became used to the nightly thunder of H&I fire in the same way that I was inured to train whistles as a child.

Our battalion continuously secured two firebases with one rifle company on each. That left two companies to conduct operations in the field. The battalion tactical operations center or TOC would occupy a large bunker on one of the LZs. The TOC controlled all battalion field operations and managed all aircraft flying within the battalion area of operations. It also coordinated our activities with higher headquarters and adjacent units. All communications, including requests for medical evacuation (medevac) helicopters, were carried over numerous radio networks managed by the TOC. The S-3 or operations officer, a major, was in charge of the TOC and he advised the battalion commander, a lieutenant colonel, and implemented his orders.

Another important function of the TOC was to record the essence of all radio transmissions on forms called the S2/S3 Journals or Logs. I have been able to obtain copies of these logs from the National Archives; they document the sequence of events and exact locations for nearly all of my activities in the 1/52. Since the logs only recorded what was reported to the TOC via radio, every action and detail occurring in the field were not necessarily captured in them. In this account, I have extensively supplemented the log summaries with my own vivid memories. It must also be stated that some actions or particulars that someone in the TOC had determined to be embarrassing to the battalion were not included in the logs; perhaps they were inadvertently omitted in the press of frenzied activity.

The TOC was very important piece of our field operations and will be referred to throughout the first half of this narrative.

Company B performed routine patrols around LZ Gator and I was able to become acquainted with my platoon and other members of the company. This lasted until March 25th when we were moved by helicopter for a combat assault further south and west. A helicopter combat assault landed Infantrymen into a field location which was not secured by a friendly unit; it could be "cold" (no enemy opposition) or "hot" (significant enemy resistance). Adding to the confusion in terminology, "landing zone" was also used to describe these locations but unlike the semi-permanent LZs described above, they were unnamed and normally used only once.

Instead of the three mortars that were authorized, the mortar platoon normally carried only one on an extended field operation due to weight. On this occasion, since the walking distances would be short, we carried two. As always, additional mortar rounds for use during operations were carried by the Infantrymen in the rifle platoons.

After landing we trudged through the flat, open terrain without incident and came to a tall hill covered with knee-high, dry grass overlooking the Song Tra Bong. It was about 10 kilometers (6.2 miles) upstream (westward) from the Binh Son bridge where I had so slowly begun my tour in Vietnam with 3d Platoon. Here we would set up a temporary company base from which to conduct local search patrols.

The top of the hill was a relatively flat area roughly 100 by 20 meters. Sectors of the perimeter were assigned to the rifle platoons and the mortar platoon began several concurrent activities to put our two mortars into action. Pits had to be dug to protect the crews from enemy weapons fire, the three-part mortars had to be assembled and the rounds had to be removed from their cardboard packing cylinders so the detonating fuses and propellant charges could be attached. Helicopters began ferrying in more mortar ammunition in three-round wooden cases along with water and C-rations for our extended stay on the hill.

As the unpacked rounds with their sensitive fuses and volatile propellant charges were being spread on the ground for assembly, someone threw a smoke grenade within the perimeter to provide the inbound helicopter pilots with a wind indicator. Smoke grenades produced billows of colored smoke and were used for a variety of identification purposes. But in this case, the burning process which generated the smoke quickly turned the dry grass into a conflagration. The wooden boxes, cardboard tubes, fuses, propellants and high explosive rounds were in the path of the wind-driven flames.

There was no way to concentrate the little water we had to quell the fire. We could only try to stamp out the flames, dig a fire break near the exposed rounds and move as many rounds away from danger as possible. It was a desperate time but the burning grass was finally extinguished with no injuries beyond minor burns. A few rucksacks and shirts which had been initially discarded in the high grass were lost. In the end, the worst outcome was the ash and bits of dry grass, whipped up by the propwash from the choppers, that stuck to the skin of the sweaty, shirtless soldiers.

Without much real success to show for our patrolling efforts, we packed up and moved from our hill on April 1 and, searching as we moved, worked our way five kilometers (3.1 miles) west. We were notified that we would be extracted from the field by helicopter on April 7, stay at LZ Bayonet in the rear area overnight and fly to LZ Colt in the northern part of the Division area of operation on the 8th. I was to go directly to Colt ahead of the company as the advanced party.

My task was to determine Colt's bunker layout, review any recent enemy contacts and generally smooth the transition from the current tenants, the 1/6 Infantry Battalion. The battalion commander was Lieutenant Colonel William D. Kelly who used the radio call sign "Gunslinger;" I thought he was very colorful--just right for a field commander.

LZ Colt, named after the manufacturer of the M-16 rifle and .45 caliber pistol, had a violent past. Six months prior in October 1967, the 5th Battalion, 7th Cavalry Regiment of the 1st Cavalry Division endured a furious Viet Cong attack there. One rifle company, battalion headquarters and a battery of 105mm artillery pieces, all led by the battalion commander, Lieutenant Colonel (later General and Chief of Staff of the Army) John A. Wickham Jr., defended the LZ. It was a desperate struggle with the defenders sustaining significant casualties but ultimately prevailing over the attackers. LTC Wickham was seriously wounded and evacuated.

In our case, Company B arrived and quickly moved into place without incident. Local patrols were sent out daily to search the area but little was found. I busied myself with gathering accumulated rusty and outdated ammunition and destroying it with blocks of military TNT which I found in a bunker. The TNT was old and considered unstable but it was too tempting to resist. We carefully stacked the ammunition outside the perimeter, placed the TNT over it, inserted blasting caps into the TNT and positioned sandbags on top of the pile to contain the explosion. To determine the quantity of explosives for each blast, I used a formula that I had learned somewhere along the way: P = Plenty. There was something very satisfying about taking an action that yielded concrete, visible results—never mind the thrill of causing tremendous explosions and prodigious mushroom clouds of dust.

We were on LZ Colt for only four nights. On April 22, we walked off of the LZ as another company arrived by helicopter to take over its security. We were to be picked up and flown on another combat assault as part of a larger operation about 15 kilometers (9 miles) north of Colt.

CPT Goldman explained the plan for this operation and distributed maps to the officers and key NCOs before we left Colt. The landing zone was in the very wide river delta of the Song Cua Dai (Cua Dai River). This would be my first large-scale combat assault.

As we flew toward the landing zone, I tried to follow our path on my map but it was surprisingly more different than reading a map on the ground, although some would say it was easier. I finally identified the river delta ahead of us and it was much larger than I had imagined. I knew the coordinates of where we were supposed to land but, from all of the war stories I had heard, pilots had a lot of latitude in selecting the actual touch-down point.

We landed and piled out, quickly moving to assemble with the rest of the company. I was guiding my platoon into our assigned position in the company formation and also somewhat frantically trying to orient the map to the wide, flat expanse of sand and water. The low hills on the edges of the delta were devoid of any prominent terrain features from which to take a compass reading and pinpoint our location. I was not a novice at this process but without some physical points of reference, I was at a complete loss.

The company began to move and within 15 minutes the leading platoon called to the mortar platoon for a fire mission. To execute a fire mission the mortar platoon fire direction center (FDC) needed two pieces of information: the map coordinates of the mortars themselves and the coordinates of the target. The FDC would then calculate the mortar sight settings and the number of propellant charges for the mission and relay that data to the gun crews. Once the initial round had been fired, an observer could make adjustments by providing additional information to the FDC.

The mortar crews quickly and expertly set up their weapons while the FDC men got the plotting board, charts and grease pencils ready. In less than two minutes, the FDC looked expectantly at me--their leader and the only guy in the platoon with a map--to give them their coordinates so they could determine the mortar sight settings for the crews. I was at a complete and utter loss. And there was no faking or fudging map coordinates when live mortar rounds were to be fired over the heads of our comrades who were located between us and the target.

It did not take CPT Goldman long to cancel our fire mission and request the artillery at LZ Colt to handle it instead.

Although no one was hurt as a result of our inability to act, this was a complete, devastating, ignominious failure for me. Not only had I let down the troops who needed fire support but I had deeply embarrassed the mortar platoon, which was helpless and ineffective without their needed coordinates.

This operation wore on for several days until about April 25th (the logs are missing for the 24th and 25th) when we found ourselves about half way back to Colt on yet another LZ—Baldy.

Over the next several days on Baldy, I worked at regaining the confidence of my platoon. I finally achieved that by skillfully supervising the handling of a misfire, in which a round slid down the mortar tube but did not fire. The entire crew knew the correct drill for this, but when I directed a textbook-perfect misfire procedure, I believe some of the frost came off of our relationship.

On April 27, I was informed that the battalion reconnaissance platoon leader was nearing the end of his tour and I was being considered as his replacement. The reconnaissance platoon leader worked directly for the battalion commander through the TOC just like the rifle company commanders. The platoon—referred to as Recon--normally operated in small independent squads in the field. The Recon platoon leader's radio call sign was "Romeo." Would I like to accompany the platoon on a patrol to get a feeling for how it operated? Who wouldn't like to try for that job?

So far, I had not had one experience in Vietnam where I had done anything "my way." Recon seemed to be the only opportunity for me to achieve that freedom of action, even more so than as a rifle platoon leader.

That afternoon of the patrol, the Recon platoon leader—Romeo--told me to meet him at a certain place on the perimeter of LZ Baldy at 6pm. When I arrived, the platoon was lined up at the exit in the barbed wire barrier and I was placed in the middle of the 18-man file. We rambled across the hilly terrain until it became dusk and when we arrived at the flat, level rice paddies we stopped to eat. Romeo gave me a rough idea of our location but nothing specific about what we were supposed to accomplish.

It was well after dark when we began to move again along the dikes of the paddies. The movement was stop and start as all patrols were and after about two hours there was a prolonged halt. Suddenly firing broke out ahead and short bursts of different types of weapons could be identified by sound. Then there was silence. Everyone was lying flat in the dry paddy and none of us in the middle or rear of the file knew what had happened.

I moved slowly up the line of men until I came to the front and identified myself. It seemed that as the patrol was moving along the edge of a small village, Romeo decided to investigate a particular crude farm dwelling known as a "hooch." Apparently he went in the door, turned on a flashlight and--lo and behold--there stood three armed Viet Cong who opened fire and blew him back out of the door. Other rounds were fired by our patrol killing two of the

VC. We were now faced with a severely wounded platoon leader in decidedly hostile territory.

The sergeant from the lead squad called for a medical evacuation (medevac) helicopter although it was unusual for them to fly at night. We moved out away from the village into the vast expanse of the adjacent dry rice paddy and the chopper came in guided by the bright flashes of a handheld strobe light.

Although I had previously only been along for the ride, I now placed myself near the center of the action and monitored all of the platoon's activity.

As the wounded Romeo was being carried to the medevac, he handed me his signal code book, map and compass and said, "You have the platoon now." The helicopter lifted and flew safely into the night, billowing dust from the arid paddy.

Naturally, many questions arose in my mind. Where are we? What are we supposed to be doing? Who are the squad leaders? Are there any more VC in the area?

Although I lacked many important facts about the situation, I was the only officer present so I assumed the leadership of the platoon without any delay or second thoughts.

My first action was to move the platoon away from the village and medevac pickup point and further into the large rice paddy. It was no use trying to hide after the firefight and commotion of the helicopter, but we could get good fields of fire and artillery and air support if we could have open spaces around us. Next I got the squad leaders to meet with me but it was so dark that I couldn't see their faces and using a flashlight was out of the question. This situation had an uncanny similarity to some of the complex tactical problems that we had been challenged with in OCS.

I decided to employ a defensive configuration previously unknown in Army doctrine: the Z-shaped perimeter. Based on the intersections of the rice paddy dikes, the direction of a possible attack and the limited visibility, I established a unique defensive "perimeter" in that shape. It seemed like a good idea at the time.

More challenging was my attempt to communicate by radio with the battalion TOC to discuss the many questions arising from recent events. Everyone knew that the reconnaissance platoon leader's call sign was Romeo (the NATO phonetic word for "R" which was short for reconnaissance). My personal call sign as the Company B mortar platoon leader was Bravo (for Company B) Four (for 4th or mortar platoon) Six (for commander or leader).

When the platoon was settled in I called the TOC on LZ Baldy via radio, identifying myself as Bravo Four Six. I was cursorily ordered to stay off of the radio network because Recon was in a serious bind and I was interfering with a critical operation. I tried several times to explain and was always rebuffed. To this day I think the sergeant on TOC radio duty was drunk.

Despite the frustration, uncertainty and potential for disaster, I discovered that in my first real combat action as a leader, I was much more comfortable than during the previous two months as a mortar platoon leader in Company B.

Sometime later that night, the battalion S-3 (operations) officer came on the radio, straightened things out and gave me the objective for the following day. As it was, given the unavoidable delay for the medevac and lack of sleep, we never made it to the objective. Eventually we took the dreary walk back to LZ Baldy--sadder, wiser and minus one good man. He would eventually recover from his wounds but not return to Vietnam.

The TOC logs don't include any of the turmoil and confusion that occurred on the radio after the medevac departed.

Three days later, I became Romeo.

CHAPTER 5

Romeo in the North

★ ★ ★

I was very pleased when I began my new job as Recon platoon leader, radio call sign Romeo, on May 1 on LZ Baldy. As far as I was concerned, it was the best field assignment for a lieutenant in the battalion or anywhere else. This was because Romeo worked directly for the battalion commander with no company commander in between. That translated into a unique freedom of action for a junior officer since the platoon would operate independently in the field. Of course, the previous incumbent had been unlucky but that couldn't be used to judge the value of the job since everyone in the field was subject to sustaining similar injuries or even death.

As soon as I fully understood that I would have much more control of my new unit's operations in the field than I would have had as a platoon leader in an Infantry company, I knew that this was a golden opportunity to do things "my way."

Nevertheless, I was baffled about receiving the assignment. I had not distinguished myself during my time with Company B and had even, in my own opinion, been deficient. The decision may have been the result of the four rifle company commanders such as CPT

Goldman being reluctant to give up one of their seasoned lieutenants to fill the Recon vacancy. It may have been that since I had been on the patrol on which the previous Romeo was wounded, it was easy to let me stay with the platoon. There is no documentation to explain the decision but I don't believe that CPT Goldman put up much resistance to losing my services.

I didn't know what the men in Recon thought of me, especially with respect to the creative but unconventional perimeter I had initiated after my predecessor was medevaced. However, none of us had been solicited for his vote on my new assignment so we all decided to make the best of the situation.

The Recon platoon was comprised of seasoned soldiers, most of whom had been working together in Vietnam for seven months. I saw my new role as providing continued competent leadership and expanding the skills of the platoon.

The mission of Recon was normally to observe and report enemy activity so that the TOC could respond to that information. This response might be artillery, helicopter gunships or Air Force fighters. As will be seen, we also took advantage of targets of opportunity by ambushing small groups of enemy that came our way. Stealth was the key to moving unobserved into and through any area to perform our primary mission. Our standing instructions were to evade if discovered by the enemy.

The standard organization for a recon platoon was three squads of five men each including the squad leader, a staff sergeant. The platoon headquarters was supposed to be composed of a lieutenant, a sergeant first class (platoon sergeant) and two radio operators (RTOs), one for the platoon leader and one for the platoon sergeant.

In actual operation, the squad leaders were Sergeants, one rank below the authorized level. The Army had a program of identifying and training qualified enlisted men (at an NCO Candidate Course or NCOCC) and giving them accelerated promotion to Sergeant. This initiative was intended to fill the NCO vacancies that occurred during the rapid increase in new units deployed to Vietnam. It also served to prevent incessant returns to the combat zone by the Regular Army NCOs with no breaks between them. The men who completed this program were universally referred to as Shake-N-Bakes or Instant NCOs.

Although the squad leaders had only 12 weeks more training than the men they led, their performance was generally exemplary in my experience. However, this was not the case universally. In Recon, the squad leaders were mature men with a steady, serious approach to the job at hand. If I ever had a gift of good luck in Vietnam, those squad leaders were a heavy dose of it.

We had a platoon sergeant for only a very short period of time as will be related later.

Everyone was authorized to carry the standard M-16 rifle, except for one man in each squad who could carry an M-79 grenade launcher. In fact, only one squad employed an M-79, a squad leader's choice which I did not contest. The M-79 grenade launcher is so unique that even Americans who grew up with firearms required substantial training to master the weapon. It's short, stubby barrel launches the equivalent of a modern hand grenade up to 300 meters to explode on contact. An alternative short-range round propels deadly buckshot like a traditional shotgun. M-79s will have a recurring role in this narrative.

No machineguns were authorized or desired. We wore the floppy, wide-brimmed bush hats, known as boonie hats, instead of helmets and no flak jackets. We obtained an additional radio and assigned one to each squad. For the first several months of my tenure as Romeo, we didn't carry the ubiquitous rucksacks but crammed dehydrated rations into the cargo pockets of our uniforms for consumption in the field. Unencumbered in this way we enjoyed rapid and silent movement.

As lightly armed and equipped as we were, it was impractical and dangerous to be assigned normal Infantry missions. There were times, however, when we were required to perform in a regular Infantry role.

My preference for deploying the platoon was by individual squads operating separately. Five or six men were by many factors easier to move and conceal than an entire platoon of any size. Normally, two squads would be operating independently in the field while one rested on a firebase; the squads would rotate periodically on a staggered basis. The enemy situation sometimes dictated that two and rarely all three squads would operate together, in which case I would lead them. Otherwise, I would accompany an individual squad, trying to be in the field as often as possible. I could not control other squads when I was in the field so each separate squad communicated directly with the TOC.

Since I considered all three squads and their leaders equally qualified, I normally would accompany the squad with the best overall sense of humor. This choice was not based on any leadership principle but simply on a selfish desire to be among amiable people. The downside of this was that the squad leader whom I accompanied was superseded by me and his authority diminished.

The northern part of the Americal area of operation was dominated by the Que Son Valley, named for an inland district headquarters town. Beginning about 14 kilometers (8.7 miles) from the beach, the valley was triangular shaped: 14 kilometers wide toward the beach and tapering inland to the west for 24 kilometers (14.9 miles) before meeting its apex. It was almost all rice paddy and therefore a massive rice producing area, making it highly desirable by both sides and the key to controlling I Corps. The NVA 2d Division moved in and out of the valley from Laos depending on the pressure put upon it by U.S. and South Vietnamese forces. American Marines had battled the VC and NVA in the valley before and would again. I knew none of this at the time.

Que Son should not be confused with Khe Sanh, where the Marines fought an epic battle against the NVA that bracketed the 1968 Tet Offensive in time.

The battalion TOC was not slow in putting me to work. On my second day on the job as Romeo, May 2, I was walking off of LZ Baldy with one squad and following a very slow-moving U.S. convoy on Route 535 headed southwest. It was the first of the many patrols I would lead. About four kilometers (2.5 miles) out, we veered away from the convoy into the rice paddies and waited until dark to set up for the night among some large boulders on a small rise. The moon was full and bright, casting stark shadows in the open air. We were careful to stay low so as not to reveal our position by being "skylined," or silhouetted.

That night we were spectators to a fantastic and deadly ballet in the sky to our northeast, probably near Hoi An, about 13 kilometers (8 miles) away. I believe that one participant was a modified U.S. C-130 cargo plane, known as Spooky, flying a circular pattern and equipped with a Gatling gun firing a 25 millimeter bullets. The other was clearly a VC with a communist-bloc .51 caliber machine gun. As Spooky orbited overhead, they performed a bizarre *pas de deux* shootout, each taking a turn firing at the other.

Both weapons fired a tracer every five or six rounds and the gunners would aim by observing the paths of these incandescent bullets. As each gunner adjusted his aim while firing, the tracers would sway in the air like a thin stream of luminous water from a high-pressure hose. Spooky's one-inch diameter rounds were raining down at the rate of 1,200 per minute and the VC's one-half inch rounds swooped upward at 600 per minute. We were amazed at the bravery and tenacity demonstrated by both sides. Eventually Spooky broke the engagement, flying off to the north, probably to the large airbase at Da Nang. With no other information, we called it a draw.

The next day, May 3, unknown to us, the United States and North Vietnam agreed to formal talks to end the war. The talks would sputter off and on for years and were effectively meaningless at that time.

We poked around southwest of LZ Baldy for six days without any significant incidents. One exception was when the TOC couldn't contact us by radio beginning just after midnight on the 5th. This was always alarming because our only means of requesting artillery and medevacs was via radio. At 2:49am, a platoon from Company C was able to contact us and relay our position to the TOC. On May 8th we returned to Baldy and, as usual when on an LZ, we manned several bunkers on the perimeter.

On the 11th we again found ourselves walking with a convoy headed southwest on Route 535, but this time we had a specific mission. A particular house was suspected of being a hub of VC activity and we were to begin surveillance on it the next day. There were 11 of us—two squads and me.

The convoy stopped briefly at Company B's command post while some road clearing activity was occurring ahead. As we waited, one of the tanks from the escorting cavalry unit was firing off to the side of the road. When we finally moved out, the tankers asked us to assess the results of their gunnery. After we surveyed the damage, I reported that they had scored one KIA and three WIA: a water buffalo had been killed and three children slightly wounded. (KIA: Killed in Action; WIA: Wounded in Action. In Vietnam, these terms were applied only to the enemy, despite the long tradition of describing friendly casualties). We left the convoy, turned off of the road and proceeded to our objective via a zig-zag route.

A saddle-back hill overlooking the target house had sufficient vegetation for concealment and we melted into the greenery in the late afternoon. I set up a command post with one squad where we could maintain surveillance on the route we had just followed and obtain good communications with the TOC. The other squad would work its way around our cone-shaped hump of the saddle to set up an observation post with an unobstructed view of the house. Although we had two squads and two radios, it was considered a single patrol so the command post radio was on the TOC network and the observer squad's radio would be only used in an emergency. The observers would send a messenger back to the command post on a 10-minute trip to report any significant activities which I would relay to the TOC. Everything was going according to plan and we spent a quiet night.

The next morning passed without incident but just after noon the observers reported an increase in pedestrian activity around the house. No weapons were observed but some of the traffic seemed to be coming from our hill although they couldn't confirm that. I sent the command post squad leader and two men to investigate. About an hour later the squad leader reported that a major trail, not indicated on our maps, passed over the low point in the saddle and led directly to the target house. Now the plan had to change.

At mid afternoon, the squad leader and one man went back to place surveillance on the newly discovered trail. Just before 5pm the command post observed six VC with weapons moving through the area we had used to approach our hill on the previous day but we soon lost sight of them. We continued our routine of observing and reporting until just before dusk. Suddenly two bursts of gunfire exploded from the direction of our trail watchers. Twenty minutes later an observer-messenger breathlessly arrived to report that the house was swarming with armed men in an agitated state. Before he could finish his account, the sweating, panting trail watchers returned with even more important news.

They had spotted two VC in uniform walking on the trail toward the house; one was armed with a U.S. .45 caliber pistol and carried a large dispatch case. Using commendable initiative, they successfully engaged the VC and retrieved the pistol and dispatch case from the bodies. The sergeant said that one VC appeared to be an important officer because his uniform had a "high Chinese collar."

Our situation was this: We had revealed our presence, killed an apparently high-ranking VC official, stirred up a large number of no-doubt vengeful enemy and found ourselves in the gathering darkness. It was time to depart.

I quickly radioed the sergeant's verbatim account to the TOC and began to direct our movement out of the command post location.

I soon realized that the terms “Chinese” and “dispatch case” must have sent alarm bells clanging all the way up the chain of command, which was apparently eager to verify a communist Chinese advisor operating in Vietnam. Before we could begin our move, I received new, imperative orders. Expressions such as “without fail,” “immediately” and other stark military terms were emphasized throughout. The patrol, with the dispatch case, was to travel directly to Company B’s night location, about two kilometers (1.3 miles) away, near where our patrol had been the day before. Upon our arrival, a helicopter would retrieve the case, an unheard-of night-time action.

I had no choice but to take the command post group and leave immediately with the dispatch case. The messenger was sent back to the observers’ location with instruction to pack up, overtake us if possible or make their way to Company B’s location independently. Both radios were switched to the reconnaissance platoon’s frequency which the TOC would monitor. A moonless but impartial night dominated the landscape.

My group picked its way through the underbrush with as much haste as silent movement would allow, knowing the enemy was already searching for us. As we neared the open rice paddies and stopped for a break, a radio call came from the observer group moving somewhere in the night.

“We hear movement ahead of us.”

This was one of the most dreaded combat situations: two friendly groups moving independently in the same area where the enemy was also moving—at night. Determining friend from foe was nearly impossible and mistakes were fatal. Everyone was on edge and no one wanted to shoot a buddy from another squad any more than he wanted to be shot by him or by a misidentified enemy. All of this did nothing to alleviate my strong dislike for night patrols that I had acquired back at the Binh Son bridge.

Then, word was whispered up the line to me from our rear-most, or drag, man: "I hear movement behind us." I radioed the observer group to stop and asked the drag man if he heard anything now. "Maybe. I can't be sure." The observers were also equivocal about what they were hearing.

Clearly, the quandary was: both squads had detected movement in the darkness; was that movement the enemy or just the other squad?

Reviewing the options, all of them bad, I had an idea from my Boy Scout days. I passed this back down the line: "Who can do a whip-poor-will bird call?" Long minutes passed before the reply was relayed that one man could perform the task. A call was made to the observer group with the same question.

Another dreary wait. The answer: Negative. OK, another question: How about a bob white? Command post group: Yes. How about the observer group? Affirmative.

Surely no VC could imitate a bob white. A bob white call was initiated by our command post whistler and we waited for a matching answer. After several nerve-wracking attempts it became clear that the observer group had coincidentally followed the same path as my group and nearly overtook us before being detected. A friendly fire disaster was averted and the two squads were reunited.

Now a very different problem presented itself: How to navigate to Company B's location quickly and quietly through the darkness. Despite the debacle during the river delta combat assault with Company B, I was a very proficient map reader on the ground. However, at night I required frequent stops and use of a red-filtered flashlight to view the map, neither of which was prudent in this situation. I consulted with the two squad leaders and they in turn checked with their men. One of the sergeants returned with a young private in tow and presented him as the solution. Since we had taken a long, circuitous route from Company B's location the day before, how could this 18-year-old find a direct path back there, in the dark, having never seen a map? The sergeant's answer: "Well, he's a Wyoming country boy."

The country boy was put on point and I followed along with the rest of the patrol. We moved quickly, stopping briefly from time to time, totally in the hands of an untried, low-ranking soldier. At last I bumped blindly into my guide when he stopped for a final time.

"What?" I asked as everyone crouched behind a rice paddy dike.

"B Company. Over there, about 150 meters. If we get any closer they'll probably shoot us up."

The Company B commander, still CPT Goldman, was radioed and, when his perimeter had been alerted to the presence of approaching friendlies, our patrol entered the relative safety of that small patch of U.S. controlled territory at 1:35am. Sure enough, the TOC dispatched a helicopter to retrieve the dispatch case as well as the two soldiers who had reported the "Chinese" uniform.

The country boy, bird callers, intrepid messengers and trail watchers melted quietly back into the anonymity of their squads, neither expecting nor seeking recognition. Immediately, I became occupied with new challenges for the platoon but was unsurprised at its depth of latent skills that invariably, unpretentiously would surface, shine and recede when necessity called.

I had been Romeo for less than two weeks and I began to wonder if the remainder of my tenure would be this thrilling.

Forty-seven years after this event, while researching background material for this book, I came upon a copy of the Americal Division's newspaper, "Southern Cross," dated June 1968. A headline startled me: "198th Infantrymen Kill Key NVA Leader." The story was an overview of this particular adventure without some of the drama and contained an interview with me that never occurred. I knew that the reporter had not spoken directly to me because I was quoted in the article as referring to the soldiers in Recon as "my men," a term I never used. The article claimed that one of the VC was the commander of the 105th Main Force Viet Cong Battalion. Main Force VC were full-time soldiers in contrast to the part-time guerillas. It also identified me as a first lieutenant, a promotion still two months off. Finding this article was the first time I had gotten feedback about the results of that operation.

The 105th Main Force VC Battalion was endemic to the Que Son Valley. Indeed, the TOC logs record that on May 5, six days before the start of this patrol, intelligence reports indicated that the VC battalion had elements hiding in three areas within eight kilometers (five miles) of the above incident. At that time, I did not know that I was in the Que Son Valley and I had never heard of this enemy battalion.

Later that morning we trudged back to LZ Baldy but would not stay long. On the 15th we were flown to LZ East in the central sector of the Americal's area of operation where we performed local patrols for three or four days. Probably on the 20th (the logs are not clear), we walked to LZ Cacti, which was closer to our new patrol area than Baldy.

From Cacti we performed the same local patrols as always, sometimes staying overnight in the jungle. Although we had no significant enemy contacts or success in the field during this period, day by day we enhanced our field craft in ways that would yield benefits later.

Recon had always adhered to strict noise discipline standards. The TOC called each unit in the field during the night for a situation report every hour on the hour. When Recon was asked for a report, the TOC would say something like: "If your report is negative (all OK), key your handset twice." By pressing the "Talk" button on our radio handset, known as "breaking squelch," the TOC's radio speakers would receive a distinctive "TSSSK" sound and we would not have to speak on the radio. Whenever we had to use the radio in the field, we always whispered. All of this was just good field practices that we used to keep from revealing our position. Sometimes, when events became exciting, it was perversely gratifying to know that the radio operators in the hot, stuffy TOC would have to turn off the fans in order to hear our whispered reports. Details of our night time radio watch procedures are in the next chapter.

I felt that we could improve the communications between individual patrol members in the field. On a typical five- or six-man patrol, each member had clear responsibilities. The point man was in the lead and had every physical and mental sense on maximum alert for the enemy, trip wires, mines and any other threat. The slack man covered the point man in the event he was engaged by the enemy. Sometimes the two would switch positions to relieve the constant stress on the point man; some point men refused to relinquish the position, thinking that they were the best for the job. Next came one or two men without specific responsibilities who could react to threats from any direction; I would normally be in this position. The radio man followed. Last came the drag man, who provided rear security, sometimes walking backwards and always facing the rear during stops.

My concern was our ability to gain the attention of and communicate urgent information with others on a patrol as silently as possible. We tested various methods and settled on signals that could be completed with one hand, leaving the other to control the rifle. For example, two finger snaps would send an alert to the next man ahead in the file, such as between the slack man and the point man. The sounds of snaps were loud enough to span the interval between men but didn't travel much further. I still go on alert today when I hear finger snaps.

With attention gained, the urgent information had to be quickly and silently passed. We could frame complete sentences with hand signals. An index finger pointed to the eye (I see) or ear (I hear) formed the subject and verb. The number of individuals sighted was formed by flashing the appropriate number of fingers; two flashes would combine for numbers above five; we didn't want to think about numbers requiring more than three flashes. The thumb indicated the combatant status of the people detected: thumb up for unarmed civilians, thumb horizontal for undetermined and thumb down for armed enemy. A hand formed in a karate chop would be thrust in the direction of the people in question. This would be followed by more finger flashes, usually three, that indicated the distance in meters from us to the people who had been spotted. So very quickly and silently, one of us could secure the attention of another patrol member and "say:" I see six armed enemy to my front at a distance of 75 meters.

On May 19, instead of returning to LZ Cacti, we walked to LZ East where we saw the crash site of a Marine CH-53, a heavy-lift helicopter known as the Jolly Green Giant, just outside the perimeter wire. It looked like a huge, dead grasshopper lying on its side. We manned perimeter bunkers and conducted day and sometimes overnight patrols.

One afternoon, I had returned from an overnight patrol wet, tired and very dirty. I was sitting in the mud in a neatly scooped out, unfinished bunker position in the side of a hill inside the perimeter, greedily wolfing down a cold C-ration. Just above me on the hill I noticed a Red Cross lady, affectionately known to all GIs as a Donut Dolly, looking down at me with an expression of profound melancholy and pity. To earn a look like that, I must have looked grungy and forlorn far in excess of how I felt.

On June 2d, Recon left LZ Cacti in the north of the Americal's area of operation and flew into the center sector to a firebase under construction called LZ Clifford.

CHAPTER 6

A Day in the Life of Romeo

★ ★ ★

The men of Recon were no different from any other Infantrymen who had only two modes of life: in the field or on a firebase. As described previously, life on a firebase was static and mostly defensive. While resting from a field operation, some squads might conduct local daytime patrols and return to the firebase to occupy defensive bunkers at night. But most of the time, this meant that we could relax during the day. Crude showers and purified drinking water were the height of luxury; there were no other amenities.

Arriving at a firebase after a long patrol never produced a calm, safe feeling for me. The firebase was a known factor to the enemy, who could, at their leisure, set up well-planned mortar, rocket and ground attacks. Since we had no helmets or flak jackets, the idea of waiting for the enemy to exercise his initiative was repellant to me. Although we were on perimeter guard in well-constructed bunkers, I felt no sense of security. My idea was that we were much safer in the vast jungle, looking for the enemy on our terms, than waiting for an inevitable attack on a denuded hilltop LZ. So as the squads rotated off the LZs on patrols, I always accompanied the first to leave.

When we left an LZ for a patrol, it was by helicopter for an insertion (a one helicopter combat assault) or by foot. Either way, we were subject to easy observation by the enemy and we had to take evasive measures to insure that our planned route and objectives were not anticipated by an enterprising foe. Some helicopter insertions are described in other chapters. But if we walked off of an LZ such as Chippewa, we quickly crossed open areas and entered the nearest tree line at a right angle and then ran sharply to the right or left with all possible speed. Many times we went up and down the steepest possible mountain sides to confuse any hostile trackers. Some of these were so steep that we had to pull ourselves up by grabbing the smaller trees.

Recon's most visible differentiation from the rifle company Infantrymen was our floppy-brimmed boonie hats and lack of flak vests. The hats allowed for much easier hearing in the jungle than the standard helmets, something that was critical for us. Although they were issued in a shapeless condition to prevent easy identification by the enemy, we managed to individualize the hats in ways that defeated that purpose. One squad leader had stiffened the brim and crown to produce a gaucho effect. I pinned up one side to the crown to emulate an Australian slouch hat.

Most men were equipped in the field in the same configuration. Naturally we carried an M-16 rifle with a few exceptions. The foundation for other gear was load-bearing equipment consisting of a pistol belt and attached suspenders. Two ammunition pouches with a capacity of five magazines each were attached to the front of the pistol belt and two one-quart canteens were on the back over each hip. The pouches were designed to accommodate one grenade on each side; I carried two hand grenades and two smoke grenades.

I also carried a two-quart canteen suspended by a narrow strap over my shoulder. Some men carried extra magazines and food in cloth pouches resembling bandoliers.

In a later chapter, I'll relate how and why we eventually began to carry rucksacks like other Infantrymen.

The best way to describe a day in the life of Recon in the field is to begin in the evening. This was the time the military calls "begin evening nautical twilight" (BENT) or the start of darkness. Two possible conditions could occur: the patrol had been moving for some time or had been static while observing some point of interest. In either case, it was important to move for at least 30 minutes before BENT.

We would then stop at a place that could not be approached by the enemy without noisy movement through the underbrush and then prepare our evening meal. In the same way that the spicy Vietnamese ngoc mam sauce gave away the enemy's locations, the aromas emanating from cooking U.S. rations must have provided Viet Cong and NVA with certainty that U.S. forces were in the area. So if we felt the enemy was anywhere close, we would eat our meals cold.

"Cooking" meant heating water to add to dehydrated patrol rations or warming the entre from a C ration meal. Both of these actions were performed by burning military issue heat tablets about the size of two Alka Seltzer tablets. Cigarettes at an evening meal could be tolerated if they didn't pose any more threat to exposure than the smell of our cooked rations.

After our evening meal and just before complete darkness (end evening nautical twilight), we would move rapidly to a new location that was well off the beaten path and unlikely to be randomly discovered. Impending darkness would prevent visual trackers from following us.

Another factor other than telltale cooking smells that might alert the enemy to our presence was difficult to control—body odor. The VC, when we captured or killed them, seemed to emanate only wafts of pungent ngoc mam sauce and had no stale smell of old sweat. We, however, would normally generate enough sweat to completely dampen a jungle fatigue shirt every day. As will be related, it was difficult enough just to obtain drinking water on patrols, so bathing was out of the question. After a 12-day patrol without a change of uniform we not only looked, but smelled, grungy.

For about the first two months of my tenure with Recon, we would simply lie down directly on the jungle floor to sleep. Since we were anxious to remain undiscovered, our resting place was normally on the untraveled steep slope of a mountain. I would reach down with my left hand to find a fairly smooth, flat area, hoping that there were no stinging critters lurking there. Then I would ease down to lie on my back; the canteens on either hip held me in that position all night—no rolling over to a more comfortable position.

During the night, each individual was assigned to monitor the radio for about a two-hour period. Naturally, the more men on the patrol, the less time each man was required to perform radio duty. We would arrange ourselves in a circle so that whoever was next on the roster would be within arm's reach. That way, we could simply nudge the next person and hand him the radio handset. Every noise we emanated in the jungle at night was a potentially compromising event so our radio was tuned to "Squelch Off," which meant that the normal hissing noise on a military radio was silenced; this also meant that the range of the radio was reduced. The battalion TOC would call us every hour for a status check.

It seemed that I had a snoring problem—a big one. Twenty years later the cause was diagnosed as sleep apnea. In the jungle, however, it was considered a hazard to everyone's safety and I was regularly poked or kicked to wake up. Despite the fatigue and stresses of each day, my nights were more sleepless than optimal due to this unfortunate affliction.

Probably because of this, I was sometimes selfish in assigning the roster for radio monitoring at night. I usually took the first and last shift. This meant that I had a chance at the most continuous period of uninterrupted sleep despite my snoring. In my defense, I felt that if I was fatigued I would not make the best decisions for the patrol during the next day.

Being on radio watch meant more than just monitoring for calls from the TOC. We also had to be attuned to the sounds of the jungle, listening for any noise indicating that the enemy was moving nearby. Since the jungle canopy blocked any moonlight, the nights were completely dark and sounds were the only means of detecting the presence of others in our vicinity. I don't remember the ambient jungle sounds being easily attributable to any specific animal such as they were in the old Tarzan movies; they seemed to produce a constant background buzzing.

Sitting in the blacked-out jungle in the middle of the night listening for a tell-tale snapped twig, equipment rattle or foreign voice was, to say the least, a unique experience. I don't remember thinking, "How did I get here," or internally reminiscing about more pleasant episodes in my life. It was mostly a constant struggle to stay awake. I had a Seiko watch with glow-in-the-dark hands which was passed around with the radio handset to each person on the radio watch roster. We would check the time often, willing the hands to move more quickly so we could end our shift and return to sleep. One man confessed to me that he had once moved the hands slightly ahead because he was too exhausted to stay awake.

In the morning, if everything felt secure, we would have breakfast in place, which would include a canteen cup of hot coffee or cocoa. The process was the same as preparing the evening meal on the day before. Then it was time to move to another location in the event we had been pursued by visual trackers who could be following our trail from the previous day. We also wanted to put as great a distance as we could between us and any lingering aromas from our meals.

Sometimes our mission was to check a specific area for traces of the enemy and sometimes it was to observe a trail or an expanse of rice paddies. Despite the universality of night ambushes by U.S. forces, most evidence indicates that contact with the enemy occurred in daylight hours during good weather. We conducted almost no night ambushes in Recon.

Although we were not tasked with engaging the enemy, occasionally, if a "target of opportunity" presented itself, we would take advantage of it. However, if two Viet Cong were observed ambling down a trail, it was unknown if they were the point element of a hundred or so of their comrades following closely behind. The decision to engage such a hapless duo was always tempting but risky. If we miscalculated, the result would have been a disaster.

For our noon meal we would repeat the procedure that we had followed the night before for our evening meal—move, eat and move. Regular food was critical to maintaining the energy level required for the stressful, physically demanding extended patrols. As always, if we felt we were close to the enemy we would not cook our meals.

Water was clear and plentiful in the mountains but not without risks in obtaining it. The enemy, after all, spent extensive periods of time there and water was always in demand for rice preparation as well as hydration in the hot climate. In areas where the purity of the water was questionable, we used iodine purification tablets liberally, preferring the nasty taste to hosting the even nastier micro organisms that lived in the water. Some of the anecdotes described later will illustrate the dangers in the constant quest for water.

Everyone had one-hundred percent immersion in the task at hand. With five or even 10 men, there was no one to fall back on or to maneuver to take pressure off if we were ambushed. In the jungle-covered mountains, there were few--and far between--landing zones for a reaction force from the battalion to swoop in to save Recon's bacon. The same restriction applied to any medevac helicopters needed during a firefight. A five-man patrol under duress might be able to carry a wounded comrade for only a limited distance in the heat.

Resupply operations involved delivering food and ammunition to us in the field so we could continue a mission without returning to a firebase. However, they created an additional set of problems: the helicopters delivering the resupplies had the same potential for compromising our locations as they did during insertions. So we had to deal with the undesirable yet essential resupply events as they occurred. Some specific examples will be related in other chapters.

Personally, I was always comfortable in the jungle, except for the presence of the unlovable critters such as leaches and scorpions. Almost immediately upon joining Recon, I felt I could quickly become tuned into the rhythms and currents of the jungle. I attribute this to the fact that I had played and camped in the northwestern Ohio woods as a child and waded, rafted, canoed and swam in the nearby St. Joseph River. Back then, we had conducted BB-gun fights in the local cemetery: 10 BBs per combatant and no shooting at the eyes. One of the strongest links between Ohio and Vietnam was the hated, inescapable mosquitoes.

On patrols, I was so intensely focused on the operational aspects that I never noticed the details of the vegetation that surrounded us. Although the plants themselves were critical for mobility, visibility and concealment, their accurate physical description and botanical names were irrelevant and I don't recall many of their specific attributes. While the jungle was certainly different in many ways from simply a damper Ohio woods, for me the details were unimportant unless they had a direct impact on our tactical situation. Thus, the most appealing aspects of the jungle became a vague background which I can't describe.

Of course the biggest difference in Vietnam was that numerous people were intent on killing me. But even this became another component—although an important one—of the complex tapestry that formed the vibrant and all-absorbing experience of operating in the field. Looking back, it was like playing in a present-day 3-D war game as seen through virtual reality goggles but with devastating, irreparable consequences for careless errors or bad luck.

And so the days would unfold in surprising and ever-changing ways as described later. No day was the same as those before and none that followed had any pattern. As time wore on, the morale of the platoon remained high and confidence continued at a level that contributed to our successes, despite the ever-present dangers. We continued to operate as directed and perform our missions while suffering no enemy inflicted casualties.

Everything we did contributed to my feeling that, at last, this was going to be my war, my way.

CHAPTER 7

Romeo in the Center

★ ★ ★

We didn't realize that our experiences on LZ Clifford would be much more exciting than the sedate patrolling we had performed around LZ Cacti. The first such event was the 40-kilometer (24.8-mile) flight to Clifford in a Marine Corps CH-46 helicopter, a twin-rotor, smaller version of the Army's medium-lift CH-47. It seemed that the Americal Division was chronically short of aircraft and perhaps it borrowed some airtime from our sister service. In any case, when we came barreling into Clifford, still under construction, the chopper sat down too close to the TOC bunker and one of its rotors whacked the tops off of several long-range antennas before bouncing to a stop. Shaken up but no worse for the wear, we moved to our assigned position on the perimeter.

Combat Engineers were busy clearing vegetation and building bunkers inside the perimeter. We would have to wait for them to help us build our bunkers on the outer perimeter. Without the entrenching tools (folding shovels) carried by the regular Infantry, we were helpless to fill sandbags for our protection; the earth was simply too hard. In the meantime we had no overhead cover from enemy mortars.

We had acquired a platoon sergeant just prior to leaving LZ Cacti. He was a staff sergeant and therefore one rank lower than authorized. I had honed my demolition skills at LZ Colt by blowing up old ammunition while still with Company B. Our new platoon sergeant assured me that he was also proficient with explosives. Not wishing to wait any longer for engineer assistance in softening the unyielding dirt to build our bunkers, we secured C-4 plastic explosives and began the process ourselves.

Everywhere on the hill were deep holes between six and eight inches in diameter; we called them snake holes but hoped we were wrong. They were handy for our purposes because we could assemble the demolition charges, place them into the snake holes and wedge (or tamp) dirt around them to magnify the explosive force. Tamping was ALWAYS completed before lighting the fuses. There was a shortage of igniters to light the time fuses so we improvised. Once the time fuse had been attached to a blasting cap and the cap inserted in the C-4 explosive, we would split the end of the time fuse and wedge a match head into the exposed powder. When the charge had been tamped, we would yell "FIRE IN THE HOLE" three times in accordance with regulations and light the imbedded match head with another match. The match head ignited the time fuse which, after burning its length, exploded the blasting cap which exploded the C-4. The time fuse was old and burned unevenly so we always used extra long sections but still ran like crazy when it was ignited.

By our second full day on LZ Clifford we had completed all demolition activities required for the Recon bunkers and felt quite proficient at this task. The troops adjacent to us, who were still waiting for the engineers, asked us to help them get started on their bunkers by blasting some snake holes. We were having fun so we agreed.

To save time, the platoon sergeant and I would set our charges in adjacent holes and time our explosives to explode simultaneously. After the charges were tamped, we would give each other a thumbs-up, yell the warning, light the fuses and run. The Army field manual specifies that after igniting time fuses, the demolitions handler should walk to safety but we ran anyway.

I knew one of the causes of what happened next and strongly suspected another. We were following our procedures and had just ignited the time fuses at two neighboring snake holes. As I began to run, I noticed the sergeant still poking at the snake hole, obviously trying to tamp it a little more. I stopped and yelled at him to run NOW and never mind if the charge wasn't fully tamped. I turned and resumed my run as did the soldier who was assisting the sergeant. When I cleared the blast zone I looked to verify that he had obeyed my order but he hadn't. As he turned to run his charge exploded.

He was lifted about ten feet into the air and thrown about 25 feet. His flying body was partially obscured by the dirt and dust from the blast so I had the dismaying impression of a shirt being blown by the wind. When my charge exploded almost immediately afterward, we scrambled to the sergeant's aid. We sometimes had a medic assigned to Recon and luckily one was on hand that day. The platoon sergeant had come to rest on his back and was not fully conscious. He had no obvious injuries but was unresponsive to the point that some of the dust had settled onto his open eyeballs.

I heard one of the helicopters that were constantly delivering supplies to LZ Clifford beginning to take off for another round trip to the rear area. I told the radio operator to call the TOC and have the chopper turn around to perform an urgent medevac. I knew that the battalion surgeon, Captain Strong, a medical doctor and a good man, was on the LZ and we requested him to treat the casualty at our location and transport him to the helipad.

The emergency evacuation went smoothly. We never heard any feedback about the sergeant except that he would live and be returned to the U.S.

In addition to the excessive tamping, the second factor in the tragedy, I believe, was that the platoon sergeant had only a short remnant of time fuse and decided to use it instead of causing a delay by finding a longer piece. I did a lot of soul searching about this incident, reviewed my actions and concluded that this was an unfortunate accident due to a lapse of judgment by the victim. Of course, the old Army adage dictates that anything a unit does or fails to do is attributable to the officer in charge. As far as I know, my superiors bypassed the adage and came to the same conclusion that I did.

Nevertheless, I was never assigned another platoon sergeant.

It might have been on LZ Clifford that the battalion surgeon confided to me that the battalion staff had formed a betting pool, the winner of which would have successfully predicted the closest date to when I would become a casualty. I had been Romeo for less than two months and I thought I was a shrewd and careful operator in the field. Apparently not everyone agreed.

On another occasion, someone suggested to me that the VC had put a price on my head. I thought this was preposterous and probably just a joke. The only connection to reality could have been the episode when we killed the VC battalion commander near Colt and the story with my name appeared in the Division's newspaper. If they sought revenge, they didn't have far to look for a victim. The VC probably had a copy of that paper the day after it came off the press while it took nearly half a century for me to finally read it.

The terrain around LZ Clifford was different from the rice paddies common to LZs like Baldy, Cacti and Colt in the Que Son Valley to the north: it was characterized by vast, high, steep mountains covered by jungle. We found that we could patrol through an area and miss a significant discovery by fewer than 100 meters only to find it several weeks later. It would be impossible for any battalion to control this huge expanse of densely vegetated terrain with available resources. We would learn this lesson many times.

There was no time to brood over the fate of our former platoon sergeant because the next day, June 5, we began to conduct day patrols around LZ Clifford.

As the firebase was still being built, there was the need to improve security by patrolling the area at the base of the steep hill. One day I took a five-man squad to check the rice paddies east of Clifford. We had worked our way down to the flatland and skirted the edge of the massive hill for three or four hundred meters when I decided to give three of the men a break and take the other two to investigate just a little farther before we returned to the LZ. I left the radio with the lucky three-man patrol base.

We went a hundred meters and were immediately out of sight of our comrades but still hadn't seen anything unusual. So I thought we'd go on a little more, and then a little more until having walked over 300 meters we came to a muddy section of rice paddy that extended well into a small valley in the hill. It was too far to go around on such a hot day so two of us covered one man while he waded across and then he covered us as we sloshed through the knee-deep muck.

On the other bank we would go a little more, a little more until the trail we were following turned to the left, following the contour of thc hill. Thc man on point had an M-79 grenade launcher loaded with a short-range buckshot round. Rounding the corner he suddenly spun to his right and BOOM! He shot downward into what was a crude bunker, killing an inept VC sentry. Reaching down he quickly snatched the AK-47 rifle which the guard would no longer need. I was covering him when the third man noticed that there was a lot of activity not far off; armed men—clearly VC-- were emerging from cover, alerted by the firing.

With no radio, no way to call for support and being clearly outnumbered, we turned and ran, knowing, or hoping, that the trail back to our patrol base was still safe. Reaching the section of flooded rice paddy, I stayed on the high ground and covered the other two as they crossed, one lugging the captured weapon. Then they took up firing positions to cover me so I could follow. Wallowing across the syrupy morass, I was about half way to the other side when my right leg sunk all the way to the hip in the mud.

I was off balance with no solid place to lever my leg from the suction of the paddy. Floundering desperately, I could clearly imagine 10 VC, incensed by the death of their comrade, charging over the high ground to my rear with weapons blazing. Finally I pulled loose from the ooze and found myself on my knees, waist deep in the water but free enough to struggle to my feet and lurch to the far side.

The three of us ran through the hot Vietnamese afternoon back to our comrades and called in artillery on the enemy locations we had observed. The lesson learned was not that you shouldn't go off with too few men; it was that you shouldn't go so far from support with too few men and no radio.

On another patrol which I did not lead, not far from LZ Clifford, a Recon squad found a cache containing boxes of hand grenades, rockets, mortar rounds and detonators. These were blown up in place by a demolitions team.

There were times when no training or experience could explain the phenomena that were presented to us in the jungle. None of our Army classes, none of the war stories--no matter how fantastic or contrived--were adequate to help us understand our encounters with the "weird."

If a patrol followed a trail, it was an invitation to an ambush. To be sure, we followed trails from time-to-time, but prudently we mostly paralleled them, keeping to the jungle as much as the thickness of the undergrowth allowed.

On at least two occasions, as we were navigating through the thickest possible jungle, I saw the point man suddenly freeze in place. When we were moving we were always on alert and this action would occur from time-to-time. Before he could turn to communicate his concern to me via hand signals, I crouched a little lower because I too had detected the presence of an alarming and threatening sensation: it was—perfume.

The aroma was very strong; none of the normal, potent jungle smells could compete. I'm no judge of perfumes but this one seemed to belong to the less expensive variety. It was as if someone had taken at least a quart of the liquid and poured it in this isolated spot in the jungle. There were no nearby trails; there were no streams; no villages; a quick check failed to reveal any bunkers or other human living arrangements.

It must have been some strange and exotic jungle plant or an animal secretion. It was quickly established that no unusual flora were nearby. It was one thing to suddenly come across the powerful smell of the universal Vietnamese fish oil condiment, ngoc mam, in unexpected locations as we had done on numerous occasions. But perfume? I still don't know why this happened.

On another occasion six of us were performing a routine patrol northwest of LZ Clifford, just to be sure that we were not building the LZ on top of an extensive enemy installation. We were following a narrow ridgeline extending from the larger hill above. The patrol had the intuitive feeling of a nice, easy walk through an enemy-free but unusually dark and dank jungle.

The point man unexpectedly stopped and so did everyone else, waiting for him to resolve whatever concern he might have. I have described our elaborate system of hand signals to quickly communicate many conditions with regard to an enemy presence, however, the point man stood still, his hands mute, with a helpless look back at me.

When I moved abreast of him, he pointed wordlessly to the trail about three feet ahead. Land mine? Booby trap? Trip wire? Punji pit? No--leeches. They were about two-to-three inches long and as thick as a shoe lace. We were no strangers to leeches; they had dropped on us from trees or crawled up our pants legs nearly every day. When they fastened onto our flesh, we disengaged them by lighting a match, blowing it out and immediately applying the hot match head to the leech.

A leech is devilishly difficult to kill. There was one preferred method and it was as vengefully satisfying as it was effective. Our rations always included a small salt packet. Apply salt to a leech and it would seem to boil into a shapeless mass of goo like the Wicked Witch of the West splashed with water. The killing of an annoying fly or mosquito was nowhere as pleasurable as pouring salt on a leech swollen with your own blood.

But here we had an unprecedented situation. The trail was covered with thousands of leeches—thousands. They were all rampant, rising higher relative to their body length than a rattle snake. To make matters worse, they were weaving eerily back and forth, cobra fashion. I stepped closer and suddenly hundreds of the nearer leeches stopped weaving and in unison bent toward me. That remains one of my most unnerving and creepy experiences.

So if our mission was to determine if any enemy were present on that particular ridge, my professional assessment was a clear and ringing "NO!" And if any VC decided to go there, they would quickly be sucked dry by those nasty, slimy little devils. Did we need to go any further down that trail to establish these facts? I thought not.

On a routine basis, we squirted insect repellant around our boot tops to prevent the little blood suckers from getting inside our boots and trousers, but the wet vegetation often diluted or washed it off. The leeches would attach themselves to places on our bodies where the clothing was tight such as belt lines and boot tops and the blood was close to the surface. At other times they would work their way into intimate places which we were powerless to protect. On one occasion I sat on a log while taking a break and arose to discover a small pool of my blood where I had squashed a leech.

Were we afraid of the VC? The NVA? Typhoons, monsoons or tsunamis? Malaria? No, none of these. But leeches....

A few days later we were on another day patrol on the northern slopes of LZ Clifford. It started normally enough as we walked through the scorching sun. After the previous episode with the

AK-47 and the rice paddy we knew that the VC were somewhere in the neighborhood.

We stopped for a break in the shade of a bit of jungle and I wandered ahead alone, but not out of support distance this time. A large grassy meadow opened up and I carefully walked into it until I was near the center. I could almost see the top of the hill where the firebase was still humming with construction activity.

Just then one of the many Huey helicopters bringing supplies and equipment to the base was taking off and it flew toward my meadow on its way back to Chu Lai for another load. As it passed over the edge of the clearing, it suddenly executed a sharp turn and began to orbit my position.

As earlier described, our platoon wore the floppy-brimmed jungle hats instead of the standard U.S. helmets. My dark green jungle fatigue uniform was, as usual at that time of day, drenched with sweat and appeared dark, even black, from a distance. I knew that the chopper crews were eager and enthusiastic about eliminating any threat to their vulnerable crafts and could sometimes be considered trigger happy with ground targets.

I froze in more ways than one. There was no place to run or hide and I was literally looking up the barrel of the left door gunner's M-60 machinegun. I slowly raised my left hand, waved and tried telepathy: "Hi guys. It's just me. Don't worry that you've never seen a GI in an open field by himself before. Nothin' goin' on here."

The chopper continued in its tight circle at about 100 feet, possibly calling back to the TOC for instructions or possibly about to make their own decision about me as friend or foe. My guess was that foe would win.

I had an inspiration born of desperation. Slowly I dropped my hand from the wave to my jungle hat and just as slowly removed it. My light brown hair had been bleached nearly white by constant exposure to the sun. If those jokers really thought that a blonde VC was lurking around the firebase, I would be toast.

The chopper finally pulled out of its tight turn and headed off toward Chu Lai. I was left wondering if they were disappointed (Damn!) or relieved (Whew!). The experience also reminded me how one of our greatest assets could easily become an unintentional threat.

A footnote to this episode: The weapon we had captured on our first patrol from LZ Clifford was a Chinese communist (Chicom) Type 56 assault rifle, a copy of the famous USSR AK-47. Against all rules, regulations, orders and good sense, I decided to carry it on local patrols instead of an M-16. I thought it was cool. Many practical reasons, including not being able to share ammunition with the other soldiers if we got into a jam, induced me to resume carrying my M-16. If that bloodthirsty helicopter crew saw someone in dark-appearing clothing holding an AK-47-like rifle in an open field, blonde or not, there would have been only one outcome.

An AK-47 and its clones, despite their legendary reliability, had other characteristics which were problematic in the field. The safety/firing selector was on the right side of the weapon as opposed to the M-16 which had it on the left. Holding the M-16 by the pistol grip in firing position, the right thumb naturally was positioned on the selector, allowing an instant move from safe into semiautomatic or automatic firing mode with slight pressure. Since the AK-47's selector was on the right side of the weapon, it took excessive pressure by the right forefinger (trigger finger) to move it off of safe.

Alternatively, the right thumb had to be moved from the left to right side of the weapon to perform this action. Either way, the action was awkward, time-consuming and accompanied with a loud, unwelcome click.

Another issue was the rear sight. It was a piece of metal about three inches long with a hinge toward the muzzle and a spring to hold it down against the barrel. In the thick jungle, the sight could be rotated up from the barrel by vines and then released to snap back down. The result was a clanging sound that seemed to sensitive Recon ears to reverberate through the jungle like a claxon.

Thanks to my time in Japan, I had learned about 200 Chinese characters, including numbers, which were common in newspapers and signs there. I was therefore able to determine the model numbers of the various Chicom weapons written in Chinese like the Type 56 and differentiate them from the USSR model numbers written in Cyrillic. Often captured rifles were reported by U.S. troops as semi-automatic SKS rifles when they might have been a Chicom Type 56 rifle copy or even a Type 53 carbine.

On June 20th, the winds of fate, in the form of UH-1H Huey helicopters, swept us southeastward from LZ Clifford to LZ Chippewa, from which we would operate for the remainder of my time as Romeo, with a few notable exceptions.

CHAPTER 8

Romeo in the South

★ ★ ★

LZ Chippewa, a well-established firebase, was 27 kilometers (16.7 miles) southeast of LZ Clifford. Like Clifford, it was on a large hill situated near the edge of tall, steep, jungle-covered mountains which crept up close to the coast, leaving scant areas for cultivation. The massive formation was split by a V-shaped valley about 10 kilometers (6.2 miles) deep. The huge ridges on the north and south of the valley were designated by U.S. Forces as the Rocket Pockets, Rocket Ridges or, my favorite, Rocket Mountains. The Southern Rocket Mountains, which Chippewa abutted, would become our new home away from home.

The Rocket Mountains were not randomly named. They provided close access for the VC and NVA to launch rockets into the Americal's brigade and division coastal rear areas, including the Chu Lai airfield. The vast expanses and the ample water sources were ideal for the concealment and comfort of nearly unlimited numbers of enemy. Our job would be to make life uncomfortable for them.

We began with day patrols around the base of LZ Chippewa for six days and on June 24th we extended our reach westward into the mountains. Because getting into our assigned areas took longer in these mountains, our patrols necessarily were normally extended for up to five additional days and sometimes longer. At this point, the TOC logs began to include the number of personnel who were active in the field even if it was only for a day patrol. They indicate that Recon consistently fielded 21 men per day, which was all three squads plus me. This did not mean that we were all in the field together; in fact two squads were usually on extended, independent patrols while one conducted day patrols around the fire base.

We liked the mountains. We would vanish into the jungle in the same way the enemy could. We never felt that the VC or NVA had any special advantage over us there. After all, most of them were farm or city boys and almost no ethnic Vietnamese normally lived in the mountains. While the jungle may have been suitable for hiding, if any efficient movement was required, it had to be done on the few but well-defined trails that only followed the tops of the ridges; the steep mountainsides and rocky streambeds weren't practical for military usage such as transporting rockets. Because of this, the enemy was channelized on these few narrow routes and that made our jobs easier.

We also experienced another situation that had nothing to do with the enemy. When we had moved to LZ Chippewa, the TOC had moved to LZ Gator, 10 kilometers (6.2 miles) east of Chippewa. This required our radio communications to be routed through the Company E Commander, who was in charge of Chippewa and the mortar and security personnel assigned to that base. All Recon personnel were assigned to Company E for administrative purposes although we received our missions from the S-3 officer and battalion commander. We quickly began to feel that the Company

E commander was beginning to take an inappropriate proprietary interest in Recon. This didn't seriously affect our operations but had a personal impact on me later.

We soon found our stride as we moved in and out of our assigned areas in the mountains. On one occasion we killed one VC and wounded another. We also found and reported the same miscellaneous items that the rifle companies would encounter in their daily field activities.

Sometimes we walked off of LZ Chippewa through the surrounding open grassy area that made the defense of the base easier. We were always anxious to reach the edge of the jungle at the base of our target mountains so we could become invisible.

A few other times we were taken by helicopter for an insertion into one of the few open areas in or near the mountains. On one such occasion we had selected an ideal spot on a grassy, steep mountainside near our objective. Helicopter aircraft commanders (ACs) sat in the left seat and the pilot in the right. Most ACs liked to do the flying in tricky situations while the pilot monitored the radio.

In this case the hillside was so steep that no landing was possible; we would have to jump out during a hover. The AC approached the target area with the uphill portion on his side; this allowed him a good view to avoid clipping the hill with the large rotor. The men on the left side of the chopper were a few feet from the ground and had an easy exit. For us on the right, the steep slope created a much longer jump and we crumpled onto the ground, bruised but not broken. This was another lesson learned.

I found an entry in the logs for July 2nd which was unknown to me at the time. The TOC radioed to all the rifle company commanders to submit the names of two soldiers to be interviewed by

Romeo for possible transfer to Recon. It's not clear if any names were actually submitted or if anyone was interested in coming to Recon but no interviews occurred.

On July 3rd, after one year as a second lieutenant, I was promoted to first lieutenant and my base pay went from $473.70 to $600.90 per month. I was paid slightly more than my contemporaries because I had more than four years of enlisted service.

On July 14, we were interrupted from our cycle of Rocket Mountain patrolling to return to LZ Chippewa for two days. A major operation was imminent and we would be part of it. It would be one of two brief absences from the Chippewa area, neither of which was pleasant for us.

We were flown to LZ Dottie on July 17th and walked off the firebase to a night location to the east. That night, the battalion's four rifle companies were providing security at the following LZs: Chippewa, Gator, Buff, Dottie, Paradise and Riverboat South. Three platoons and one squad from various companies were conducting ambushes. The Company C commander was on LZ Dottie, 23.4 kilometers (14.3 miles) from one of his platoons. It was unusual for the battalion to be protecting so many widespread LZs and to have so few units operating in the field.

On the 18th, the dispositions remained much the same with only a few platoons changing locations. On the next day an operation was planned near the Batangan Peninsula south of Chu Lai not far from the coast, an area new to Recon. The Company C commander with two of his platoons, Recon and one platoon of H Troop 17th Cavalry would participate. The 17th Cavalry was attached to the Americal and its main missions were road clearance and convoy escort. The Cavalry was equipped with M-113 Armored Personnel Carriers (APC).

APCs were large aluminum boxes with tank-like treads and a capacity for carrying 11 soldiers. They were originally designed to transport troops across the plains of Europe with protection from small arms fire. One of the VC's main weapons against APCs was the land mine. The combat engineers and the Cavalry worked together on road clearances to eliminate this ubiquitous threat but would inevitably detonate at least one mine accidentally in the process. The other threat was from rocket powered grenades launchers which fired B-40 armor-piercing rockets. These weapons were common among the VC and NVA and were used against personnel as well as vehicles. Because of the potential threats from mines and rocket powered grenades, the APCs were never used to carry troops but instead became heavy machinegun and mortar carriers.

On the 19th a log entry at 7:50am contained information about a VC KIA (Killed In Action) by Recon the previous day. He was apparently an enemy official carrying documents naming local VC who were to receive commendations. A blacklist would be prepared by local government forces based on that information. That was the last mundane log entry of the day.

In the next entry, at 8:49am, the battalion commander reported that Company C was in contact with a platoon of VC in camouflage uniforms. Helicopter gunships on standby at LZ Dottie were scrambled and began firing rockets in support of the two platoons of Company C at 9:04am. At 9:08am, CPT Ebert, commander of Company C, requested an air strike. At 9:50am, CPT Ebert and one other man were reported wounded by a booby trap and evacuated by dustoff (another term for medevac).

As the action escalated and Company C came under increased enemy fire, CPT Larson, Company D commander, and two of his platoons were inserted by helicopter into the area to assist the troops in contact. The enemy was using small arms, automatic weapons, captured M-79s and rocket powered grenades. The U.S. casualties began to mount. In addition to the rockets from the gunships, Air Force fighters dropped napalm and strafed the attackers, artillery was fired from nearby LZs and a Navy cruiser and destroyer provided additional fire support. At 11am the TOC reported that CPT Ebert had died of his wounds.

In the meantime, Recon and two separate platoons of H Troop, 17 Cavalry were proceeding independently to the area of contact. In the process, one of H-Troop's APCs was hit by an rocket powered grenade resulting in severe casualties. We hitched a ride with another group of APCs from H-Troop and we sat with our legs completely on top of the vehicles to avoid any blasts from mines.

As we were roaring along toward the embattled Company C, I listened on its radio frequency and could not tell who was in charge as I could only hear CPT Ebert's radio operator speaking. He was clearly overcome with emotion. In one transmission to the platoons of Company C, he said: "Don't worry, Romeo is coming. Romeo is coming and everything will be okay." It was the saddest and most compelling transmission I have ever heard on a military radio.

At 5:29pm, Company D, which had also been in heavy contact, reported that CPT Larson and six-to-11 others had been wounded and required a dustoff.

As we neared the Company C perimeter, we dismounted from the APCs and followed them on foot, walking in the impressions that their treads made in the sand to avoid land mines. By this time the internal command structure of Company C (the platoon leaders and sergeants) had coalesced and no action on my part seemed appropriate. The battalion commander was overhead in a helicopter and all units were ordered to move a short distance to a huge dry rice paddy where no mines normally were placed by the VC and some respite could be assured for the rattled Company C.

We formed a large circular perimeter with Company C, Company D's two platoons and the APCs of H Troop. I had 19 men with me and we had no helmets, flak jackets, entrenching tools (shovels) or extensive ammunition; we were not used to being in such a known, exposed position. The question arose as to who would command this ensemble and it happened that the lieutenant commanding the APCs outranked all of the Company C and D lieutenants and I outranked him by three or four days. Since he had five behemoth APCs with .50 caliber machine guns and armor plating and I had never led such a large contingent, I deferred command to him. Recon borrowed spades from the APCs and enthusiastically dug spacious foxholes, something we had never done before.

For a comforting period, a four-engine C-130 aircraft orbited overhead and ejected high-intensity flares that illuminated the surrounding rice paddies so that no enemy could surprise us. Knowing the burden of the H Troop commander in assuming control in such an unusual situation, I toured the perimeter, visiting each foxhole and offering encouragement to the Company C soldiers who had suffered such a great loss.

At one point, someone, probably a bold local VC, fired a B-40 rocket which harmlessly swooped over the perimeter. As I continued my rounds from foxhole to foxhole, nearly everyone swore that the round had passed not more than three feet over his head. No further action occurred that night.

> The cost for the day to the 1/52:
> Company C: 2 KHA*; 6 WHA**;
> Company D: 2 KHA, 11 WHA;
> H Troop, 17 Cavalry: 5 WHA;
> *Killed as a Result of Hostile Action
> **Wounded as a Result of Hostile Action
> The verified cost to the enemy: 8 KIA and 1 WIA

That night our perimeter was located 5.6 kilometers (3.4 miles) from the hamlet of My Lai, which had paid an even greater price four months earlier at the hands of a different Americal brigade.

On the 20th, we were moved back to LZ Dottie, probably on the APCs, and immediately flew back to LZ Chippewa where we were idle for two days. During this period, the powers at the TOC were planning another brief absence from Chippewa for Recon.

We were flown 17 kilometers (10.5 miles) south-southeast to LZ Buff, another firebase new to us, on July 23. That night we were to move to search an area about six kilometers (3.7 miles) from the firebase on an extended patrol. After studying the map, I identified a route toward a fairly prominent hill which would aid our navigation in the moderate moonlight.

The TOC was still located at LZ Gator and was too far away for us to communicate with directly by radio. Therefore, we would remain under the operational control of the Company E commander at LZ Chippewa. I was uneasy with this arrangement.

Late on the afternoon of the day we were to leave, I ran into a sergeant I had known in Company B when I was the mortar platoon leader. He invited me to his very spacious bunker for a dinner of C-Rations. As we ate, he handed me a canteen cup half-filled with a purple liquid saying, "Try this. It tastes just like red wine." Sure enough, it did.

I ask him where he had gotten it and he explained that it was grape juice with some vodka added. As we were reminiscing about B Company, I finished my dinner and drink and asked for another since it tasted so good and he complied.

At 8pm it was nearing time to leave on the patrol and I rejoined the two squads that were to accompany me. The principal unknown on this mission was a medic we had borrowed to replace a man who was on R&R. Although he had field experience it seemed clear that he wasn't a volunteer. I was uneasy about this as well.

Also, there was a roving ambush from the security forces on Buff somewhere in the darkness near our line of march. They had been apprised of our movement but as we knew from the Chinese collar incident, two nearby friendly groups operating in the dark presented a potential for disaster. It was an additional worrisome situation.

At 9pm, we departed through a gate in the barbed wire and began the descent to the rice paddies below. After about 30 minutes there was a commotion near the end of our file which violated our very strict policy of noise discipline. I stopped the patrol and investigated.

The borrowed medic had stomach pains and, according to his professional opinion, was too ill to go any further. In broad daylight I might have been able to make my own examination and render my assessment but using a flashlight under these circumstances was out of the question. One option was to return to the firebase which would mean that we could never resume the patrol and reach our objective under darkness. In addition, this choice was just plain embarrassing for the platoon.

The other option was to locate Company E's roving ambush, deposit the medic with them and proceed with the mission medic-less but with minimum delay. Since the roving ambush was moving in darkness on the featureless sides of the large hill and we were doing the same, neither of us knew precisely where we were so such a linkup seemed to be against the odds.

As I sat in the stillness of the night pondering our next move, one of my most acute faculties came to my aid: sensitive hearing. This ability certainly contributed to my insistence that the platoon adopt the most strenuous noise discipline measures. If you are sneaking around in the jungle and trying to avoid detection, idle chatter and clanking equipment work in your enemy's favor.

But the roving ambush definitely had no such scruples about noise discipline. Nearby, I could hear their radio, loud talking and metallic clanks as they tripped along the hillside. I radioed the Company E command post and had it call the ambush and instruct them to stop, stay put and don't shoot me when I brought the hapless medic to join them. In no time we were on our way again.

I know now that the roving ambush patrol was from the security platoon assigned to Company E and its purpose was to operate close to the firebases to protect Company E headquarters and the 4.2 inch heavy mortar crews, also from Company E. We wondered if these noisy ambushers might someday become the ambushees because of their lack of common sense and field craft.

We quickly were at the bottom of the hill and stopped to get our bearings. From my map study I knew the specific compass bearing that would take us to the prominent hill that was our first objective. But in the low fog I could make out only one large terrain feature resembling our hill and it was significantly to the right of that bearing. In the planned direction, everything seemed flat and featureless.

I conferred with the squad leaders and they confirmed my visual assessment. Perhaps we had come to the bottom of the hill at the wrong place due to the problem with the medic. Maybe I made a mistake when checking the map. But there was the objective, dimly visible in the murk. I decided to go with our eyes instead of our brains. Besides, it was easier to just walk toward the visible hill than trying to use a compass to navigate at night.

As a result, at daybreak, we discovered that we were 400 meters from where we should have been. Of course there was no way to sugar-coat the mistake. If LZ Buff decided to fire the 4.2 inch mortars for any reason and we weren't where we were supposed to be, it could be fatal for us. I called up, fessed up and we moved toward our assigned area.

Was it the "wine" that made me choose such a wrong-headed path? I think it was more likely overconfidence in my intuition. However, nothing could mitigate the stupidity of that decision.

That night we settled into our new position, assigned radio watches and fell asleep. Everyone was exhausted in trying to recover the ground we had lost through my error. I could sense an atypical lack of rhythm in the functioning of the patrol and a feeling of disquiet.

Later than usual, we awoke and began breakfast. The man who had been on radio watch at twilight hesitatingly reported that he had seen what might have been a large, white tiger less than 50 meters from our location. Everyone quietly jeered him and I wrote it off as the effect of too little sleep. While not densely populated, this area had too many people to still be inhabited by tigers of any color.

We saddled up and listlessly began the day's patrol. We hadn't moved very far before I heard the alerting two finger snaps from behind. I passed the signal up to the point man and, when everyone had stopped, I went to the man who initiated the alert. He silently pointed to the side of our line of march where three massive paw prints were clearly defined in the mud.

There are times when a leader faces a series of setbacks and then rallies his men to continue the mission under adverse conditions. This would not be one of those times. We tried for two more days to get back into synch and into the flow of the mission but we could not regain our balance. Finally, I took a highly unusual step and radioed to LZ Buff for permission to return to the firebase early.

The Company E commander on Buff replied with some dismay. "You are Romeo. You are the elite. You can't come back before the mission is finished." I think that he somehow felt that our early return might make him look weak and would adversely reflect on him; he was reluctant to act on my request. Although we had been in much more dire straits in the past, I had never requested assistance or early extraction, so I felt that we were owed at least one pass, especially if our present lack of normal functioning could cause a fatal mistake.

The company commander, unwilling to take the responsibility, forwarded my request to the TOC and it was approved. As we trudged back to Buff, an M-79 gunner spotted an individual about 150 meters away on a parallel track to ours; he shouted "VC" and began firing at him. Everyone else turned and also started to fire, blazing away at the man as he began to run, never changing course, never trying to evade or take cover. After an Olympian effort he finally disappeared into a wood line, apparently unscathed.

It was another ignominious performance in an already embarrassing episode.

In another recent discovery in the logs, I noticed that the day before we began this ill-fated patrol, two artillery pieces were airlifted to Buff solely to support our mission. This was unknown to me at the time and was no small undertaking, requiring approval at a level above the battalion. Even if I had had this knowledge, I still would have spent all of my carefully accumulated moral-high-ground chips to bring about our early return to Buff.

I'll describe much later in this narrative how this episode impacted me with regard to the Company E commander

If, after returning to Buff with our tails between our legs, we thought we would spend some time sorting out the problems and soothing our nerves, we were very, very wrong. The next day was July 29 and 19 of us were inserted on a combat assault seven kilometers (4.3 miles) northeast of Buff and three kilometers (1.8 miles) from the hill where Company B and my mortar platoon had fought the grass fire not far from the Tra Bong River.

This was an area of villages, low hills and rice paddies with no clear-running streams like we were used to in the mountains. We patrolled the area without any significant success.

However, during this patrol, another incident occurred that did not make it into the logs. It was evening and we were looking for a place to set up for the night. We thought we could pass through some eight-foot-tall elephant grass with little effort. Although vegetation is seldom accurately represented on a map, we had a feeling that this patch of thick, tough stalks with long, sharp-edged leaves would not extend far, so we charged ahead.

The point man was a good, solid soldier and an asset to Recon. His nickname was Stumpy, a reference to his height. The elephant grass was so thick that it was impossible to edge between the stalks and we couldn't use machetes because of the noise. We had to physically push them down and step over them. This was accomplished by holding a rifle above your head, jumping toward the grass and letting your body weight push the stalks forward to the ground; they would bend but not snap off at their roots. This would gain about four feet and then the process had to be repeated. It was a hot, exhausting procedure and the dry, crumbled bits of grass worked their way into every opening in our uniforms and stuck to our sweaty skin.

Night had fallen and the progress was maddening, not only because it was slow but also because it was noisy. Despite everything, no one suggested that we retrace our steps. We might break out of the grass in only a few more feet, but we couldn't tell that because the darkness and thickness of the leaves severely limited our vision. Of course, we also knew that if we turned right or left we might be only a few feet from open spaces, but it was just as likely that such a move could add a hundred meters to our trek.

Stumpy was soon worn out and I didn't want a heat exhaustion casualty in these circumstances. Others stepped forward and were overcome in their turn. I did my share and fell to the side like the rest. We had been low on water to begin with and were hoping to find a small stream running down from the low hills. But now everyone was using more water than usual due to the heat and demanding effort. We finally broke out of the thicket and we were a collective mess.

There are few more dangerous conditions for a competent unit in a combat zone than for exhausted men to be led by an exhausted leader at night in an unfamiliar area. We needed rest but we needed water more. The Tra Bong River was only 200 meters away.

I tried to picture the map in my head. I knew that our position on the Tra Bong was about 20 kilometers (12.4 miles) from where it emptied into the South China Sea. More significantly, the river probably extended over 100 kilometers (62 miles) upstream with farms and villages located all along its banks. It was like an open sewer carrying agricultural chemicals and human and animal waste downstream toward the open sea.

Knowing this, could we drink from it? In our condition, the answer was "yes" because there was no alternative. I cautioned everyone to use extra water purification tablets. I don't know what they actually did but we suffered no reportable adverse effects.

On August 4th, we were extracted by helicopter and returned to LZ Chippewa.

CHAPTER 9

Return to Chippewa

★ ★ ★

Our stay on LZ Chippewa lasted one day and we walked off the firebase on August 4th to return to the Rocket Mountains. We began with two squads patrolling with me and one squad operating independently, all in the field simultaneously. Later one squad would rest at Chippewa while the other two patrolled, as was our normal practice. A wide range of events—from the routine to the exciting and quirky--ensued in the mountains beginning at this point, the order and times of which are not important.

Sometimes, when patrolling in the Rocket Mountains and elsewhere with Recon, strange associations would pass through my mind and some of these were associated with music.

We would move smoothly through the jungle like a silent, well-coordinated, efficient machine. Everyone was alert and attuned to the environment. At these times a melody would begin a loop in my head, pleasantly repeating over and over. It was a song that we had played in the high school band and had been popularly recorded by Glenn Miller in 1942. It was "American Patrol" and had a catchy melody that, once heard, remained unforgettable. There we were, an

American patrol, with "American Patrol" providing me with continuous background music.

Another time, at some distance from LZ Chippewa, six of us heard some unusual tapping sounds. We moved closer to investigate and the sounds became sharp, pounding whacks. One of the men had encountered a similar situation before and identified the sounds as the activities of wood cutters, who were normally civilians. It was highly unusual to encounter civilians this deep in the mountains.

We moved closer to check them out and were crossing an open, grassy area. Suddenly the point man froze, snapped his fingers twice for attention, pointed to a wood line about 50 meters away and we all went prone in the eight-to-twelve inch high grass. Walking along the wood line was an old man with a white beard and a woman, both carrying long poles and axes. What were the poles for? Making shelters for the VC? Reinforcing caves for the NVA? Antenna supports? Or some other purpose we could not guess? In any case we did not want to be spotted by anyone so far from help.

As I lay in the dry, brittle grass, some pollen went up my nose and I had to stifle a sneeze. Suddenly a thought flashed into my head: holzhacker—the old man and woman were holzhackers, the German word for wood choppers. Somewhere I had picked up that word but never had an occasion to use it; now it was so perfect for these people. As the holzhackers moved slowly along the wood line, another association took over. "Wood chopper" gave way to "Woodchopper's Ball," a Woody Herman song recorded in 1939 which I had played again and again on my old hifi record player as a teenager. Lying immobile in the grass, with nowhere to go for the time being, "Woodchopper's Ball," upbeat and lively, began to play from my memory. For the remainder of that patrol, the "Holzhacker's Theme" replaced "American Patrol" as the unquenchable musical loop.

It may have been on that same patrol that we came across an old night location of an American Infantry company. The standard procedure for a unit the size of a company was to form a ring of foxholes (the perimeter) and to place the mortars, company headquarters and reaction force somewhere in the middle. The company could stay there for several days to conduct local patrols or possibly move on the next day. This night location was about 40 meters in diameter in a fairly large open field, an unusual feature in the mountains.

It was easy to determine that this was an American encampment because the enemy never set up in the open. We were leery about checking the area because sometimes American units booby-trapped their old positions.

When we finally moved in, we found a bonanza. When in the field with five men, a resupply was always a tricky event. As described in a previous chapter, we were always loathe to receive a resupply and took great pains to evacuate immediately from an area where we had to have one. It was clear that this American unit had been resupplied during its time at this location.

First we found discarded, unopened C-Rations in plentiful supply; this meant we would not need an unwanted but essential resupply for ourselves as soon as we had expected. The squad leader discovered a clean, unused towel which he immediately used to replace the ragged one he used as a sweat scarf. I found a recent copy of the Chicago Tribune and discovered that my Boeing stock was still in the doldrums. More exciting were some letters that the soldiers had received and simply discarded on-site. They were from wives and girlfriends and verged on the pornographic, brightening our day and putting to shame the paperbacks that we read as will be described later.

I was puzzled by the thought that an American commander had allowed so many usable supplies to be abandoned for inevitable use by the enemy. I was equally puzzled by why the enemy or even civilians had not yet scavenged the position as we had. Nevertheless, we gathered all remaining usable items and destroyed as much as we could.

At some point during this period, the summer monsoon arrived but I was so focused on all other details of our operations that I didn't see it coming. It dawned on me one night in the mountains.

Previously I had acquired a four-foot square piece of green plastic from a VC who would no longer need it. It folded neatly and took up little room in my jungle fatigue pocket which it shared with my rations for each patrol. I used it for a ground cloth and as partial poncho during light rain.

But that night the monsoon had descended in force and I was shivering beneath my small square of plastic, unable to sleep. We slept clustered around the radio so we could each take a share of the nighttime watch. A new man was lying beside me and, unlike the rest of us, he carried a rucksack which allowed him to have a waterproof poncho and a lightweight, warm, easy-to-dry poncho liner. Without any fanfare, he slid part of his poncho over me and I had a reasonably comfortable night.

This event reinforced the validity of the old Infantry saying, "Travel light, freeze at night." From then on we all carried rucksacks. Not only did we sleep dryer and warmer in the rain but we could carry more food and ammunition, allowing us to stay in the field longer and increase the interval between the risky resupply operations.

On another day we were taking a break from walking on the steep slopes and filling our canteens in a clear mountain stream. I was restless and decided to check the terrain upstream by myself. I knew the enemy needed water too but would never build a camp near a stream because of our nightly harassment and interdiction fires.

I climb noiselessly (I thought) up the streambed for over 100 meters. It was under the jungle canopy and refreshingly moist and humid but dimly lit by occasionally shafts of sunlight. I approached a slightly level area which had some boulders clustered together.

Suddenly, among the boulders there was a large splash, obviously from a pool formed among the boulders by the stream. Moving quickly, a figure emerged from the pool and crawled uphill away from me and was out of sight in seconds. It was too late to aim and fire even though I was on alert.

The figure, as I saw it then and can see it now in memory, was of a large, greenish lizard with a long tail, short snout and body the size of a young child.

But could it actually have been an enemy soldier in a green uniform taking a solitary bath and scrambling away at my approach? Since I discovered no evidence of human presence around the small pool, I settled firmly on the lizard theory.

Returning to the patrol, I described the incident which was unique in everyone's experience. I was cheerfully jeered for inventing an implausible ploy to achieve the cherished but fictitious goal of the entire platoon: to be removed from the field due to a physical or mental impairment. It was a constant game to invent new reasons why one must be returned to the rear area permanently and escape field duty. My attempt was considered weak and implausible.

Another event in this same vein occurred when we were on a rotation back at LZ Chippewa. Because of the heat, we always rolled up the sleeves of our jungle fatigue shirts above the elbow. This exposed our forearms to the sharp leaves of elephant grass, miscellaneous thorns and rough surfaces of the unavoidable wait-a-minute vines. The resulting long, narrow scratches would fester quickly and narrow tunnels of pus would form under our skin. Routinely, we would scratch the skin off one end of the tunnel and run our fingers along it to squeeze out the pus without giving the process much thought.

One day after a long patrol, I was in the TOC briefing the battalion commander on our findings as we bent over a map. I was tracing a trail with my right index finger when a leech emerged from my shirt sleeve and began working its way down my arm. I hated leeches so I swept it off of my arm onto the floor and stomped it repeatedly. With more time I would have used the preferred method and poured salt or insect repellent on it.

As we returned to the map, the colonel noticed the pus-filled scratches on my arms and offered to apply some disinfectant ointment from his personal tube. My normal response when in Recon mode would have been to recoil and exclaim: "Are you crazy? How else am I going to get out of the field unless these scratches get more infected?" Luckily, tired as I was, I was able to choke back that reply and graciously accept his offer.

Of all the resupply episodes, my favorite occurred in-flight when we were picked up by helicopter from one field location only to be inserted into another in the Rocket Mountains. We had to open the C-ration cases in the air, fairly distribute the choice along with the undesirable meals and pack them in our rucksacks. Everything was made more difficult by the jostling of the helicopter as it executed deceptive maneuvers. The pilot would swoop down into four or five different clearings to confuse the enemy as to which one was our actual insertion point.

It happened that some kind soul had included a case of canned beer in this resupply package but we didn't realize it until we were descending onto the final landing zone. Hoping as always that the landing zone would be cold, we leaped from the chopper and dashed to the nearest wood line. I was carrying the case of beer under my left arm and brandishing my M-16 with the right.

Having entered the trees, we continued at full speed toward our objective, putting as much space between the landing zone and us as possible. Despite the false landings it would be obvious to the VC or NVA that any helicopter landing in this remote area could mean only one thing—and they would be correct.

After about three or four hundred meters—a long distance in the jungle—we stopped to catch our breath and to gulp down a warm but highly satisfying can of beer. I distributed the remaining cans, probably three to each man, which we packed up for later, and we moved out to our objective.

On one of our resupplies in the field there were no landing zones available so the C-rations had to be dropped from a hovering chopper. I was carrying the rucksack with our radio and standing on a huge boulder trying to direct the aircraft to our position so it could drop the cases of C-ration through the trees. I used the engine noise to determine the Huey's position and to guide toward us but it was a slow process. The engine noise would also alert any enemy as to our location. At one point it hovered directly above me as I teetered precariously on my narrow perch on the boulder and I didn't want

25-pound C-ration cases to fall 30 feet onto my head. The crew was rightfully getting antsy about the vulnerable position they were in. So I shouted into the handset over the high-pitched engine noise for them to move 15 feet to the right and dump the resupply. We grabbed the cases and moved as far as we could with the dead weight of the C-Ration cases before we could safely distribute the food.

Soon after we had returned to the Rocket Mountains, we developed a technique to perform trail watching in a more enjoyable manner. With five men including me available, two men would watch the trail and, if the enemy were seen, they would either engage them or, if there were too many, sit tight and report. The other three would be 30-40 meters away with the radio. If there was an engagement, we would advance to reinforce the trail watchers as a reaction force. If the enemy was too numerous, the trail watchers would silently move back to us and we would call in artillery.

A pattern developed when we were trail-watching but encountering no enemy. The reaction force, including me, began to read paperback books to while away the time as we waited for something to happen. Since the reaction force was always in a position where we couldn't be surprised, I saw no problem with this arrangement.

On one particular mission, after some days of inactivity, a sudden flurry of firing broke out on the trail; from the sounds the firing seemed to be exclusively from our M-16s. I ran from the backup location to the trail, sensing that the entire reaction force wasn't needed.

The two trail watchers were standing on the trail nervously looking to the east toward Chu Lai. One of them was holding an NVA helmet, which was similar to the old British sun helmets used in India.

Their story unfolded as follows: Two NVA soldiers were observed coming down the trail from the direction of Chu Lai. The trail watchers engaged them and they fled back down the trail. They were unarmed but were observed wearing empty harnesses of the type used to carry rocket components. One had dropped his helmet.

So the question was: how did two unarmed NVA escape from easy capture or death from the mighty Recon platoon members who were clandestinely monitoring the trail?

The answer was ugly. The two idiots had actually been sitting ON the trail instead of being concealed nearby. Worse, they were bored and reading their paperback books. When the two NVA, trudging head down, nearly stumbled on them, all four men reacted in surprise. The NVA fled back down the trail. The two recon heroes jumped up to engage them but encountered a problem. The man closest to the NVA leaped to his feet only to discover that his leg had fallen asleep and began hopping back and forth on the narrow trail. The other man was on his feet with his M-16 at the ready but couldn't manage a clear shot because his buddy was bobbing and weaving between him and his target. Quickly the NVA had vanished around a turn in the trail.

Ironically, the only prize from the encounter—an authentic NVA helmet—offered a small slice of humor. A date was written in ink on its outer cover, 21-8-1968 or August 21, 1968, the date of the encounter. Apparently, the NVA soldier was following a tradition almost universally embraced by American GIs by writing the date of his last duty day in South Vietnam on his helmet. We had interfered with his plan. Although he had survived, undoubtedly his fate was to return helmetless with his empty rocket harness to an NVA supply depot in Laos, Cambodia or even North Vietnam, get another rocket component and hump his way back to the Rocket Mountains or another launching area.

This was another example of where Romeo had screwed up by not checking on his men. I followed the lead of many angry tyrants by banning books in Recon forever.

CHAPTER 10

Romeo s Last Hurrah

★ ★ ★

After our return to LZ Chippewa we conducted as much surveillance on the major trails in the Rocket Mountains as our limited numbers would allow. Patrols lasting 10 days were not uncommon and we had periodic contacts with the enemy, capturing some weapons. It was not long before events began to gain momentum and drama.

Late in August we were five kilometers (3.1 miles) west of Chippewa and called for a medevac for one man with a badly sprained ankle and another with dysentery. One of our most valuable assets—mobility—was compromised by these periodic and unavoidable medical conditions. We were immobilized to the extent that we couldn't search for a large-enough landing zone for a medevac helicopter so we needed a chopper with a jungle penetrator.

The area we were patrolling was thick with very tall trees, commonly known as triple-canopy jungle. When the medevac was approaching our vicinity, we threw a smoke grenade and watched the smoke rise slowly in the hot, moist air and dissipate through the dense branches. In the end I had to guide the chopper pilot by the sounds of his engine and rotors to an overhead hover.

The jungle penetrator was lowered through the thick canopy on a steel cable from a winch operated by a crewman. It was heavy enough to push its way through the interlocking branches on the top one-third of the trees. I had never seen one of these but a squad leader had had a previous experience with it. It was about four feet long and 14 inches in diameter. Three narrow steel plates were hinged at the bottom and spaced evenly around the base; they folded down to form seats for the evacuees.

Although the helicopter pilot tried to keep the craft at an even hover, it nevertheless made unavoidable jumps and jerks which were transmitted down the cable to the penetrator and made loading the evacuees a dangerous procedure. Finally, after we had attached the safety straps around the two men, I radioed the crew to winch them up to the chopper. As I watched them rise up through the canopy on what must have been a 40-foot ascent, I thought I would rather complete the patrol on a broken ankle than to take that ride.

The seemingly eternal period that the medevac had been hovering over us must have alerted every VC and NVA within several kilometers that U.S. personnel were on the ground in that vicinity. We had to move and more quickly.

From that day onward, throughout the patrol, we had daily contact with the enemy.

On the day following the medevac, we were watching the intersection of two heavily travelled trails. This junction was a typical target of harassment and interdiction fires and recent barrages had shattered many trees; leaves and broken branches were scattered everywhere. We had taken a position behind some fallen trees and large boulders so we could both observe the junction and ambush anyone travelling through it. It was noon and we were preparing a meal.

With no warning, one of the men on the right flank began firing and others soon followed. I crawled over and the man explained that he saw two VC walking directly toward our position and he had fired at them. I had an impression that, contrary to our procedures, more men were preparing their meals than were on alert for just such an event. Was this another case of Romeo's lax supervision that had been reprieved by sheer good luck?

We had no way of knowing how many enemy were actually on the trails just out of sight or what was the fate of the two known VC. We had to resolve those issues before I could decide our next step. Finally, I rose and cautiously moved out into the junction and began to check each trail. Others came out and we discovered two dead VC and recovered one AK-47 along with one hand grenade and some documents. We quickly packed up and moved to another location; lunch could wait.

Later I had another, longer conversation with the man who had engaged the two VC and this is what he told me: "I looked up and saw the two VC, one behind the other. The man behind had an AK-47 but the one in front was not armed. The man in front was bent over peering at the ground and the path he was taking was the same one we used to come into our position." The VC with the AK-47 couldn't bring his weapon to bear in time to save the man he was covering and he was quickly hit himself by the fire from the other Recon soldiers.

It was clear that these two VC were visual trackers who had somehow found our trail and were following us. While it was always nice to be recognized for our accomplishments, this was not the kind of attention we were seeking.

The next afternoon we engaged three armed enemy in two separate incidents; as sometimes happened they all escaped.

As evening began to fall, we were in a stream bed with very steep banks filling our canteens before moving to our night location. One man spotted a VC at the top of a 30-foot bank and opened fire on him. A few others followed suit. The VC disappeared but another Recon man, directly below the bank was showered with dirt and bits of vegetation torn loose by the impact of the bullets.

While all of the excitement was occurring, the rest of us took cover until we could sort out the situation. I wedged myself into a small fold or crease in the opposite bank and looked for a target. One of the new men, finding himself completely in the open, ran over to my modest shelter and, with surprising strength, elbowed me out into the streambed. When the firing had ceased, I received a quick report and decided to vacate the vulnerable area immediately.

We found a feeder stream with a grade shallow enough to climb and were soon free of the point of contact. We hadn't gone another 100 meters in the six-foot-high grass when more firing erupted at the head of the file. I hurried forward to the point man who adamantly insisted that he had fired on three armed NVA in the grass about 30 feet to the right of our column. He claimed he had hit them all and wanted me to check for their bodies so he could claim credit for three kills.

I reminded him that we didn't keep track of individual kills in Recon. Then I assured him that no one, especially me, was going to be thrashing around in the tall, dry grass, 30 feet on the flank of a group of edgy Infantrymen fresh from an enemy contact, just to satisfy his need for validation. We then moved with prudent speed to distance ourselves from the scene of the commotion.

On the August 25th we encountered another NVA but were unable to successfully engage him. I called the TOC with my assessment of our situation. It appeared that the enemy was dispersed in small groups to avoid casualties from nightly harassment and interdiction fire, perhaps living in deep streambeds. They would then converge on any firing they heard in their vicinity, knowing that U.S. forces would be involved and would probably be in small numbers like us. In this way they could outnumber whoever was operating in their area but still benefit from dispersion. If that wasn't enough, we knew that they were using trackers, although they were now one team short.

The next day I called in to inform the TOC that we were down to four meals and low on ammunition. We received no specific reply about a resupply or extraction.

On the following day we unsuccessfully engaged another VC and called in artillery. Later we heard two shots fired not far off and then another nearby seemingly in answer. We knew that the VC never fired their weapons for no reason and these were probably signals. Since we were running short of food, we all dug into the bottoms of our rucksacks so we could pool whatever food that had been overlooked there. We came up with a few tins of peanut butter, some cans of crackers and packets of dehydrated coffee, cream and cocoa. We had a frugal meal that evening and even less in the morning.

We were resupplied in the field the next day (August 28th) and five more Recon men were on the helicopter which brought our strength to 15. We were operating near the maximum range of supporting artillery.

One specific member of that patrol stood out and I remember him clearly. He was very young, very pale and new to Vietnam. We always tried to recruit experienced people but some were reluctant to join us. This kid had thick, yellow hair that stood straight up due to the perpetual sweat. Thus he was called "Straw Head" and would remain so until he could contrive a more personally pleasing nickname that everyone would accept. To make sure that Straw Head was tough enough for Recon, I gave him our radio to carry on this, his first operation.

On the 29th I received an urgent radio message in the late afternoon instructing us to depart our location immediately and proceed eastward as quickly as possible. Moving fast while trying to remain undiscovered by the enemy was never a good option and doing so in the impending darkness was even worse.

Eventually it was revealed why this haste was necessary: a large B-52 bombing raid was scheduled for that night dangerously close to our location. My reaction was, "Why can't you cancel the bombing raid?" The answer was that such a request would have to travel up the chain of command all the way to MACV (General Westmorland's headquarters) and then over to the Strategic Air Command, etc. There just wasn't enough time. And anyway, we (the TOC) would look like dummies for letting Recon go out to that area in the first place when we knew a B-52 mission was scheduled. The TOC didn't actually articulate this last statement.

My plan was to follow a deep, narrow streambed that ran generally east. It would be fairly easy to travel in but, of course, that meant that the enemy might be using it as well. In addition, the easier-to-use trails on the ridge lines, as we well knew, were always frequented by our armed opponents. On the other hand, on the best day, determining one's location on a map in such a restricted, narrow area was difficult, but at night with strict light discipline, it approached the impossible.

There was also the issue of maintaining unit integrity in a defile where no moonlight could penetrate. First everyone stopped and you blindly ran into the man in front and when everyone moved out you might not realize that you were standing there alone. Noise discipline, one of our platoon's most cherished techniques, was impossible in a brush ridden streambed. Everyone was in a strung-out line and control in a crisis would be nearly nonexistent. I realized that I had been trapped into leading a hated night patrol.

Every 15 minutes the battalion TOC was on the radio asking for our position. I was reluctant to use my red-filtered flashlight to read my map, even assuming that I could have ascertained our location based on terrain features I could not see. I began to report our location as a reference to our previous position: "We've moved 300 meters due east since our last report."

As time wore on and the time over target for the B-52s approached, the TOC became more demanding of our progress and I began padding an extra 50 and then 100 meters onto my reports. Today I strongly believe that the TOC and every intermediate headquarters did the same so that at some point our actual position was at least 500 meter short of what was reported to MACV headquarters.

Worse than the possibility of being bombed by our own B-52s was an alarming event occurring about midway through the trek. Everyone in the inky darkness was essentially an individual with no communications with anyone except the men immediately to his front and rear. Nevertheless, I knew that every experienced soldier in that line felt a sudden jolt as we passed through a particular point. The streambed seemed to widen and there was the feeling that smaller streams branched off on either side. Then, as unmistakable as the strong, distinct aroma from a bakery, came the pungent smell of ngoc mam, the Vietnamese fish sauce condiment.

There could be only one explanation: VC and/or NVA were living somewhere nearby, using the deep ravine to provide shelter from harassment and interdiction fire and for plentiful water. Ngoc mam doesn't lie. Maybe they were more afraid of us than we were of them because they had no way of knowing how many of us there were. They were certainly surprised by their nocturnal visitors and no one likes to fight unprepared in the darkness.

My mind was whirring through possible scenarios—none with pleasant outcomes—until I felt that our last man had moved through that dangerous spot. Despite the hundreds of ugly possibilities that might have occurred, we passed unmolested. It was one of the most lavish and overwhelming gifts of luck I have ever known.

Exhausted as we were from a full day of patrolling and now this nerve-wracking forced march, we still had to put some distance between us and the ngoc mam. The B-52s became quite secondary.

During all of this, Straw Head carried my radio and was always directly behind me. As we all were nearing our physical limits, I heard him quietly weeping. The man behind him took the radio without prompting.

We found a suitable ledge about one-half way up the side of the ravine and everyone, completely spent, flopped down on the dirt and rocks to sleep. I don't remember setting up a radio watch roster.

The B-52 raid went on as planned and not one man on that patrol heard the not-far-off, earth-shaking explosions. I know I didn't.

Straw Head didn't go to pieces or commit dangerous, rookie errors on that patrol despite the tremendous uncertainty and pressure he must have felt on his first operation in the field. He would eventually be accepted as a valued member of Recon. He chose to keep his nickname unchanged.

A review of the log reveals a radio message earlier in the day warning us of the bombing raid. I know I never received it because I didn't take any action to protect the platoon from certain disaster. There are no references to our nighttime travels, the constant requests for our position or our final night location.

We were extracted by helicopter on the 30th and I gave an extensive briefing to the S3 officer about the terrain in the mountains and my assessment of the enemy activities there. We were given the next two days off, if performing perimeter guard duty in a LZ bunker is considered time off.

There is an interesting side story to the fairly intense activity we had experienced over the previous two weeks. The Americal Division, like most U.S. divisions, had a small unit called Long Range Reconnaissance Patrols or LRRPs (pronounced "lurps"). These five-man patrols would sometimes operate in our battalion area of operation, making them no more vulnerable by size or no more "long range" than us. Like us they were restricted to operating within artillery range. They seemed to be excessively sensitive about being "compromised." Some log entries record them requesting, and receiving, an extraction for merely having been seen by an old woman in a village.

By contrast, during our patrols, we would have almost daily contact with armed VC or NVA and report the action to the TOC only to be told to continue with our mission. On the few times when we felt truly "compromised" and anticipated an extraction, such as after having been detected and tracked, we were instructed to carry on. I decided to take these situations as a complement to our resourcefulness and ability to handle dicey operations without ever suffering a single casualty.

A September 1st log entry records instructions for me to report to the brigade commander to brief him on the situation in the Rocket Mountains. I'm positive that this did not occur. One reason was that I had a huge, non-regulation handlebar mustache which would not have advanced my career or anyone else's if I had sported it at the brigade TOC. The other reason was that on September 2 we were back in the field. Perhaps the two reasons were related.

We were inserted back into our old area but this time we were to be under the operational control of our sister battalion, the 1st Battalion, 6th Infantry or 1/6 (1st of the 6th). As we were moving to our objective we came across some NVA telephone wire strung across a trail and disappearing into the jungle on either side. Since it was grey we knew it was NVA because U.S. forces used black commo wire

Quickly I assessed the situation. There was probably a large NVA headquarters nearby because smaller units weren't supplied with the scarce wire; they used couriers. The NVA never left valuable resources like commo wire behind. Elements of that headquarters were therefore on at least one side of the trail. Such a high-level headquarters would have seasoned security forces for protection. It was unlikely that we could get any of our battalion's already committed companies there in time to mount an effective operation.

In the meantime the 1/6 had a specific objective for us and we had little time to get to it. I decided to report the wire and proceed with our assigned mission. I have rehashed that decision many times and wondered what would have transpired if we had remained to find what was at the ends of that wire.

That night we were unable to make radio contact with the 1/6 TOC so we reverted to our own TOC frequency and it relayed our traffic.

The plan was for the 1/6 to conduct a large operation that was expected to flush out a substantial number of enemy. Some were expected to evade to the east along the mountain trails. Our assignment was to set up a blocking force on one of those trails. A blocking force physically places itself in the enemy's path to deny their movement. This is very different from an ambush where, if the enemy is too numerous, the ambush isn't sprung. When this mission was relayed through our TOC, a brave lieutenant informed the 1/6 that Army doctrine for reconnaissance platoons didn't include performing blocking force missions. Somehow the brigade commander intervened and firmly overruled the lieutenant.

On September 4th, a new and ominous situation arose. This was the arrival that night of Typhoon Bess with 50-knot winds. We were in such thick jungle that the wind didn't directly affect us but it ripped a great many leaves from the trees and scatter them on the trails and underbrush. The heavy rain added a sheen to the fallen leaves and to those remaining on the trees so that the entire jungle took on a shimmery quality. Looking down a trail was like peering into a kaleidoscope which had only glassy shades of green. There was another issue: Due to the storm, all aircraft would be grounded so there would be no medevacs, resupplies, extractions, reinforcements or gunship support.

On the 5th we duly set up our blocking position astride the assigned trail amid scattered, glittering shreds of vegetation. There were 10 of us and one man was a newly assigned medic about whom I had second thoughts. He told me he was conflicted about shooting enemy soldiers, which was one reason he had become a medic. He said he wasn't sure he could fight when the time came. He related all of this after we were two days into the operation.

I set up our position with two men on each side of the trail facing west, the direction from which we expected the enemy to approach. Since we knew that the VC and NVA were constantly using the trails from both directions, I place four men in the same configuration facing east toward Chu Lai about forty meters down the trail. The squad leader and I were half way between with the radio. We would be the reaction force if needed and anyone else not in contact would be the backup.

At 11:55am, the 1/6 TOC reported to the 1/52 TOC that their Recon platoon had heard AK-47 fire and hand grenade explosions from our direction. They had no communications with us. The 1/6 commander decided to check our area in his helicopter and gunships were requested.

Just after noon I called in the following report, some details of which did not find their way into the logs: Three VC with AK-47s were walking cautiously on the trail coming from the west toward our position. The dubious medic was sitting beside the trail with his back against a tree and facing in their direction. Two other men began firing at the enemy trio and the medic rolled into the prone position, bringing his weapon into firing position. In the meantime, the VC on point executed a shoulder roll off of the trail and came up firing; the other two VC were immediate struck down.

As soon as I heard the firing, I began a low, fast crawl towards the action. I hadn't gone far when the leaves 10 feet in front of me were kicked up by five or six rounds. I executed a reverse crawl, something I had not done before, and tried a different route toward the action.

About this same time, the bark on the tree which the medic had lately vacated was splintered with four or five rounds, clearly aimed at him. Incensed, he returned fire at the VC and later assured me that he had most likely scored several hits and that the VC's body was probably somewhere back down the trail. He insisted on being credited with a KIA or at least a WIA.

We could confirm two VC KIA and two AK-47s captured along with ammunition, rice and a diary. We moved to a different location where we established another blocking position.

After settling in, I debriefed the four men involved in the action. All of them swore, with no prior collusion, that the VC point man was, in fact, a female. That meant that the near miss I had had was the closest I have ever come to being killed by a woman, although I could be wrong. I'm sure that the medic, based on his own narrow escape, felt the same.

The next day I called the 1/52 TOC, asking when we would be returned to the control of our own battalion. September 7th, the following day, was set for the turnover. In addition, we were directed to return to the location of the NVA commo wire that we had not pursued and to check it in detail.

We had some distance to move on the 7th to follow this directive. On the way, we came to a "Y" in the trail and the point man stopped to wait for me to indicate which fork to take. He was standing in the open in an exposed position and was anxious to move on. Not receiving a response, he turned to me and made an impatient gesture.

However conceited it may seem, I had always felt that I had a good intuitive sense about trails and when and when not to use them. This was reinforced by outcomes that showed my choices had always been correct. But now I was at a loss; my intuition was failing me as well as the other men of the patrol.

They were shocked when I loudly ordered, "Go Left!" thus breaking the most sacred rule in Recon with an unprecedented verbal outburst. The squad was very subdued for the remainder of the patrol. For the first time since I had joined the Recon, I began to doubt my ability to lead it as I thought it should be led.

From the day my predecessor had been blown out of the hooch door at the end of April, no one in Recon had been killed and only one man had been wounded, and that was with a squad on an independent patrol. Now, so it seemed to me, I was losing my ability to maintain that streak.

On the 8th we were back in the area where we had seen the commo wire but it was gone. Instead we found a platform in the trees that was clearly an observation post. When I reported this, the TOC informed me that we would be extracted the following day. On the 9th we were back on LZ Chippewa.

It was a policy in most divisions that officers would spend one-half of their tours in the field and the other half in the rear area bases performing support roles, if possible. This policy served two purposes. It allowed all of the available officers to gain at least six months of combat experience during their one-year tour in Vietnam. This would insure that our entire officer corps would be better prepared for any future conflicts. It also served to prevented burnout. In the field, officers were just as vulnerable to enemy fire as the enlisted men but they also had a heavy responsibility to make correct decisions on an uninterrupted 24-hour basis. Without actually counting my accumulated months in the field, I reflected on my loss of personal control on the last patrol and began to wonder about my own potential assignment in the rear area.

This was the first time I had ever doubted that things were going my way.

CHAPTER 11

A New Assignment

★ ★ ★

During my four-and-one-half month tenure with Recon, I spent every possible moment in the field with at least one of the three squads. Rarely would the entire platoon go on an operation together as a unit and only sometimes would I take two squads with me. Usually, the squads would operate in the field independently, returning at irregular intervals to our assigned firebase. I would accompany a squad on an operation, return to the firebase for a short rest and then accompany whichever squad was to depart on the next mission. Almost always, we had at least one squad in the field.

This created a lot of wear and tear, literally. Although operating in the field with only a few men meant that we could usually move nimbly and undetected, it also meant that we could easily and quickly find ourselves overwhelmed by a relatively small enemy force. Although we had been lucky, no one knew when the odds would change against us.

After that last patrol and as we were winding down, I was informed that I had indeed been in the field for six months and it was time for my mandatory R&R but there was no mention of a new job. After the unfortunate ending of that patrol, R&R couldn't have come at a better time for me or for Recon. I was flown to LZ Gator as the first leg of my journey to the rear area to begin my R&R.

Coincidentally, our new battalion commander was touring the firebases and was on Gator getting to know his officers and making some changes in assignments. He was LTC William C. Stinson Jr., certainly an unsurpassed commander and true gentleman about whom I will have more to say.

It was about September 10th when I was called to the TOC for my interview with the colonel before departing on R&R. It was the end of the day and he had had nonstop meetings throughout. He had a stack of index cards with notes on each officer and he pulled one out as we began our conversation sitting on a pile of sandbags outside the TOC. First he complimented me on my performance with Recon and informed me that I was to become the battalion S-4, or supply officer, which was definitely a rear-echelon position. I thought, "Wow, after all of the close calls with Recon, I'm going to make it through my tour."

Then he frowned and seemed embarrassed. He shuffled the index cards and selected a different one. The colonel apologized and admitted to a mistake. "Ah, you're Lieutenant Lockhart and you're not going to be the S-4. You're going to be the Company A commander."

WHAT!? Company commander? All of the battalion's company commanders had always been captains and I had been a first lieutenant for only two months. I had been a strap hanger as a mortar platoon leader in Company B and then had run around in the jungle with five or ten guys in Recon. A rifle company had as many as 120 men.

He read the stunned, are-you-sure-this-time look on my face and assured me that there was no mistake. Since LTC Stinson was new and didn't know me, LTC Fuller, the outgoing commander, must have thought enough of my performance as Romeo to recommend me for this new role. That was confirmed by log entries from a month before, which I had not seen at the time.

Combat command assignments were essential for the career advancement of Infantry officers. "Command" was different from "leadership." Command occurred at company level and above while leadership, such as I had performed with the mortars and Recon, was at the platoon level. Therefore, every Infantry captain who had not previously led a company in combat would be hungry for this type of assignment. This concept worked side-by-side with the six months/six months policy so that the average captain would command a rifle company for six months and then move to a support assignment so another captain could experience a command position. It was known as "getting your ticket punched."

Lieutenants with career aspirations had to serve as a rifle platoon leader in the field to get a check mark in the correct box before moving to the rear areas. This was considered to be a minimum requirement. However, after promotion to captain, an assignment as an Infantry company commander became the new hurtle to overcome in order to remain competitive. This led to most career officers serving multiple tours in Vietnam to insure that they had the platoon leader and company commander credits in their records to enhance their retention and advancement in a now-crowded field.

Since I had already led a mortar platoon and a reconnaissance platoon in combat, commanding Company A during the same tour--as a lieutenant--would be the equivalent of a golden ticket.

Although it would mean another six months in the field, I was deeply honored by this confidence in me. As I departed for R&R, I left Recon and my comfort zone behind and pondered my future with Company A. I thought I could reset whatever had gone wrong at the end of my time with Recon and function successfully in this new assignment.

And, unless I had miscalculated, it seemed that with the skills I had developed, the experience I had gained in the field and some massive luck, I would continue to experience my war—my way.

PART THREE

VIETNAM ACT 1.5

CHAPTER 12

New with Company A

★ ★ ★

On September 25, 1968, I signed the order assuming command of Company A, 1/52 Infantry, thereby giving up the call sign Romeo and the Recon Platoon to become call sign Alpha Six with Company A. I had been a first lieutenant for less than three months. On the next day at Americal Division headquarters, another officer was assigned to a much-sought-after job which was also authorized at one rank above the one he held: Major Colin Powell became the Assistant Chief of Staff, G-3 (Operations).

Company A had sustained about the same casualty rate as other rifle companies in the battalion since arriving in Vietnam in October 1967. Snipers, mines, automatic weapons fire and mortars took their toll by individuals and twos and threes. Occasionally, a terrible loss would be suffered. This happened to Company A on June 6, 1968, in an NVA ambush which cost six KHA and 23 WHA in an area known as Dragon Valley. I was quickly assured by several men in Company A that they could never go into Dragon Valley again.

I arrived at LZ Bowman late in the afternoon on September 26, 1968, and physically assumed command of the 88 men of Company

A who were present for duty. I was the "old man" in more ways than one. At age 27, only a few NCOs were older.

Early the next morning, the company was moved by helicopter to LZ Young, a nearby firebase. Unlike most firebases, LZ Young was on a low rise amid rice paddies, very different from the hilltop bases from which I had operated with Recon. I did my best to meet everyone with whom I would work directly: my three radio operators, the company medic (like all medics he was always referred to as "Doc"), the artillery forward observer (FO), the mortar platoon sergeant and the three platoon leaders. I don't remember getting a briefing on the strengths and weakness of these key personnel.

This would be my first time in command of other officers, in this case the platoon leaders. In Recon we didn't have a forward observer, normally a first lieutenant, to call in artillery support for us—one of the squad leaders or I did that. Recon didn't have a dedicated medic and now in Company A there were four: one for each platoon and one for the company overall. Of course, Recon did not have mortars, machineguns or many M-79s. For me, taking command of a rifle company was like going from playing checkers to competing in three simultaneous chess games.

Later that morning I received a mission from the battalion TOC: move the company north to a specified area where an Air Force fighter jet had crashed and retrieve the pilot's remains and any sensitive material. It was not the most exciting or pleasurable task for my first assignment as company commander. I called the platoon leaders together to explain the mission and how we would accomplish it. As we stood in an informal group someone pointed to the FO's shirt collar where a nasty-looking black scorpion was leisurely crawling.

The FO wisely froze; the next moves were out of his hands. Naturally, everyone else stepped back and looked to me for the first important decision of my tenure as commander. As would happen so many times, my thoughts raced through all of the training, war stories, war movies and Army publications to which I had been exposed to find a precedent that promised a successful outcome. Nothing appropriate came to mind.

As I carefully watched the ugly insect, softly murmured suggestions were proposed from the onlookers: put a rifle as near as possible to the little devil and blow it away, squirt insect repellant on it, hit it with a rifle butt, etc. None of these actions seem to bode well for the FO, either due to the reaction of the scorpion or from the remedy itself.

As I recall, we cleared an area to the FO's left and I took my map case, neither too pliable nor too stiff, and swept the critter off the collar onto the ground where it was duly crushed. I believe the map case, made of a thick, clear plastic, caused a small scratch on the FO's neck, a small price compared to the alternative and which was soon treated by the company medic. I had passed my first test but more were pending and came due on a daily basis.

Then a radio call came from the battalion TOC and I was harshly upbraided for not having already left the LZ for the aircraft crash site. No excuse, sir. I quickly gave the platoon leaders the order to move out. I had previously provided the instructions that were a daily necessity—the order of march. This was not a time to be creative, so I had given a standard sequence for the company to move in column in this order: first platoon; command group (my radio operators, medic, FO and his radio operator and me); second platoon; mortar platoon and third platoon in the rear. This was a flexible and maneuverable placement of the company assets and each day the order of the rifle platoons would change.

When we arrived at the crash area, I designated two platoons as security and one platoon as the search element. We could clearly see the debris from the F4C fighter: large and small pieces along a narrow, long path, which seemed to indicate an impact at a shallow angle. The search platoon walked abreast and examined everything that was scattered in their zone. No one was glad to perform that task since we knew that the pilot had not ejected before the impact. However, not one objection or complaint was uttered in retrieving the remains of an unknown comrade as we knew he would not have shirked in supporting us in time of need.

I awaited the results of the search at my first field command post as company commander and they gradually came in. Of the objects, I remember a revolver with its long barrel bent into a U-shape by tremendous forces. Singed, classified bombing tables were also retrieved. I will not describe the nature of the pilot's remains that were found and brought to me except that they were few and we could not understand why. A helicopter was dispatched to return our findings to the rear area.

Later, I received a touching letter from the dead pilot's commander thanking the company for our efforts in recovering the remains. I shared the contents with the men, and I still have the letter since there was no place in our crude headquarters building in the rear area to retain such a valuable item.

There was no joy in accomplishing this mission, and the men of Company A and their new commander moved out to meet their fate in other places.

I believe that most of the men in Company A thought that I would try to remake them into a large Recon platoon with all of the seemingly undesirable aspects that would entail. I knew that such a course of action was both impossible and unnecessary. Some simple changes were needed and they revolved around a basic combat principle: don't make the enemy's job easy. Another way to put it is: neither side had an inborn advantage in the jungle and rice paddies. Although the veterans among the VC and NVA had extensive experience hiding in the local area, their recently acquired replacements were no more jungle dwellers than we were. Therefore, the side which made the most mistakes gave the advantage to his adversary.

In order to make real changes in an Infantry unit that had been in Vietnam for eight months and felt themselves to be competent and experienced, a combination of gravitas, demonstrated competence, a rumor of mystique, pure honesty and rational justification were required in varying measures. I also felt that if I added a moderate dose of arrogance to that mixture, it would be preferable to timidity.

Any changes I desired to make would have to be implemented as we operated in the field—there would be no "time outs" for such fine tuning. It would be like making modifications to an airplane while in flight.

The main selling point for my new ideas was that any improvement, however small, would contribute to our success and, more importantly, our survival.

My first and most difficult task was to instill the need for noise discipline. When soldiers are used to being in a group as large as 120 men, they can easily and understandably develop a false sense of security. Shouting, clanging equipment and random discharge of weapons were common. While it's impossible for such a large group to move silently, excessive noise could alert an enemy at a distance and eliminate surprise. He could set up a hasty ambush, having been alerted to our line of march. I was very gratified at the speed with which noise discipline became a habit in the company. In a later account, the depth of that adaptation will surface when I grossly violated it.

Several other reforms were implemented over time. No large group of men could always move unobserved in the open rice fields where we were operating no matter how perfect their noise discipline. This applied to U.S. forces as well as the VC and NVA. So if surveillance was inevitable then it was necessary to present the unit as an unappealing target for ambush or attack.

One way to accomplish this was to keep all weapons at the ready for instant use while moving, with half pointed to the left and half to the right of a column. This way, fifty percent of the company's firepower was immediately responsive to an ambush from either side. Unbelievably, some Infantry companies permitted soldiers to carry their rifles grasped by the barrels and resting on their shoulders or uselessly by their sides, gripped by the carrying handles. Innumerable souvenir photos and movies taken in Vietnam record this breach of basic Infantry practices.

Another important technique in dampening the enemy's incentive to attack also dealt with demonstrating preparedness. When choosing and preparing a night location, we assumed that we were under observation. Therefore, we always paid due diligence to every defensive measure within our capabilities. These will be described later by specific examples.

Probably the basic combat principle that soldiers most often violated in Vietnam was bunching up. Walking in a file, with many stops and starts and the human need in stressful situations to seek companionship, it was easy to take two or three more steps to where the man in front had stopped and chat during a pause. An ambusher loves to fire on a group because it gives more of a chance of hits than firing at a single man. This concept is eloquently described in Leo Tolstoy's short story "The Cossacks" when the old Cossack, Eroshka, explains it to the hero.

This principle is also valid with regard to land mines and command detonated mines, such as our claymores. If a mine is tripped or detonated, the more people clustered near it, the more casualties will occur. Again, photo archives contain extensive evidence of violations of this basic principle. Vigilant leaders were kept busy enforcing this most difficult of rules.

We established a minimum interval between men that would avoid bunching. This interval would increase or decrease depending on visibility as determined by terrain and vegetation. For example, in crossing a large rice paddy, the interval between men would increase so that the number of men exposed in the open would decrease.

The men of Company A responded quickly to the logic--and self preservation--at the core of these changes. Not long after these behaviors had been perfected, we were assigned to secure a pickup zone for another company in our battalion that was being extracted by helicopters, a fairly standard operation. As the other company approached our perimeter, they were obscenely bunched up and carrying their rifles on their shoulders. Our soldiers were incredulous and I heard many comments about the lack of professionalism and poor discipline in this careless mode of operation.

I had an idea about why these types of poor tactical behaviors were tolerated in some units. I felt that some leaders thought that the troops were deprived by being in Vietnam: many had been drafted, they existed day-to-day in mortal danger, the climate was hot and humid, the insect were voracious, their work was demanding and exhausting, etc. Therefore, these leaders were reluctant to insist on "tough" discipline and field techniques, although these were actually less odious than they seemed. In these cases, weak leaders felt they could gain the respect of the men by being lenient. In fact, such forbearance was dangerous to the troops because these bad habits encouraged the enemy to attack any inept-seeming unit.

Although some theories of leadership claim that a leader should know all of his subordinates' names, their family history, etc., I did not subscribe to this idea. I was so busy learning the trade and focusing on leading the company on a 24-hour-a-day basis that I couldn't become familiar with an ever-changing group with an average strength of 100 men. I felt that the platoon leaders' job was to be knowledgeable about their men and their capabilities and to be their direct motivational leaders.

With regard to the platoon leaders, we were not the best of buddies. I wasn't sure of their attitude about a junior first lieutenant assuming command of the company and, frankly, I didn't care. I didn't know what arrangements, if any, had to be made with the existing lieutenants in the company for me to take command or if any of them actually had a senior date of rank. I didn't know if the sources of their commissions were West Point, Reserve Officer Training Course (ROTC), Officer Candidate School (OCS) or direct commission; that was irrelevant. In addition, they were of varying degrees of experience and competence, which were my primary concerns. I can say that I always consulted them on important matters and respected their input while reserving all company-level decisions to myself.

Overall, my leadership objective was to mould the company, which was already by no means inept, into a quietly competent unit with confidence in its professional abilities. There was no need for ego-enhancing, macho unit calling cards to be left on enemy bodies. No catchy mottos, special symbols (ala the Star of David and swastika from Company B), alliterative nicknames or other artificial contrivances could substitute for the feeling of being a part of a high-functioning military machine.

Notwithstanding all of these best efforts, as everyone knows in these circumstances, nothing is certain and even the most disciplined, field-tested Infantrymen can be bested by a vastly superior force. This was where our individual and collective luck was invoked and it served us well.

In terms of permissiveness on my part, this next event happened early on and did not result in a massive breakdown of discipline. One of my radio operators (RTO) was to complete his tour in about 45 days. I eventually noticed that his boots were in shreds and told him to order another pair on the next resupply. He glumly acknowledged the order and later one of the other RTOs spoke to me in private. It seemed that some time before, an RTO had ordered new boots just before the end of his tour and he was wounded shortly thereafter. The connection between a cause and effect was established and a superstition was born. It seemed to me that it was better to have an RTO with his full attention on his job than one who had a constant distracted worry about a hex or curse. I relented and both the RTO and the ragged boots survived to return home.

In another situation within days after I had assumed command, we were moving through a narrow stream bed and the command group was standing aside to let one of the platoons pass. As one soldier, easily identified as a medic by his distinctive bag, moved through, I noticed that he had no weapon and asked him about it. He replied, "I'm a CO," and moved on. I thought, "I'm a CO (commanding officer), too, but I still have a weapon." Seeing my perplexed look, an RTO nudged me and whispered, "Conscience Objector." This was my first experience with this kind of CO. It was not my place to begrudge this man his beliefs; the Army policy was clear. My thought was that in a firefight we would have one less rifle, but then, as a medic, he would be too busy to fight anyway. Also, what kind of courage did it take to walk without a weapon in an environment where deadly encounters routinely took place at close range?

Another change I instituted involved tactics. Army doctrine dictated that when moving in a combat zone, flankers should be used. Flankers are two or more men who move evenly with the point man but are spaced far out on each side. Their job is to flush out ambushes. This proved very difficult to implement in a jungle or in an area that alternated between jungle and rice paddy. The flankers tended to be constantly delayed, out of sight or too close to the main column to be effective. Another flaw with this concept was the potential for flankers to be misidentified and fired on by their comrades as well as being in the line of fire if an ambush occurred. For these reasons I stopped using flankers.

This change was related to the previously described minimum interval between men. If the company was in a file with the correct interval between men, the chance of everyone being caught in the killing zone of an ambush was reduced. Those not in the killing zone could then maneuver against the ambush force. However, if the ambush was very large, there were not many viable solutions anyway.

Another ambush avoidance technique was never to move on a fixed course. This would prevent the enemy from anticipating our future position and setting up a hasty ambush.

I also instituted the concept of an "out" platoon. Even with noise discipline, it was difficult for a large group of men to move clandestinely. One platoon would be designated as "out" and it would operate independently from the bulk of the unit. In this way, if enemy attention was focused on the main body of the company, the out platoon's movement would be less obvious. That platoon would then set up ambushes at night with less likelihood of detection. It would also be available to maneuver against ambushes on the company and vice versa. Every three days a different platoon would rotate "out."

So in terms of tactics and techniques, I employed the best of those I had learned in OCS and added a few that would keep the enemy guessing.

My experience so far in Vietnam told me that the soldiers' primary expectation of their leaders was competence; everything else was extra. To them, this meant that the mission would be accomplished but no unnecessary chances would be taken with the men's lives.

As I had first learned in NCO Academy and later in OCS, everyone could be motivated by actions that were collectively known as leadership. This quality was fostered when most men thought their leader was special in some way: intelligent, dedicated, physically strong, calm under fire, funny, etc. Although my policy tasked the platoon leaders with the principal responsibility for the motivation of their men, I strove to project a compelling, overall command image that would serve as a symbol of unity and authority.

I felt that if the platoon leaders had shortcoming that I had not detected but were obvious to their men, those deficiencies could somehow be mitigated by my own accumulated personal credit. By the same token, I hoped and expected that the platoon leaders would enhance their own credibility with their men by grumbling about, but obeying, some of my unpopular orders.

In Recon I found that the soldiers responded to off-beat or quirky traits in their leaders. When I first became Romeo, I grew a very large, non-regulation mustache. I had also acquired a small gold pinch-on ear ring which I always wore. Both were affectations. Combined with the bush hat, the overall effect was indeed quirky. I think that these things were important to Recon's morale because they exaggerated the aura of differentiation, mystery and danger that the platoon liked to foster. On one occasion I forgot to remove the ear ring while briefing the battalion commander and elicited a mild reproof.

I also believed that humor was important in leaders. If a company commander had solid respect from his troops, he could criticize or poke fun at himself with more good than harm resulting. I was reminded of such an event by Jim Anderson, a fine soldier with whom I have reconnected nearly 50 years after these events. After sending a captured VC nurse back to the rear area, we discovered her meager cache of clothing that she would never use again. I appropriated a small, polka-dotted green bra and mounted it on my helmet like the goggles worn by desert troop in WWII movies. This may have been more goofy than quirky but no one minded.

Since I was now wearing a helmet instead of a bush hat, I followed the tradition of others in Company A by adorning it with graffiti. Most soldiers had their DEROS (Date Estimated to Return from Over Seas)--their day of departure from Vietnam--boldly displayed on the camouflage cloth helmet cover. Other, more witty and profane notices were popular. I decided to take it up a notch and inscribed the Chinese characters for "Good, Bad and Ugly" from the Clint Eastwood movie on mine. It seemed to become another catchy morale builder. Of course the local Vietnamese civilians were completely mystified by these runes which weren't part of their normal alphabet or they failed to make the cinematic connection.

It was obvious that the men in Company A did not want to be commanded—they wanted to be led. I tried to meet this challenge by combining my training, experience and personal creativity—my way.

CHAPTER 13

The Daily Grind

★ ★ ★

I was now leading Company A in the field and it was a 24-hour-a day, total immersion experience.

On October 2, five days after joining my new company, we were set up in a night location less than 900 meters from Company D. I had listening posts of two or three men set out in front of the perimeter to detect any enemy approaching our position. This was another standard procedure to detect surprise attacks.

At 11:55pm, Company D began to receive mortar and small arms fire directed at one of their squad-sized ambushes and the company perimeter. The squad returned to the perimeter with many wounded. Helicopter gunships and a flare ship were dispatched to the area. My first act was to offer Company D support of our mortars which would fire illumination, or flare, rounds to help them see the enemy. We did this until the artillery from the closest LZ began firing illumination and later a flare ship arrived.

My next action was to contact the helicopter gunships that were firing miniguns at suspected enemy locations. We were close enough that a small error would have had severe consequences for us. I had a high intensity strobe light that I used to mark our position; it was a choice between alerting the enemy to our position or marking us for the gunships.

Normally, we in the company headquarters section dug one large foxhole for the seven of us. As we stood watching the nearly continuous stream of tracer rounds from the gunships, suddenly one of them began to jitter and the stream of bullets swayed toward our perimeter. The headquarters personnel all piled into the lamentably small fox hole, and, in the light of the flares, arms and legs could be seen protruding at various angles like a Beetle Bailey cartoon. I still held the strobe light above the tangle.

I can still recall that red stream of tracers as it edged closer to our perimeter and then seemed to bisect it. I was on the radio to the gunships while simultaneously receiving status reports from the platoon leaders on the perimeter. No one was injured.

Company D's losses that night were one killed and six wounded; all were medevaced. The next morning two more men were airlifted out with concussions from the incoming mortar explosions.

Periodically, as we were patrolling in the field, we would receive intelligence reports via radio that originated at the "highest level." We never knew exactly what that level was nor did we care. These reports nearly always predicted attacks by large enemy forces over a fairly extensive geographic area and they were seldom contained specifics. We called these messages the "Asian horde alerts."

Three days after the attack on Company D we received another such alert. An NVA regiment was expected to be moving along an axis which included the area in which we were operating. A regiment consisted of several battalions and was therefore considerably larger than our company. We received no instructions other than to be "on alert." We were moving at a right angle toward this suspected axis, which the map indicated was most likely along a major trail we had yet to cross. I had selected a steep, cone-shaped hill on the other side of the trail as our best location for defense during that night. It seemed reasonable that we could cross the trail, climb the hill and prepare our defensive perimeter before being threatened by any potentially large enemy force.

We walked down a slight incline through the thick jungle and soon the point platoon reported crossing the large trail and beginning to climb the hill toward our night location. We were all following in single file and for some reason the company medic and the mortar platoon brought up the rear, an unusual situation. The mortar platoon's radio was completely dead. It was late afternoon and I crossed the trail at twilight.

As we began setting up the perimeter by moonlight, it immediately became clear that something was very, very wrong: Doc and the mortar platoon were missing. Apparently they had lost contact with the platoon ahead of them in the dark at the trail. The only explanation was that they had mistakenly turned onto the trail and were following it with a fifty-fifty chance of a head-on collision course with the Asian horde. And their radio was dead.

I instructed a platoon leader send a squad back down to watch the trail. Their orders were these: 1. Look out for Doc and the mortar platoon and don't shoot them up. Make contact with them in a way that, nervous as they surely will be, they don't shoot you up. 2. If you see the Asian horde, don't provoke an entire regiment of NVA since you only have eight men.

Then I did the unthinkable. I stood at the pinnacle of our hill and, as loudly as I could, yelled into the night: "HEY DOC! HEY DOC! COME BACK! COME BACK!"

I have already described how the implementation of strict noise discipline was wholly embraced by the company to the extent of becoming self correcting. Immediately I heard from many quarters of the perimeter low-spoken, unkind phrases admonishing me to shut up. I was gratified that my rule of silence had taken hold so firmly and I knew that not everyone knew about the missing men, but I had no choice but to repeat the call several times in spite of the protests.

I reported the situation to the Battalion TOC as an unplanned night activity, which was no lie or exaggeration. I knew that if something went wrong--or worse—as commander I would bear the responsibility as indeed I should. I wracked my brain as to how I could have prevented this mess while I waited to learn the fate of the "lost patrol." I have no frame of reference as to how long the suspense lasted.

Finally, finally the squad returned with the errant group, shaken but intact. When we analyzed the situation we discovered that one of the mortar platoon men had lost sight of the man to his front in the dense underbrush. When he came to the trail in the waning light he mistakenly assumed that everyone has turned right onto the trail so that's what he did. Everyone behind followed him down the trail toward the reported NVA regiment. We all agreed that, on this one occasion, breaking the rule of silence was acceptable. The lessons learned through this episode were lost on no one, especially me.

Later that night, a loud explosion occurred on the perimeter, on the steep side of our hill farthest from the trail. The men claimed that they heard noises like someone scrambling up the slope and then a sigh as if someone had breathlessly reached the top. They detonated a directional claymore mine that they had judiciously deployed at that location. Then they produced a pair of rubber sandals and said that the former owner had been blown out of them by the claymore and fallen back down into the ravine far below. I had never known anyone to detonate a claymore without good cause so I took their story at face value. When reporting this incident to the TOC, I omitted the detail of "capturing" a pair of Viet Cong sandals.

On the eighth of October we were back on LZ Bowman as part of our rotation. Three of the RTOs and I were assigned to a very small bunker, perhaps seven feet wide, 12 feet long, and under six feet high. A makeshift table for radio watch was located at one end and four bunks were at the other; one of the bunks consisted of wooden boards two inches above the bare earth. The doorway (with no door) was between the table and bunks.

On my return trip from R&R between Recon and Company A, I had briefly stopped in Taiwan. There I purchased a short sword, with a 24-inch blade and a wooden handle and scabbard. Upon joining Company A, I had given up my gold ear ring but added the sword. I strapped it diagonally across the back of my rucksack, ninja style, so I could draw it with my right hand. I felt this added to my quirky persona.

That first night in the damp bunker was not easy in terms of getting to sleep. My bunk was across from the doorway and I received the full force of the noise and constant flashes of light from our outgoing mortar rounds. I finally dozed off but within the hour

I sat bolt upright in my bunk for no apparent reason and looked over at the door. There, looking around the bunker with seeming curiosity, was an ugly looking snake with colored bands ringing its body. I could never remember how to differentiate venomous from safe snakes by their marking so I had adopted the attitude that "no snake is a good snake." It was about three feet long and the thickness of a walking cane.

If the snake turned to its right, so to speak, it would crawl directly into the bunk of a sleeping RTO; if it turned left it would be headed toward the RTO seated at the radio table about three feet away. It turned left. I yelled at the man on radio watch to vacate the table and the snake quickly slithered behind it. Since shooting weapons in a bunker is never a good idea, I took my heretofore unused sword, dug the critter from behind the table and dispatched it. I now felt that possession of the sword was more than mere posturing.

On the 18th we walked off Bowman and began operations to the east. I can see by the logs that we were in the same static location for three days. This was something I would never do unless ordered to do so because it gave the enemy an opportunity to study our position and make plans for an attack. We were to act as a blocking force for another unit and there was some type of delay.

I remember this because we were kept stationary for so long that I developed a high level of frustration and anxiety. When an RTO told me that the TOC had called with a request for a complete inventory of every round of ammunition, I had had enough. I radioed the TOC and asked for a confirmation of their last transmission. They repeated it and I replied that their signal was breaking up and I could not make out the message. They repeated it again. I replied that they were still breaking up but I understood that the next resupply helicopter would be bringing six cases of beer and ten cases of soda. No one at the TOC was amused and the request for the inventory was quickly changed to an order, which I could not ignore.

Company A was patrolling in the rice paddies on the north side of the Rocket Mountains, my old Recon stomping ground. We would never operate in the mountains as I had done in Recon. We didn't have any enemy contacts and were getting bored.

There were many smaller spurs extending out from the massive spine of the mountains, forming valleys between them. Most of the spurs, instead of a smooth, even descent from their intersection with the larger ridgelines, formed a series of saddleback humps. In these lower areas there was no jungle; instead they were covered with densely spaced, low-growth trees about 10 to twelve feet high.

I sent a squad to investigate one of these ridgelines as part of our search of the area. There were three distinct humps between our position in the rice paddy and the point where the spur met the main mass of the mountain. The squad had to climb up, dip down slightly, climb up again, etc. over each hump to reach the top. From our vantage point below we could follow their progress as the tops of the thickly growing trees were disturbed by their movement.

Suddenly their progress stopped and quickly reversed followed by a radio call: on the third hump they had come across a large, freshly constructed bunker complex. No single squad would or should take on bunkers alone. We watched as the vegetation was shaken as they backtracked to the lowest of the three humps.

By a fortunate coincidence a group of Air Force jet fighters, or fast movers, were nearby and looking for some work. This had never happened to me before when we needed an objective to be softened up before we moved in. The battalion TOC contacted the Forward

Air Controller (FAC) and put him on my company radio frequency. The FAC was flying in a small, slow-moving, propeller-driven plane from which he could see the terrain from the perspective of the jets. When the FAC identified a target, he would fire smoke rockets to mark it and direct the jets in a way that was impossible from the ground.

As he orbited in a slow circle, I described the situation: the small spur had three humps; my squad was on the lowest hump and the bunkers were on the top hump and there was a sufficient margin of safety between. OK, roger. The FAC fired a marking smoke rocket at the top hump and brought the fighters in. They came in at a right angle to the ridgeline so that if the munitions fell long or short, they would not land on us or the squad.

Whoosh, BANG. Whooosh, BANG. BOOM! BOOM! Rockets and napalm erupted from the fast movers and created palpable heat and a voluminous cloud of white smoke over the spur. However, somehow their attention had been diverted to the MIDDLE hump, which now had most of its foliage engulfed in flames while the top hump was unscathed. It is easy to imagine the reaction of the squad who felt the intense heat of the napalm and ensuing fires.

I called a "check fire" to the FAC; this is a term used to stop artillery and mortars from firing but it did the trick with the USAF. We had a discussion about the location of the target being on the top hump of the spur and, in the FAC's mind, that was where the munitions had been delivered. To clarify the target location further I dug deeply into my OCS training and military vocabulary and now described it as being at the "tippy top" of the spur. Ah, much clearer.

The fast movers came around again, delivered another scorching punishment—on the top hump—and flew off into the wild blue yonder. I was glad that the much afflicted squad could hear the radio transmissions so as not to think that their company commander was careless with their safety.

When we could pass the flames on the humps to search the bunker complex, it was empty. The Viet Cong were not stupid and they had taken advantage of the delays to "un-ass" their bunkers and were back on the main ridgeline to fight another day.

The term "tippy top" passed into the lexicon of Company A as a means of indicating the maximum height of any terrain feature or object.

Normally, the jungles and rice fields in Vietnam were lush and verdant, giving off a feeling of vibrant life despite the ravages of the war. At the opposite end of the spectrum were the results of spraying Agent Orange, the widely used defoliant. As we moved into one such area, no one could doubt that it had been the target of that chemical. The vegetation appeared burned and stunted; no greenery was to be seen. It must have been what J.R.R. Tolkien had in mind when he envisioned Mordor in "Lord of the Rings."

In the middle of this devastation was a large bomb crater, probably from a 500 pounder. Water had accumulated in the bowl-like hollow and it had a poisonous green color that looked and smelled like distilled evil. It was the most depressing place I have ever seen.

A more positive event occurred as we were patrolling on our way back to LZ Professional. We had stopped for a break in a valley just east of Professional and I called one of the long-time RTOs over and asked him if he knew where we were. Of course he didn't so I pointed to our location on a map but that didn't enlighten him either. Finally I informed him that we were in the middle of the dreaded Dragon Valley (sometimes called Death Valley) where the company had been badly mauled in an ambush prior to my arrival. He had been one of the men who assured me when I took command that he would never set foot in there again. At first he looked startled but then took a moment to slowly survey the surrounding terrain. Then he smiled and nodded with obvious understanding and satisfaction. He went down the line of the resting soldiers and had a jolly time by surprising the other ambush survivors about their location. I'll always cherish that tacit expression of confidence in my leadership more than any medals or written commendations.

CHAPTER 14

A Day in the Life of Company A

★ ★ ★

One of the advantages of being the commander of an Infantry company in Vietnam was the commute: there was none. Not only were you immediately at work the moment you awoke in the morning, you were at work during the night when problems frequently arose that demanded your attention. A disadvantage was that no commander ever wanted to take a sick day: he never wanted to leave "his" company in someone else's hands. Fortunately, Doc was always immediately available with some powerful remedies for the inevitable aches, pains, bumps and bruises.

The "work day" often began at first light unless exhaustion from some troublesome night-time issues pushed us into sleeping late. My first awareness upon waking was of lying in the pup tent-like shelter made from three plastic-coated ponchos snapped together. Two RTOs and I inhabited this "hooch;" I was in the roomier center section due to my exalted rank. We slept on air mattresses about two and one-half feet wide and it was sheer luxury compared with sleeping on the jungle floor in Recon. Even in a queen-size bed today, I still sleep on my back and occupy that same amount of space.

In my opinion, the camouflage-patterned poncho liner was the best innovation of the Vietnam War. It was lightweight, quick drying and always provided sufficient warmth no matter how cold the nights. I always slept with my poncho liner pulled over my head to insulate myself from mosquitoes. I have never overcome my hatred for mosquitoes.

There was no need to dress: everyone slept in his jungle fatigue uniform even if it was wet from the previous day. In the field, I never took my boots off because I never knew where I might have to walk or run to within the perimeter during the night. That meant sleeping in wet boots and socks with all the potential for damage to my feet, but the alternative was not acceptable. The best I could manage was to loosen the boot laces. Surprisingly, I never suffered anything more than mild athlete's foot.

Next was breakfast, do-it-yourself style. Unlike my early days in Recon, everyone had a rucksack and carried his own C-rations. Most of us carried a canteen cup in which we brewed packets of cocoa or coffee from the C-ration boxes; some men used a large C-ration can for this purpose. My cup was crusted with residue from previously heated beverages and I would knock the big chunks off from time-to-time. We would heat the water and our main course with heat tablets if they were available. Otherwise we would use the forbidden method of burning a small amount of the explosive C-4. C-4 burned with intense heat but wouldn't explode without the use of an imbedded blasting cap. Everyone had a small C-ration can with air holes punched in the side that functioned as a stove.

Usually about 8am, the TOC would call to see if we had departed from our night location for another day of searching and destroying. Of course, no one had had a decent night's sleep because everyone had spent some part of the night on guard duty or radio watch. I knew it was useless to explain this obvious drawback to beginning our workday this early so I devised a method to satisfy everyone. I would designate one squad to pack up and leave before breakfast and move about two hundred meters toward our objective for the day. They would halt there and prepare their breakfast while we finished ours and leisurely packed our rucksacks. When the TOC called for a report, I would answer, "My lead element has already left the perimeter." This implied that we were all following immediately. It was a thin subterfuge but I was never challenged.

As we were packing up our gear, the mortar platoon would distribute the excess rounds that they could not carry to the rest of the company. We wanted to have as many mortar rounds as possible available in an emergency, so everyone in the company, including me, carried a round. RTOs and medics were exempt because they already had heavy burdens.

Everything we needed day-to-day was packed in or strapped onto our rucksacks, which weighed at least 60 pounds. Only food and ammunition were brought to us by helicopter; however, we received clean uniforms on an unusually long patrol. We had no assigned area on any LZ in which to store personal items to be retrieved at a later time. When we were in the field, we didn't know which LZ we would "return" to. We were homeless.

In Recon, I had spent most of my time in the mountains. With Company A, we were mostly in the lowlands and rice paddies, which were dotted with villages and patches of jungle. A full company simply was not efficient in the thick foliage of the mountains.

The company was normally assigned a grid square each day to search. A grid square was formed by the vertical and horizontal parallel lines printed on military maps. Each line was numbered and they were used as references to identify physical locations. With the reference lines printed at 1,000 meter intervals, each grid square was 1,000 square meters. If there were many villages or dense foliage, one day was about the correct amount of time for us to search each grid square.

The concept of controlling a 1,000-meter square of terrain, even if imperfectly, was to me a practical approach. The two considerations were line of sight and range of weapons. In other words, to shoot at somebody or something, it has to be visible. If all politics are local, to an Infantryman, all combat is local. What happens out of sight in the next province or district is irrelevant unless the enemy forces involved there are moving into your province or district.

If we had an indication of enemy presence on our planned line of march or if we just had an uneasy feeling, we would conduct reconnaissance by fire with artillery. This involved firing onto likely ambush locations along a planned route out to about 1,000 meters. If this didn't stir anyone up, it would make a potential ambusher realized that we had targets already registered from which we could easily adjust fire if we were attacked.

In order to avoid setting a pattern that could be anticipated by the enemy, we would occasionally use reconnaissance by fire on a route that we didn't intend to take. Early in the morning, the FO would walk high explosive rounds down a narrow valley even as we prepared to travel along a different path.

If we were moving over a long distance, we would take one or more breaks in the morning and afternoon, depending on the temperature and terrain. On one such occasion, as we had just stopped and were organizing security, a VC came along an intersecting trail and blundered in the command group, catching us unaware. Annoyed at being embarrassingly surprised, several RTOs opened fire and pursued him back up the trail but to no avail.

When we were searching, we would periodically stop and the platoons would check areas that I would assign, then we would reassemble, move on and repeat the process.

At noon we would stop, set out security and have lunch. We all sought shade for this short respite. The cooking ritual was the same as at breakfast. After a decent interval, we went back to work.

On one occasion the First Sergeant, who managed company affairs in the rear, had thoughtfully arranged for hot chow to be airlifted to us in the field. On the surface it seemed like a good idea: give the troops a break from the constant diet of C-rations. In practice it was something else entirely--from my point of view.

First, the chow had to be flown in by helicopter, which, if the VC hadn't already determined our exact position, would now leave them no doubt. If they had a clue about this being a hot meal in the field, they would then know that we would be immobilized for at least 90 minutes and they could make plans for mortar attacks and ambushes. Then the thermal cans that kept the food warm had to be arranged in a line with one man dispensing servings from each can. Next, everyone had to line up in some fashion to receive their portions. Finally, the helicopter had to come again to retrieve the thermal cans, confirming that we were still in the same location.

Without any deep thought process, I determined that the security of the company was infinitely more important than hot chow and we never enjoyed that experience again. No one complained.

We were normally resupplied by helicopter every three days and the experience was similar to the hot chow event but somewhat shorter in duration. We received the normal C-rations as well as fresh batteries for the radios which were our lifelines for medevacs and artillery support as well as internal communications.

C-rations came in sturdy cardboard cartons bound with a horizontal and vertical length of thick wire. The first time I saw a soldier use the barrel of his M-16 to snap the wire, I started to protest but that procedure seemed to be effective and harmless. The individual meals were arranged in the cartons in 24 flimsy cardboard boxes and they consisted of mostly balanced meals with meat, vegetables, fruit and condiments. Some meals were more prized that others (beefsteak and potatoes vs. ham and lima beans).

Since I was the arbiter of all things in the company headquarters group, I devised a method to insure that everyone would get an equal chance to select one of the more desirable meals. When the carton was broken open, I would turn it upside down so that the description of the meals printed on the individual box tops were not visible and each person in turn would choose a meal randomly. It was soon clear, however, that some of the craftier men had memorized the location of each meal in the carton and could always select the choicest meals even when upside down. I had not wisdom enough to satisfactorily resolve that issue.

With the helicopter-borne resupply of C-rations came the mail. Normally one of my radio operators would segregate the envelopes into piles for each platoon and headquarters and then call the platoons to pick up their mail. He would then separate the headquarters pile by individuals and distribute it as appropriate.

One day, when the radio man was otherwise occupied, I decided to give out the headquarters mail myself. I came across a name I didn't recognize and asked the medic who it was. He replied with embarrassment, “That’s Bogie, your battalion radio operator.” I had been sleeping beside Bogie in the commander/radio men’s hooch for over three months and was never farther than arm’s reach from him during the day. I was stunned that I didn’t know his real name: he was always “Bogie.” His nickname originated from his remarkable resemblance to the actor Humphrey Bogart.

Water was a constant concern, more so than food. Read Rudyard Kipling’s “Gunga Din” for a better description of this need than I can provide. In the lowlands—rice paddies—water was everywhere during the rainy season but it was tainted with mud and fertilizer; in the dry season only the large streams were flowing and they were still none too desirable. I yearned for the mountains that always had clear running streams.

Due to several confrontations with the enemy while gathering water when I was in Recon, my personal supply was probably excessive. I had two one-quart canteens on my pistol belt and a two-quart canteen on a strap over my shoulder just as I had done in Recon. This arrangement insured that if I had to drop my rucksack, I would still have sufficient water. Two two-quart canteens were attached to the rucksack. With eight quarts at two pounds per quart, this amounted to 16 pounds of water and I was happy to bear the extra weight.

Every day one or more helicopters would fly over what I considered “my” 1,000 square meters of Vietnam. As I have expressed before, the helicopter crews were extremely sensitive to anyone on the ground that remotely resembled enemy troops. While we could never express our gratitude for the indescribable bravery that these men displayed on a daily basis, I was always leery about their ability to restrain themselves from shooting first and asking questions later. So the instant I heard the whop-whop of a helicopter’s rotors clutching at the air, I was on the radio to the TOC to find out what business it was about. Even today, that sound makes me uncomfortable.

In the lowland rice paddies, the countryside was not wide open territory such as found in the plains of Midwestern United States. There were tree lines, patches of jungle, villages and low hills that obstructed long-range vision. Otherwise, we could have settled in one central location and picked off the enemy with artillery and mortars. This terrain contributed to our daily surprise confrontations with the VC and NVA: none of us could see far enough away to gain an advantage on the other.

Because of this restriction in long range visibility, one of the platoons would randomly encounter VC or NVA as individuals or small groups. There would be a spate of gunfire in either or both directions and the enemy would disappear. Occasionally, he wouldn't be so lucky and was killed. Rarely were any captives taken. Artillery was always fired in the direction of any enemy evasion but seldom yielded results.

This situation led to persistent tension whenever we stopped and the platoons went on independent searches away from the company headquarters. When moving, everyone was on hyper-alert: what lies ahead? There was no constant in the possible threats and anything known and unknown could be waiting to kill or maim the careless or unlucky trooper. Eventually, luckily, all of the patrolling platoons would return unscathed to the company command post.

My challenge was to keep the nervous soldier with his hair trigger from killing his buddy from another platoon or squad due to lack of knowledge about his proximity. In the same way I kept zealot helicopter gunners from machine gunning our troops, I spent at least forty percent of my time keeping Company A troops from shooting each other.

When I first came to Company A, the radio call signs were simple: I was Alpha Six (the Company A commander) and the platoon leaders were Alpha One Six for first platoon, Alpha Two Six for second platoon, etc. The radio operator for each leader would add "Kilo" to his call sign. When there was something afoot, it was easy to remember the call sign for the appropriate element.

Then, someone decided that it was too easy for the enemy to monitor our radio transmissions and determine who was who. The result was that everyone was assigned a randomly determined call sign consisting of two words, which changed periodically. This meant that in a crisis, I had to remember the latest iteration of the call sign assignments in order to contact the platoons and the TOC. I think this procedure imposed a greater inefficiency than it reaped in confusing the enemy.

One of the daily issues that we all faced regardless of rank was handling bodily functions: bowel movements and urination. I have never, among the many accounts I have read about service in Vietnam, come across any description addressing these needs, although I understand a reluctance to do so. Nevertheless, the reality was that 100 men generated a large quantity of bodily waste which could not be ignored.

Ideally, one could perform these functions within the perimeter in a slit trench latrine in the morning or evening or at the stop for the noon meal. Unfortunately, nature and gastro-intestinal disturbances did not always allow for such fortunate timing. If we had followed a trail into our perimeter location, the platoon covering that sector would use the trail as an open latrine, hoping to surprise any enemy trackers with this variation on land mines. Of course there was never any privacy.

When on a firebase, basic, open-sided outhouses were provided and the waste dropped into 55-gallon drums cut in half. At some point the drums were pulled from under the wooden structures, partially filled with diesel fuel, set alight and stirred until the contents were completely burned. At first I thought that such a job would be a detail assigned as a punishment for minor offences. But surprisingly, this seemingly odious task had regular volunteers who insisted on being chosen repeatedly. Maybe they felt that they could see their efforts come to a definitive, positive outcome as compared to the often inconclusive patrolling that they experienced on most days in the field. In any case, like the men who insisted on walking on point, they seemed to take pride in their one-of-a-kind achievements.

In the field at mid-afternoon, it was time to decide on a night location. Of course, this was limited by the nearby terrain, vegetation and the best guess about the enemy. Sometimes a grassy hilltop which gave good fields of fire for defense was ideal but it would, at the same time, offer the enemy easy observation for planning an attack. Other times a tangled jungle location would prevent the enemy from observation and silent night-time approaches but had poor fields of fire and limited ability for us to fire our mortars. Occasionally, we would set up our perimeter half in the jungle and half in an open meadow just to confuse any enemy trying to size us up.

Timing was also important. If we set up for the night too early, it would be easier for the enemy to plan an attack and to move easily into attack position in the daylight. If we set up too late, we would not be able to fully develop our positions and everyone would be too tired to do their best job in preparing the defenses. Also, in preparing our evening meal, we did not want to display flames from heat tabs (or C-4) at night when they could be exploited by the enemy. Inevitably, despite our best efforts, sometimes we set up after dark. Flashlights were prohibited without red filters. The mortar platoon, the FO and I all had paper-related tasks to perform and it was always more difficult after dark.

Once we had selected a night location (often know as a Remain Over Night or RON), everyone had specific duties to perform. I would designate sectors of responsibility on the perimeter to the platoon leaders by indicating a bush or tree as a dividing point. Foxholes were dug, fields of fire cleared, claymore mines deployed, trip flares installed and listening posts (LPs) sent out. LPs were three or four men who were outside the perimeter to detect any approach by the enemy. The mortar platoon dug in and set out their aiming posts, plotted potential targets, assembled their rounds including the all-important illumination.

Sometimes the site I selected for the night was so rocky that we couldn't dig proper foxholes. By then it was too late to move elsewhere and we were stuck with inadequate shelter from enemy small arms or mortar fire. Fortunately we never suffered casualties due to this error in judgment.

I would get the locations from the "out platoon" and any ambushes we had deployed and encrypt them using a code pad for that day. The battalion radio operator would relay that information and the company's position to the TOC. Later in my tour, instead of manual code pads, we used voice scramblers for the radios. This required an additional man in the headquarters group to carry a scrambler, equivalent in weight to a radio. These scramblers significantly lowered a user's voice and the S-3 officer's normal bass voice came across as a deep rumble.

Then the artillery forward observer and I conferred about preplanned defensive fires. We would select points on the most likely paths that an attacker would take and assign a number for each of them. The forward observer would have the artillery battery fire a smoke round on those targets for confirmation. A smoke round didn't explode like the normal high explosive rounds; the final portion of its trajectory was marked by a stream of white smoke. Therefore, if a mistake was made, no friendly troops would be in danger and if the actual impact was not visible at least the forward observer could reasonably detect where it landed by the arc of smoke.

These preplanned fires had two important objectives in my mind. The first was that if we were attacked in the night, we could readily call in artillery on targets that had already been plotted and fired, thus saving precious calculation time even if we had to make some adjustments. The second was that if the enemy had discovered our location and was contemplating an attack, this obvious and effective defensive action was an indicator that we would not be unprepared. Taken with everything else that we had demonstrated and projected as a professional military unit, it must have given the VC and NVA a reason to reconsider the benefits of a night-time attack.

As evening twilight came, those who were inclined would light a last cigarette; none were permitted after dark. The C-ration meals included cigarettes and full cartons were distributed via another method. Although I was a non-smoker, I frequently enjoyed a free cigarette as one of the few amenities available in the field.

On the perimeter, there were normally three men in each foxhole. This meant that each one would have to be awake for one-third of the night. The platoon leaders with their radio operators and medics were positioned behind their portion of the perimeter for control and, if necessary, to act as a reaction force. Every hour, the person on radio watch at the company command post, located in the center of the perimeter, would query the platoon command posts for a situation report (sitrep). The platoons, in their turn, would query their squads and the listening posts in front of their positions for a sitrep. The TOC would request a sitrep from the company on the hour.

An ideal situation would have been to have a senior NCO who would act as the Field First Sergeant. Since we had almost no senior NCOs and those we had were properly employed in the platoons, I performed the mostly administrative tasks that a Field First would have done. One of these was to assign each company headquarters individual to radio watch during the night. In this I gave myself a rare privilege. I always assigned myself to the first and last shift, as I had done in Recon, so that I could get the longest stretch of uninterrupted sleep during the night. In this way I thought I would not be too tired to make good decisions the next day. Although this seems selfish, to my knowledge, no one disagreed with this logic.

The company headquarters radios were always physically near where I slept and I could easily hear the sounds coming from each handset. Because we were in the middle of a large perimeter, it was not necessary to use the Squelch Off settings as we had done in Recon. Nevertheless, I always slept soundly. The exception was when I heard my specific call sign, Alpha Six. Normally, during the night all calls to the company command post from the TOC and the platoons were to Alpha Six Kilo, the call sign of the Company A radio operator. Whenever a call was made to Alpha Six, I would wake up from the deepest sleep.

Sometimes during the night, emergencies would arise to be handled in easy or difficult fashion. These are recounted elsewhere in this book. Then the morning would come and the cycle would begin again.

We alternated between the field and a firebase every ten to 14 days. On a fire base, life settled into a routine of lazy days and nights that required continuous guard duty at each bunker. This pattern would be interrupted with periodic local day and even night patrols by squads and platoons as dictated by the TOC.

There was always clean drinking water and primitive showers available and the opportunity to dry out field gear if the weather allowed. We would conduct mandatory classes in first aid and related subjects, but the emphasis was on resting from the constant stress of being in the field. While never completely relaxing, bunker duty at night within the barbed wire and other barriers was less nerve wracking than in the field.

Life on a firebase was no guarantee of safety. Periodically, the enemy would mount serious, determined attacks on these bases with dire consequences for U.S. personnel. My only experience with such an event was just after relinquishing command of Company A on LZ Professional and observing a mortar attack on the base. The mortar rounds came in and primarily impacted in the vicinity of our own mortar pits, wounding some of the gunners. We had counter-mortar radar activated which identified the location of the enemy mortars but the damage had been done by the time we could react.

Mortar rounds do not normally create the upheaval of earth represented in movies. While devastating to nearby soldiers, their visual impression is somewhat whispy.

One of the most time-consuming and, probably, most bothersome initiatives for U.S. forces was the anti-malarial campaign. Without doubt, malaria was a major casualty-producing factor, particularly among the enemy. Some NVA units were rendered non-effective with one-hundred-percent afflicted soldiers. While not normally lethal, it was debilitating to combat units, resulting in sick-days which reduced unit effectiveness.

The VC, NVA and Americans used head nets, sleeping nets, repellants, and anti-malarial drugs in a never-ending struggle to control this disease that still kills millions today. It's not a stretch to say that the U.S.'s superiority in logistics effectiveness provided our forces with sufficient countermeasures, but the disease was far from eliminated as a factor in the eyes of senior commanders.

The on-the-ground effect was that American soldiers had a regimen of a daily tablet of Dapsone (little white pill) and a one-a-week tablet of Chloroquine/Primaquine (big yellow pill). These requirements were rigidly enforced not only because there were sensible and humane but there was an implied threat of adverse evaluations for commanders whose troops had a high incidence of malaria.

It must be said that a very small group of soldiers thought that malaria, and its resulting removal from combat, was worth the suffering it promised. However, diligence from the dedicated medics and platoon leaders effectively eliminated this scourge from Company A. Non-malarial fevers of unknown origin (FOUO) were short lived and less debilitating.

Without doubt, the next most dangerous non-enemy-inflicted threat was heat injuries. Again, the best approach was prevention. This meant insuring adequate quantities of water and managing physical demands on the troops. Another facet was the initiatives of the medics who distributed salt tablet to their buddies. During a rest stop on an especially hot day, while everyone else had flopped down to rest, the Docs would check each man for early signs of heat injury and distribute salt tablets.

Personally, as a profuse sweater, I took up to 10 salt tablets per day and carried extensive quantities of water despite the extra weight. My reasoning was that it was better for me take my chances with the side effects of too much salt than to be sidelined by a heat-related injury.

Another, more common but less publicized affliction, was diarrhea. As described elsewhere in this memoir, in the field, water was where you found it and in the condition you found it. Liberal use of iodine tables probably prevented more widespread occurrences. Sometimes known as Ho Chi Minh's revenge, diarrhea became, like mosquitoes and leaches, another annoyance of daily life.

Much has been made about drug use among U.S. troops in Vietnam. My experience as a commander consisted of a single incidence. One of the soldiers had been discovered smoking marijuana while on guard duty and was reported by one of his comrades. This wasn't a case of being a snitch: no one wants his safety in the hands of a stoned sentinel. Luckily this was a time when we had a senior NCO as a platoon sergeant in the offender's platoon. I spoke with that NCO, and "old Sarge" had a "chat" with the young man in question with no further ado or recurrence.

I am not so naïve as to believe that no other drugs were consumed under my watch. However, the powerful motivation for self-preservation in the troops was sufficient to prevent the widespread use like that which would further tarnish the Americal's reputation in the disaster at LZ Maryann near the end of the war.

All-in-all, the health of Company A remained at a high level despite the many threats to its wellbeing. This was a testimony to the diligence of platoon leaders, squad leaders, medics and the riflemen themselves.

CHAPTER 15

Dealing with the Mistakes

★ ★ ★

As we continued our rotation between the field and firebases, some unpleasant and troublesome events occurred. Most of these are not listed in the logs so I can't put a date to them but their details remain perfectly clear to me. They fell into the categories of accidents and outright mistakes and sometimes a mixture of the two. Without doubt, Company A's luck was at work in minimizing the damages. Except for a few of these incidents, as commander, I bore the ultimate responsibility.

Our maps weren't always accurate and, of course, this was frequently cited whenever anyone misread a map or became lost. However, on one occasion we were in an area where I had previously operated with Recon and I knew that navigation was going to be tricky. It was even more so because that was the area where the "out" platoon would rejoin the rest of the company.

My plan was to meet at a certain point on a river. We would purposefully intersect the river somewhere upstream and then travel downstream to the rendezvous point instead of trying to hit it directly. This technique of offset navigation was often used in such uncertain situations. The uneven, 12-foot-tall vegetation made the process even worse.

When I felt that both elements were getting close, I called a halt for everyone. I instructed the platoon leaders to personally go to each man and explain what we were doing and the direction from which they could expect the other element to approach. When I received confirmation that this had been done, I gave the order to proceed.

It was not long until firing broke from the platoon behind our headquarters group. I called cease fire and the radio operator called the platoon leaders to halt. Moving back along the file I quickly found the cause of the firing. The point man of the "out" platoon had come in at a right angle to our group and when he burst through the underbrush, a rifleman unloaded a full magazine on automatic fire at him at a distance of 15 meters.

A miracle trumped stupidity and the point man was unharmed. His canteen, poncho and some C-rations cans were full of holes and a hand grenade had been split open without exploding. Needless to say the point man had a bad case of jangled nerves but to his credit he had the presence of mind not to return fire.

As for the trigger-happy soldier, I gave him a large dose of crazy ex-Recon platoon leader in a towering fit of rage. In the end, we found that the man had poor English skills and may have been mentally deficient. It was another lesson that I learned the hard way.

Back on one of the firebases, perhaps Bowman, we had been doing some housecleaning and found some unserviceable mortar rounds in the permanent mortar pits. Naturally, it was time to have a little fun by destroying something with demolitions. We gathered the rounds, some C-4, blasting caps and fuses and we were in business.

The base was on a very high hill and at one end a ridge sloped down to the valley far below. About 20 meters outside the perimeter wire, another lower, short ridge jutted to the left; this was where the separate perimeter of the 105mm artillery battery that supported us was located.

We took our defective mortar rounds out along the ridge past the artillery perimeter and set everything up. Naturally, I used an extra long time fuse for obvious reasons. We called the TOC to get clearance for the blast and to advise the artillery battery of our plan. Then we lit the fuse. We had the luxury to leisurely stroll back to the perimeter.

As we waited at a safe distance we heard a sound that I had begun to associate with trouble. It was the whop-whop-whop of a helicopter in the distance. It seemed to be coming along the broad, deep valley that bordered the base to the north but we were unable to see it. Finally someone point downward to the east into the valley while the rest of us had been looking up. Our hill was so high that the chopper, flying at normal altitude, was actually below us.

It seemed on a course that would pass the base several kilometers to the north but I called the TOC to check on it anyway. They had no knowledge of its origin or purpose.

Then the craft changed course and began to climb; it was heading directly toward us and the large pile of yet-to-explode demolitions. I called the TOC again with urgent concern but was powerless to do anything else.

We had no signals for warning helicopters away, only for bringing them in. Could we shoot at them as a warning? Would they shoot back? Would they even know it was us shooting?

Relentlessly the chopper came on and on. We tried waving frantically, doing jumping jacks and anything we could think of. Why couldn't the crew see us? They leveled off and reduced speed for the final approach to the artillery helipad and seemed to slowly float over the pile of explosives.

The craft settled onto the helipad inside the artillery perimeter and began to shut down. Pause. Pause. Ka-BOOM.

Perhaps the lesson here was that explosives are just too dangerous to fool around with.

At the same spot where we waited in anguish as the chopper crew blithely, miraculously cheated death, on another day we were conducting mortar observation and adjustment training. The mortar crews were in the fixed pits behind us and we would practice adjusting the fire when the rounds impacted far down the ridge.

We stood in a small group at the edge of the perimeter wire and strained to observe the rounds. Mortar ammunition does not include the easy-to-see smoke rounds like the artillery and the high explosive rounds were sometimes difficult to observe. We had some success but some rounds fell out of sight on either side of the narrow ridge.

We communicated with the mortar crew via radio and we ordered another round to be fired after our last adjustment. We could hear the report as the round shot out of the tube and began its high-angle trajectory. We peered down the ridge expectantly.

Within seconds we heard the unmistakable sound of an incoming round—some defect had caused the round to fall short. We scrambled away from the wire and fell flat before the projectile impacted about 50 meters outside the wire. No one was injured and we were unable to determine the cause of the short round.

Another unfortunate event occurred while we were on a firebase. As always, our mission on the bases was "defense and base development." On this particular rotation I specified two days of rest and then improvement projects to begin on the third day. I conducted an inspection of the perimeter on day three to check on the progress.

At one four-man bunker, the inhabitants were still lounging in the sun. That particular bunker was especially undeveloped and yet no one seemed anxious to improve it. This was despite the fact that the bunker would not have protected the men from a direct mortar round impact. It had only one layer of sandbags on its roof.

Since it was still morning, I gave the four heroes until dark to add two more layers of sandbags for their own protection. I made it clear that I would be back to check. One of the men seemed to verge on stepping out of line with me but I let it pass.

As the sun was setting and before I had a chance to perform my reinspection, I received a radio call from a platoon leader who requested me to come to—the delinquent bunker. When I arrived it was clear why I had been invited early: the bunker had collapsed. The center support had failed and the roof had split in the middle with the two sides falling inward to form triangular compartments on each side.

Now we had an unusable bunker that had to be repaired immediately. But that wasn't the big news; it seemed that one of the men was pinned, unharmed, in one of the compartments formed by the falling roof. As fate would have it, it was the wise guy from that morning.

I called to him to be sure he was not injured and he calmly informed me that he was fine. I decided to supervise the "rescue" so that if something went wrong it wouldn't be the fault of a platoon leader or squad leader. It was ironic that we were removing sandbags from the bunker instead of adding them. It was a delicate task and only one man could stand on the collapsed roof at a time to throw off the sandbags and I took my turn at the job.

I would talk to the trapped man from time to time to keep him calm but he didn't seem to need my help. In fact he displayed some of the cocky attitude from that morning. It then occurred to me that if the roof had collapsed when sandbags were being added to it, why was this guy laying on one of the bunks that lined the inside of the bunker instead of helping.

So I varied the trend of my helpful comments and informed him that I hoped that the rats, snakes and nasty insects which typically inhabited the bunkers didn't bother him while he was immobilized. After a while he seemed to get my drift and became much less obnoxious.

The men were able to repair the bunker to the extent that there was at least minimal protection for the four men that night. It was in much the same condition that it had been in that morning.

During a patrol in early December near LZ Professional, yet another ill-fated action took place. In accordance with standard procedures we had detained a young man in his late teens without an ID card. Because it was nearly evening and helicopters were unavailable, we had to keep the detainee in our perimeter overnight. In my wisdom, I decided to hold him at the company command post instead of burdening a rifle platoon with the task.

The plan was for the detainee to be securely but comfortably bound and to sleep in the command post foxhole. The person on radio watch would maintain surveillance on him. This worked well until sometime after midnight when I was awakened and informed that the detainee was missing along with one of our M-16 rifles.

I immediately alerted the perimeter since this was a potentially deadly situation. We conducted a search and determined that the individual had escaped completely. Within the company, this was a huge embarrassment to the company headquarters for allowing him to get free and to the rifle platoons for letting him penetrate the perimeter, even if it was from the inside.

I didn't punish the RTO who had let this catastrophe happen but I know he was wracked with guilt. I had to report the incident to the TOC, as much as I preferred not to. The logs read that the detainee escaped and took an M-16. This was followed by a request for a replacement rifle. As with other blunders for which I, as commander, held ultimate responsibility, I wasn't chastised by the battalion commander.

On December 28, again back on Bowman, the company headquarters was assigned a much more spacious bunker than usual. It was probably 15 feet by 20 feet and had a large radio desk built in. I received notice from the TOC to provide a platoon for an ongoing operation beginning early in the morning. The platoon would be opcon to, or under the operational control of, the TOC; this meant that the platoon would not be under my command for that operation.

I had been up frequently during the night with minor alarms and taking my turn at radio watch so I was sleeping late the next morning. Suddenly the radio came alive with the opcon platoon leader frantically shouting my call sign. I woke up and tried to understand why he was calling me since he was opcon to the TOC.

From his voice it was clear that he was very upset, even desperate. He explained that he thought that the helicopters which were participating in the operation were dropping some kind of explosives onto his position and he implored me to make them stop. Some of his men had been wounded in the action.

I didn't know where he was located because his unit was being controlled by the TOC so I called on the field phone to find out the situation. The TOC was as clueless as I was about what was happening to the platoon. Eventually, the matter was resolved: two men had detonated a mine and been killed. Nothing had been dropped on the platoon by the helicopters.

This was devastating to the platoon leader as well as to me. In the three months I had led Company A, no one had been killed and only a few wounded. This was not a matter of a career enhancing statistic because body count was only maintained on the enemy. It was a matter of pride to me that the men who performed so well in Company A could expect their leadership to have a relentless concern for their wellbeing. Although this operation had been out of my hands, I took the deaths of these two men personally.

I learned shortly afterwards that the operation in question had been going on for some time. My platoon had been sent to a position that had been occupied several, if not many, times before. This was not uncommon but nevertheless a profound mistake. Whenever the enemy detected a pattern of any kind, such as repeatedly occupying a position, they were not slow to exploit it. These two deaths, in my opinion were completely preventable.

The chaplain came to Bowman a few days later to conduct a memorial service for the two men. At the end of the service, I indicated that I wanted to speak to the assembled company, although the chaplain didn't seem eager for that to happen. I was still livid about the senseless loss and probably should have stayed silent. I used this opportunity in addressing the company to reinforce the importance of maintaining a separation between men to avoid this type of tragedy. Of course it was difficult in a static position for men to always keep a prescribed distance from others; in fact with machine gun crews it was impossible. So I must have sounded as if I was blaming those men for their own deaths. That outburst was yet another of my blunders that I believe was forgiven by the men of Company A.

Another less-than-stellar event occurred about one week before the one just described when the company was flown to LZ Bayonet for a three-day stand down. Bayonet was the brigade's huge rear-area base camp and as such was relatively secure. A stand down was granted every three months and this was my first. In addition, the Bob Hope USO show was at Bayonet for Christmas. The First Sergeant received the troops and relieved them of all ammunition and hand grenades, then assigned them to tents by platoon. Hot showers, clean uniforms and sit-down meals were the priorities in everyone's mind.

For many of the men, getting a full night's sleep without being awakened for a shift of guard duty was the best part of the stand down. For others, it was the chance to relax in one of the clubs on the base, have a cold beer, or more, and listen to current, popular music. A well-stocked PX provided some delicacies for immediate consumption as well as for future use in the field.

I was given an allocation of 15 men to attend the USO show, of which I apportioned four each to the rifle platoons and three to the mortars. The platoon leaders all responded that no one wanted to see the show; they just wanted to relax without any pressure or control. When I relayed this to the higher ups, I was told to furnish 15 men, period. I instructed the platoon leaders to provide the prescribed number of individuals from their malcontents and trouble makers as a sort of disguised punishment.

The base, like all Army installations, had three levels of clubs based on rank: enlisted, non-commissioned officer and officer. They were all very dark inside and featured loud music. I decided to take the platoon leaders with me on a tour of each club to check on the behavior of the troops. Since no one ever wore rank insignia, I felt that we would not be challenged for violating the taboo of crossing rank barriers.

As it happened, when we entered each of the three clubs, a different platoon leader was challenged as being unauthorized to use the facility. I was never challenged and I wondered why. I still do.

We entered the officers' club and went to the bar. Without hesitation, the bartender, an off-duty NCO I didn't know, came directly to me and informed me that one of my enlisted men was seated at the rear of the club but as long as he didn't make a fuss he could stay. I'll never know how he knew immediately that I was the man's commander but it made me feel a little better for not having been challenged as an officer when we went to the enlisted club.

Of course, even in the rear area, there was no lack of some fateful event that caused stress and anxiety. In this case, one of the M-79 gunners had a round stashed in the bottom of his rucksack that was missed in the initial screening. He was either unused to alcohol or had not had any for such a long time that he became quite intoxicated. Back at his tent, he had a fight with another man, became enraged and fired his secret round.

M-79 rounds are basically like hand grenades in that they burst and send over 300 small metal fragments in all directions. A safety feature of the round is that it can explode only after it travels 30 meters. This is what saved everyone in the tent from injury or death as the round bounced inside for only a short distance. The man was taken into custody and dealt with by higher command authority as we were leaving for the field the next day. My command level judicial power was not equal to addressing this offense.

There were times when heavy-handedness, no matter how well-justified, did not fare well with the troops. Near the end of my tour we were being airlifted to a firebase, perhaps LZ Bowman. The helipad was on a part of the base that was slightly lower than the rest. The standard operating procedure for exiting a helicopter was to jump out, bend over as far as possible and quickly move to the side of the craft to a point 15 feet beyond the ends of the whirling rotor blades. The reasons for this were stark and simple: when taking off, a helicopter sometimes teeters side-to-side, dipping the rotor blades dangerously close to the ground. It will always tilt forward when a few feet above the ground to gain forward momentum, again posing a danger to troops in front of it.

I had already landed on Bowman and was observing the last load arrive. This load contained some new men who apparently had not been trained on procedures. In any case, one of them jumped out, stood upright and walked up the incline in front of the chopper, one of the deadliest places except for near the tail rotor blade. It looked to me like the man was going to be chopped into pieces when the craft took off.

I might have been frazzled from a year of leadership in the field, sometimes struggling to overcome a few men's reluctance to do what was best for their own survival. Maybe I was just furious at such a blatant disregard for procedures. I could have just been exceptionally tired that day. In any case, I accosted the man and in a profanity-laced tirade berated him viciously in front of his buddies. I'm sure my message was lost in the passion of its delivery.

The man in question was a black soldier. Today he would be an African American, but then he was black and happy to be called that. It was clear from the look of sheer hatred on his face that he was deeply offended by my outburst. I think we were both quivering with rage but he maintained his silence and stalked off to his platoon area. In retrospect, I realized that he was new to the company and probably had not been properly indoctrinated by his leaders, but it was too late.

I believe that he was convinced by his buddies that I was colorblind in imparting that impromptu behavior counseling, however inappropriate it may have been. Nevertheless, I had again used up a large store of my carefully acquired moral currency. It seemed provident that my time in Vietnam was nearing its end when this incident occurred.

CHAPTER 16

Interacting with the Local Civilians

★ ★ ★

There were many incidents in Company A's relationships with Vietnamese civilians that spanned a range from humorous to sadly dismal. They are presented here in no particular order.

For us, the Vietnamese villagers fell into three categories: innocent civilian, VC sympathizers or active VC. We could never accurately separate them into the correct classification unless we caught them shooting at us or hiding weapons and supplies. We never had a chance to spend time or get to know them individually because we were constantly on the move and could not speak their language. But there were several Vietnamese that made an impression on me despite the short and sometimes indirect periods of interaction.

Detainees were a frequently encountered group. Any adult without an ID card was detained and extracted to the rear area. According to the rules of engagement, anyone who "evaded" was considered the enemy and fair game to be fired upon. Of course, this rule always had to be interpreted by the lowest ranking soldiers.

It doesn't take much imagination to imagine a situation where a peasant farmer in his field may not have an ID card. After all, he doesn't have a wallet. Maybe he lost his ID. Maybe it was taken by the last group of clueless GIs who went through his village. Maybe the government district chief wanted a bribe to issue him one. In any case, when detained, he got a free helicopter ride to the rear area, perhaps 50 kilometers (31 miles) away, for interrogation. If he was declared an innocent civilian, he was escorted to the gate with no return ticket to his far-off farm. On his way back home, he could be detained again with the same result. If he got home safely and didn't get an ID card quickly, he could relive the process. Naturally, the next time he encountered American troops, chances were that he would "evade" and become a legitimate target according to the rules of engagement.

We were moving on a routine search patrol through the rice paddies and villages of the lowlands. In an unusual circumstance, we had a Vietnamese interpreter with us, probably a Hoi Chan--a former VC who had voluntarily surrendered. Also unusual was a group of three older women standing on the trail as we passed instead of giving us the wide berth that was typically afforded. One of them singled me out and began speaking to the interpreter.

She claimed that the soldiers in the leading platoon had stolen 1,500 piasters, about $10, from her. Piasters or "P" was a holdover name from the French colonial days for Vietnamese money; the actual denomination was called "Dong." This was not a great deal of money for us but it was a significant amount to her. I halted the column, radioed the lead platoon leader and asked about the situation. He claimed innocence for his men but, having been focused on the terrain ahead, could not personally verify that a theft had not occurred.

The situation was a distraction and yet seemed worthy of a Solomon-like judgment. Although I had complete faith in the men's dedication to their duties, I knew that some of them had a mean streak when it came to the Vietnamese and sometimes mischief got the better of them. I therefore ruled in favor of the woman and instructed the lead platoon leader to collect 1,500 piaster from his men and give it to the woman. This produced much grumbling but the order was followed and we continued with the patrol.

Apparently I had enough leadership capital built up so that, even if I have been in error, no lasting resentment was manifested by the troops. Later it occurred to me that I—and the men—may have been the victim of a bold and cunning con artist who tried this same ploy on every American unit who passed through her village. I also wondered how many commanders were as soft hearted as I was in this situation.

One day we came upon a small V-shaped valley about 300 meters deep and 100 meters wide at the opening. It was terraced with rice paddies on each side ranging from the size of a basketball court to half a football field. Each paddy was of a different, vibrant hue of green, indicating that they had been planted at different times. It was the most idyllic rural scene I have ever come across.

As we entered the valley we saw a dwelling on the right occupied by a young Vietnamese woman and two small children. The woman was very pretty as young Vietnamese women can sometimes be, but she was clearly careworn, aged beyond her years. She wore the helpless, resigned expression that we had come to expect when we encountered war-weary civilians in these remote areas. No male was in evidence.

It seemed like this was a paradise for a young farmer and his family. The rice could be harvested and used for sustenance and the excess sold for necessities. I stood in the valley and imagined myself in that environment and I felt that I could be happy there. In time of peace it would have been a wonderland. I thought about the husband: Where was he and what was he doing?

We passed through the area without interacting with the woman. The tableau of this disconsolate, incomplete family standing in front of their humble home was a powerful symbol of the everyday misery perpetuated by the war.

Another civilian whom I encountered was unique. We were moving toward a village that had just been shelled by our artillery and was still smoking and burning. Another unit had just swept through the village so we stopped on the outskirts in order not to cause confusion in the wake of whatever action had occurred there. I walked alone into the partially destroyed area to get a feeling of what had happened.

Almost immediately I saw a figure—a man—seated cross-legged on a square of concrete. We often saw these unfinished foundations and I never understood why they remained incomplete. I approached him from his left rear so he didn't see me until I was almost directly in front of him about 30 feet away. He could have had his eyes closed while I approached.

He seemed taller than most Vietnamese, even while sitting. His head was completely shaven and may have had a topknot but that could be a product of my imagination. Although everything about him seemed to indicate he was a monk, his robe was not the ubiquitous saffron; it was of a grey material and from my vantage point seemed of a rich quality.

Why was he sitting so serenely in the midst of such devastation? He must have been there during the shelling. He stared straight at me without making any movement. I stared back.

Tiring of the game, I reached back and drew my Taiwanese short sword, expecting some reaction from this strange man. I was sure he had never seen an American brandishing a sword but his expression never changed. I had an M-16 in my left hand and he could not have known if I might have been a revenge-crazed GI out to even the score for the loss of my buddies in the earlier action.

Logic told me that if this man was a VC official or NVA officer, he wouldn't be betting his life in this fashion. And of course, whoever this was, he was betting his life.

In my adept ninja fashion, I sheathed the sword and stood for a few more minutes contemplating my companion. At last I gave him my best man-to-man Asian bow: not too deep so as to imply his superior position but enough to signal my respect. I would like to report that he bowed back but, alas, it was not to be.

I probably should have sent him to the rear area as a detainee, but I didn't. I returned to the company and gave directions to give my new friend a wide berth.

Some interactions with the locals were not close encounters. On a routine patrol with Company A half way between LZs Young and Professional, we approached a large, grass-covered saddleback hill. We never encountered a hill or ridgeline that was flat or smooth on the top; they always had a series of humps. I sent a squad to check the hill instead of requiring the entire company to climb it for no reason. They reported finding unexpended artillery rounds scattered in the waist-high grass. This was important because the enemy would use such rounds as mines and booby traps. So the remainder of the company trudged up the hill to gather the ammunition.

It soon became clear that a large number of rounds—hundreds—littered the hill and we began to gather and stack them in a double row until they were about four feet high. It was obvious that this was an old U.S. firebase that had been hastily abandoned, not only from the ammunition but from the 1/4 ton trailer and other equipment that we found. We were troubled that an American unit would abandon such deadly material that the enemy could easily find and use against us.

Since the ammunition was too old and rusted for normal use, an Explosive Ordnance Disposal (EOD) team was flown in to destroy the huge pile with plastic explosives. After setting the charges, they ignited the long time fuse as they boarded the helicopter and departed. We quickly moved off of the hill to about 900 meters away where we would set up for the night and wait for the monster explosion.

Late in the afternoon while the fuse was still burning, the artillery forward observer and I were idly standing in the perimeter and I asked to borrow his binoculars since I had none. There was a clear view of the hill and when I focused the glasses on the crest I experienced a stunning surprise. There, in plain sight, was a man looking back at me through a pair of binoculars.

Astonished, I turned to the artillery forward observer, quickly explained the situation and said: "Larry, do something."

Larry, without hesitation, turned to the hill, and, with a large swooping gesture, gave the finger to the interloper.

"No, no, I mean shoot some artillery at him!"

It was a very difficult shot because the long axis of the hill was perpendicular to the trajectory of the artillery battery at our firebase. That meant that it would be easy for the rounds to overshoot or undershoot the top of the hill instead of landing on top of the narrow ridge.

As Larry was ginning up a fire mission, I wondered if the intruder or intruders had disabled the time fuse and perhaps made off with the EOD team's plastic explosives. One way or another, we certainly would not go back on that hill until we were absolutely positive that the demolitions had exploded or that the fuse or blasting caps were defective or inoperable. If Larry could keep the bad guys off the hill until the demolitions exploded, everything would be fine. At the same time, if the artillery rounds landed in the wrong area, the time fuse or other apparatus could be disrupted and cause yet another problem.

Rounds began landing on and around the hill and no more sightings were made of the man with the binoculars. In theory, time fuse has a predictable burn rate but in practice no one would trust life or limb to it as I had learned in Recon. So we continued to wait for the noise and dust of the explosion while we speculated on the fate of the man on the hill if he chose to remained there too long. This was the only time I had been eye-to-eye with an enemy soldier when neither of us could take any direct personal aggressive action against the other.

It was after dark when the big moment came and it was as large an explosion as any of us had ever observed. Unbelievably, a quarter-sized disc of metal was propelled about 1,000 meters from the hill into our perimeter, penetrated a poncho tent and lodged in the thigh of one of the soldiers. Luckily, it wasn't serious enough for an urgent medevac; the patient was flown out in the morning along with another man with a high fever.

No further information was discovered concerning the man with the binoculars.

Some weeks later, another company patrolling nearby came across mortar and artillery rounds that had had the explosives removed, indicating that the VC had in fact been using the abandoned ammunition for improvised weapons.

Back in the field about five kilometers (3.1 miles) southeast of LZ Professional, Company A had another interesting experience. We were moving through medium density vegetation when we crested a hill that provided excellent visibility on the curve of a river and the far bank.

The leading platoon observed seven VC on the opposite bank moving toward the river. When I got to the hilltop I could see them clearly, moving carefully, slightly crouched, clearly on the alert. I instructed the lead platoon to proceed quickly but carefully to the near river bank and deploy for an ambush. I instructed the mortars to set up just behind the crest of the hill.

I asked the artillery forward observer to set up a fire mission to place fire on the opposite bank along which the VC had come. Now, the lead platoon could ambush them as they crossed the river and any retreating survivors would be addressed by artillery. I wanted to use proximity fuses on the artillery rounds which would explode in the air and rain down shrapnel on the target, a much more effective method that the "quick" fuses that exploded on impact. However, it was a cloudy day and the rounds would pass over our heads. Sometimes the sensing devices in the proximity fuses that detected the ground would instead be fooled by the clouds and explode prematurely, in this case directly above us.

Everything was going smoothly when the lead platoon notified me that a village was located between the bottom of the hill and the river bank. This meant that they had to slow their movement to the river to provide security while passing through the village. This caused a delay that somehow allowed the VC to detect the presence of U.S. troops and quickly move back the way they had come. I called for artillery fire which came too late. The VC disappeared up a small valley on the far side of the river.

LTC Stinson, the battalion commander, having heard the radio traffic about the incident arrived overhead in a helicopter. When the VC ran up the valley he followed them with both door guns blazing. Although it was a very bold move, my feeling was that if the chopper was shot down, we would move immediately to rescue the colonel and the crew and it would certainly be in enemy controlled territory. I didn't like to make such moves unless it was on my terms.

When it was obvious that the results of this encounter were unsuccessful, we moved down to search the village. I chose a site for the command post in front of a hut near the river bank. The hut was unusual in that it was not deep and there was no wall on the side facing the river. Also strange was a large, multi-drawer wooden cabinet against the rear wall. We began to remove our rucksacks to set up a command post until the situation could be resolved.

Suddenly there was a commotion coming from the cabinet and before we could bring our weapons to bear, a door swung open and a young woman fell out onto the hard-packed dirt floor. Someone restrained her and everyone else began to closely check the hut and surrounding area.

Our search of items in the hut revealed that the site seemed be a VC PX or R&R station. Personal hygiene supplies and other amenities were located in the cabinet and other containers in the hut. Soon a tunnel was discovered a short distance away. One man volunteered to check it using a flashlight and a .22 caliber pistol that I carried for such purposes. He went down and disappeared except for his boots. He had come to a barrier and couldn't proceed. We pulled him out and called in Vietnamese for anyone inside to come out. After ten minutes of this, we dropped several hand grenades into the tunnel but this produced no tangible results.

Upon close inspection, the woman was very dirty. This was unusual because the Vietnamese seemed so fastidious about personal cleanliness. It was also remarkable because the river was with twenty steps of her hiding place. Another woman was detained in the vicinity and both were picked by helicopter. A later entry in the logs identified both as "VC nurses," although their sanitary conditions seemed to belie that.

As I write this, I wonder if, instead of a VC PX, it was a small, remote store which provided minor necessities to the villagers and the "nurses" were really small-time entrepreneurs.

On another occasion we had a close encounter with a Vietnamese woman which illustrates some of the dilemmas of the war and the boundaries which reasonable people can approach and sometimes cross.

On that patrol we had been given a specific objective, which was unusual for a search mission. Intelligence had reported that one Mrs. Phu had strong VC connections and knew the location of a substantial arms cache. We were assigned an interpreter, given the location of the lady's house and told to find the cache.

The house was located on a low hill amid extensive rice paddies, so it was easy to secure when we arrived there. It seemed to be more elaborate than most residences we had seen in rural villages. We found Mrs. Phu and her two daughters, probably aged 12 and 13, at the house. The interpreter was to conduct the interrogation.

The two Vietnamese began their conversation by squatting Asian-style outside the house, but soon Mrs. Phu became agitated and upset, standing and pacing from time-to-time. Judging only from her demeanor and tone of voice, she was hostile and aggressive toward the interpreter, who soon expressed frustration with her actions.

I was no stranger to the plight of Vietnamese civilians. They were aggravated and annoyed at best by both sides of the conflict and frequently suffered property losses and casualties. I always took care, within limits, to prevent careless and unnecessary harm to the innocent civilians. Mrs. Phu, however, seemed to be a different case.

I had never seen a Vietnamese civilian so shrilly defiant. Normally, they would point to themselves and exclaim "No VC!" and relapse into glum silence. She, however, seemed intent on venting her frustration and antagonism on us despite her very vulnerable and disadvantageous position.

I reluctantly decided to take a hand in the proceedings and I have no pride in my actions. When she would storm away from the interrogator I grabbed her and forcefully shoved her back, a process later ruefully referred to as "flinging Phu." She struggled and shrieked and my actions were to no avail. Finally, I told the interpreter to inform her that if she didn't talk, we would kill one of her daughters, who were being detained just out of earshot. She replied as defiantly as before.

I gave a platoon leader my knife in full view of Mrs. Phu and instructed him to take the older daughter to the other side of the hill, out of sight, make her scream and then gag her. While still unobserved, he was then to kill one of the free-roaming chickens and return with the knife covered with blood. After about 15 minutes he returned and I displayed the bloody knife to the woman.

She was visibly stunned and her bravado crumbled as she seemed to shrink into herself. Not even the most sadistic Vietnamese Army interrogators would kill a child to obtain information and she clearly thought an American would surely recoil from such a deed. After a brief interchange between the interpreter and Mrs. Phu, we were stunned when the interpreter said he felt that she knew the location of the arms cache but still would not reveal it.

Getting her attention, I returned the knife to the platoon leader and pointed to the remaining daughter. This time she went completely to pieces and I had had enough of the cruel charade. I ordered the "dead" daughter restored to her mother and called for a helicopter to evacuate all three to the tender mercies of the Vietnamese authorities.

In the book of unintended consequences, there is a sequel to this unsavory story. The platoon leader who pretended to kill the daughter on my orders, was later badly wounded and returned to the U.S., where he was retired due to disability. He left the Army and married a school teacher. He was haunted by his actions, although they were performed under my orders. So he decided to confide his participation in the episode to his wife, expecting sympathy and comfort for his uneasy conscience. She, however, was incensed by what she deemed his moral weakness and unmanly behavior. This, along with other factors, resulted in their divorce.

He shared this news with me when we reconnected 46 years after that unhappy event in Vietnam. I accept my culpability but I wonder about the devotion of a woman for a man who had done an unpleasant, dangerous job and felt guilt for his unavoidable actions. I also wonder about Mrs. Phu and what she really knew about the arms cache.

There was a point where search and destroy gradually morphed into the mission of rice deprivation to the enemy. This was particularly true in the fertile Que Son Valley. It was a different kind of searching and it brought us into more direct contact with the villagers and farmers.

There are numerous instances in the logs where large "caches" of rice were discovered by battalion activity. As much as possible, the rice was bagged and evacuated by helicopter to the Vietnamese district headquarters; otherwise it was ordered to be destroyed.

Company A discovered its share of rice in the villages. Normally it would be stored in large pots, three feet across and two or three feet deep. However, I was in a quandary about this entire procedure. Other companies would report so many hundred pounds of rice "captured." How did they know how to estimate the weight of rice based on its volume? No one had instructed me in this calculation.

Additionally, if we were depriving the enemy of this rice, how much of it should be left to the villagers for their own use? Again, there was no guidance. If the rice was to be destroyed, what was the most effective means? We would urinate into the pots and place smoke grenades on them in an attempt to spoil the contents. It seemed sinful to destroy food in this manner. Were the pots that we found actually decoys to satisfy our objectives while the bulk of the rice was hidden in a more sophisticated concealment?

The entire rice deprivation program left me with strong feeling of dissatisfaction. It seemed to be replacing body count as a metric for success with all its potential for abuse.

CHAPTER 17

End of the Tour

★ ★ ★

The last day of my last patrol with Company A was January 29, 1969. We were walking back to LZ Professional with 90 men. The low numbers were due to the battalion retaining our mortar platoon on the firebase. It would be a sad day in several ways.

As we neared the base of the hill on which Professional was located, firing broke out from the point. In the very thick vegetation the point man had detected movement to his front and gave the command in Vietnamese that we all knew so well: 'Dung lai—Stop!" Whoever it was didn't stop but began to run away through the brush. The point man, following the rules of engagement, opened fire. When I investigated, I found a young Vietnamese woman dead at the scene.

I knew the point man to be a careful, competent soldier who would not have maliciously shot anyone. He was clearly regretful but we all knew that in other circumstances, if he had hesitated, he might have been lying dead or dying on the ground. Because of our line of march every man in the company passed the body as we began the climb up to Professional.

On February 11, I left the fire base on my end-of-tour journey back to the U.S. On the following day, Company A departed LZ Professional by helicopter for an extended operation in the field with its new commander. If I had accepted the offer from LTC Stinson, the battalion commander, to extend my tour, I would have retained command of the company. I was still a first lieutenant and deeply honored by the colonel's confidence in me but I declined. This was not a decision to be made lightly and I can try to explain my thought process.

During my one-year tour I had had a 10-day R&R and a three-day stand down at the brigade base camp. The other 353 days I had been on-duty in a 24-hour-per day schedule leading an Infantry platoon or company in the field. I was burned out and afraid that my judgment would be affected by this malaise. I had gladly stayed in the field for six additional months instead of accepting a customary assignment in the relative safety of the rear area.

The tactical nature of the war was markedly different from World War II and Korea, both of which were characterized by well-defined front lines separating each side and across which attacks would be launched. Those wars usually had a fight-rest-fight rhythm that tended to limit the continuous pressure on the soldiers. None of this implies that those struggles did not have their own particular levels of stress.

In Vietnam, there were no front lines or no-man's-land which separated enemy from friendly territory. Instead it was like wading waist deep in a swamp, unable to detect the perils, human and otherwise, that lurked unseen beneath the murky water. The idea that the enemy was always more or less all around us instead of across a clearly defined boundary added an extra layer of tension to our everyday psychological strain. If we cleared one-thousand square meters of land today, within a week, day or hour the enemy could reclaim it.

The pressure on a combat leader was especially unrelenting in Vietnam. On one level he had to constantly be prepared to react to any threat to his personal safety. As a company commander I had as much exposure to all enemy threats as anyone except the point man. It would have been ridiculous, if not impossible, for me to have a special, personal guard detail. And it was always clear to the enemy that anyone followed by two soldiers carrying radios, easily identified by their short floppy antennas, was a prime target. A subset of this level was to avoid any personal injury, without regard to the enemy, caused by exposure to the harsh terrain, vegetation, weather and critters that were daily threats.

On another level he had to control his unit's current activities to accomplish the mission while anticipating the unit's overall response to any ambush or nighttime attack. In these situations, all requests for external support travelled through the company commander.

At a third level, he had to be planning several moves in advance for issues like availability of water, night locations, supporting fires, emergency helicopter landing zones, etc.

This was multitasking where a mistake could imperil anyone in the company.

In short, I decided to leave Vietnam and a great job in Company A because I thought my luck had run out.

CHAPTER 18

Reflections on the First Vietnam Tour

★ ★ ★

The Big Picture

Since the Eisenhower administration, the U.S. policy in southeast Asia had been based on the domino theory. This posited that if one country in that region fell to communism, then the rest would necessarily follow and that would be harmful to the interests of this country. So when the French returned there after World War II, reestablished their colonial administration and eventually withdrew in defeat, the American government decided to fill the vacuum to prevent the spread of communism. This was done initially by providing advisors and materiel to the South Vietnamese military forces in gradually increasing numbers and quantities.

General William C. Westmoreland began his tenure as COMUSMACV (commander of all U.S. forces in South Vietnam) in June 1964. He soon decided that his mission of advising the South Vietnamese armed forces would be inadequate to attain U.S. goals in the region and he requested combat units to be sent to the country, initially for base defense. Eventually, under his direction, American combat units moved from base defense missions to aggressive actions aimed at destroying the VC and NVA throughout the country. At his urging, more and more divisions and support units were sent there to strive for success with this new strategy.

One consequence of this action was that the South Vietnamese government had less necessity and incentive to recruit, train and deploy its own combat forces: Big Brother would take care of everything. The unexpected and unfortunate reality of increased U.S. combat successes, measured by the number of enemy dead known as "body count," was that enemy casualties were being rapidly replaced. This meant that the VC/NVA had no effective net losses in combat troops no matter how high the body count. This was abundantly demonstrated after the 1968 Tet Offensive in which the NVA and VC were soundly defeated, only to resurge quickly to their previous personnel levels.

The replacements for VC/NVA casualties came from conscripted citizens in North Vietnam and from disaffected citizens of South Vietnam. The latter group experienced the callousness of the South Vietnamese authorities and the often egregiously brutal treatment from U.S. field forces and seemingly indiscriminate bombing.

South Vietnamese officials were mostly arrogant and dismissive of the "peasants" and especially ethnic minorities. Even their own soldiers were treated with varying degrees of contempt. This seemed to be a manifestation of the age-old Asian caste system wherein pride of position and enrichment of self and family was dominant over the welfare of the country. Not all leaders were guilty of this behavior but there were sufficient numbers of them to make the communists, despite their harsh discipline, seem more palatable.

The American soldiers were, by training and inclination, wary of the Vietnamese populace, especially in rural areas. In their minds, everyone was a possible sniper, mine layer, VC supplier or grenade thrower. Even children were thought to be potential threats. Every GI was not a sophisticated judge of the populace, but every GI did not want to be killed or wounded if he misjudged a seemingly harmless farmer who was really a hard core VC.

Thus, the rural population was generally not thought of by U.S. forces as neutral but as probable enemy agents, which, in fact, some were. Therefore, Americans, when passing through a farming village, were likely to treat the inhabitants roughly and damage their property in search of incriminating evidence of collusion with the VC or NVA. Some villages were subject to this process many times as U.S. Army and Marine units frequently swept through the same area.

Given this process, so common throughout South Vietnam, who can be surprised that the VC found a fertile field for recruitment in the countryside, not so much from their communist ideology but from the complete rejection of their own government and the abusive foreigners who supported it?

While the Americans pursued a strategy of attrition, that is, measuring success by the metric of dead enemy, ultimately the loss of nearly one million enemy dead did not deter them from their pursuit of ultimate victory.

The Little Picture

So if you can understand that no matter how many of the enemy are killed, that number will be replenished, then the concept of attrition is unsupportable. Further, attrition was not a ratio that included our losses as a factor. Reduced to its simplest form, if every dead enemy soldier was quickly replaced then every American killed represented a net loss. This assumed that a value was placed on the lives of our soldiers.

If we could kill one hundred enemy soldiers for one of ours killed and the one hundred would be quickly replaced, who would accept that bargain?

It seemed obvious to me in my microcosm of the war that we were making no progress despite the reports of our "victories." It was equally obvious that trading casualties with the enemy in hopes of a securing a favorable death ratio was criminal and dishonorable. There was no acceptable kill "ratio" in which one American life was to be traded for any—any—number of enemy lives.

It was incomprehensible that Infantry units would conduct assaults on well-protected enemy positions knowing that American soldiers would be killed and wounded in the process. Such attacks may have resulted in high number of enemy casualties (or not) and our ownership of their abandoned fighting positions for short periods, but in the end: so what?

These ideas didn't suddenly flash into my consciousness as a vivid epiphany. They were percolating below the surface, slowly bubbling and congealing into a unified perspective. Intuitively, by the time I took over Recon, I knew that no American soldier's life should be expended to support the now-discredited domino theory or the failed strategy of attrition. This conviction guided every decision I made in Vietnam during that first tour of duty.

Tragically, some commanders believed that trading American lives for enemy body count was an acceptable execution of their duty and behaved accordingly--just following orders. Such behavior can be attributed to ignorance, stupidity or, unforgivably, desire for career advancement.

For a detailed account what was happening during my first year in Vietnam, read "After Tet, The Bloodiest Year in Vietnam," by Ronald H. Spector.

The quality of the American soldier in general

During this first tour, I assumed that most of the soldiers with whom I served in were draftees, meaning that they were involuntarily enrolled in the Army for two years. Those who voluntarily enlisted had a three-year service commitment. In the final analysis, a soldier's service commitment was immaterial when he arrived in Vietnam: everyone was in it together.

Although only 25 percent of the U.S. military personnel who served in Vietnam were actually draftees, no one in Recon or Company A discussed their own or others' status vis-a-vis the draft.

Roughly 30 percent of the soldiers who died in Vietnam were draftees in contrast to their 25 percent of total numbers. I believe that this is due to the ability of volunteers to select less dangerous jobs while draftees were unable to avoid assignments such as Infantry duty and its perils. I could be wrong.

All soldiers entering the Army, draftee or not, would spend four or more months in training in the U.S., depending on their specialty, with another month of leave leading up to their ultimate assignment. This meant that, if sent to Vietnam with its maximum one-year tour of duty, they would never return there due to insufficient time remaining in their service commitment. This relatively short period in Vietnam meant that they never accumulated the combat experience of their World War II and Korean War predecessors who were drafted for the duration of the conflict. Therefore, they had to ramp up their combat skills quickly; this was accomplished by the constant exposure to enemy forces instead of the fight-rest-fight schedules in previous wars. The old dictum that war was long periods of boredom punctuated by short periods of terror did not apply. Upon return from Vietnam, if they had a minimum time left on their service requirement, they might be discharged early.

Overwhelmingly, these soldiers were excellent, considering the limited training and military experience they had had upon arrival at their combat units. The nonprofessional sergeants also included a significant share of draftees, but with somewhat more training, maturity and sometimes civilian leadership experience as I have discussed earlier.

I know that the overall quality of the Army in general changed during the later years of the war in Vietnam and not for the better and that is beyond the scope of this book.

Nevertheless, I know, without any fear of contradiction, that the men I led in Recon and Company A were equal in every way to those from the "Greatest Generation."

Motivation, Why did we go

Before and during wars, much is always said about defending freedom, whether ours or that of the countries in which we fight. Freedom sounds much more inspiring in speeches than "implementing the foreign policy of the United States." I don't believe any of the soldiers I knew felt compelled to keep the Vietnamese free. I don't believe that they thought the malaria-ridden, cave-living NVA would be landing on the shores of Oahu, as President Johnson predicted, if we did not stop them in Vietnam. However, it is not out of the question that some of them believed that our mission in Vietnam was to somehow defend freedom in general and they were willing to participate in that quest.

To me it seems much more likely that these men, volunteers or draftees, understood that their national leaders had made a commitment to a war in a foreign country and needed soldiers to prosecute that war. Following the honorable American tradition, still in living memory from World War II and Korea, they chose to serve the flag, trusting to the honor and judgment of those leaders. In other words: "...when duty whispers low, thou must, the youth replies, I can." (From "Voluntaries" by Ralph Waldo Emerson.)

Once in Vietnam, no one I knew ever mentioned protecting freedom as his motivation. His loyalty was to his unit and his fellow soldiers and his every action revolved around that loyalty. All valor and heroism was exclusively directed to the survival of the individual and his buddies. While this was all within the framework of the unit's mission, the real priorities were clear.

It is a sad distortion to say that the sacrifices made in Vietnam were in the name of freedom. It is a much, much higher tribute to say that those killed or wounded paid that price while serving honorably, sometimes heroically, protecting their comrades in a war created by erroneous assumptions

Beware of men who will start wars with ill-defined benefits, in which their sons will not fight and which will benefit their supporters.

The Americal Division

This was not a prestige unit. Officers in the know or with connections would secure assignments to the 101st Airborne Division, the 82d Airborne Division, the 1st Infantry Division, the 1st Cavalry Division and other premier units. The Americal Division was the largest division in the Army at that time and seemed unwieldy. I had been assured that the ratio of troops in the rear areas to those in the field was 10:1 which was clearly excessive but not necessarily unique.

The division's reputation suffered severely from the aftermath of the My Lai incident. Although the officers who were closest to the action were, for the most part, not materially affected, the commanding general at the time was later demoted by one star rank and stripped of the Meritorious Service Medal. Another disaster at LZ Maryann further tarnished the division's image near the end of the war.

Several prominent future leaders' careers were not adversely affected by serving in the Americal, including Chairman of the Joint Chiefs of Staff and Secretary of State Colin Powell, Secretary of

Homeland Security and Congressman Tom Ridge and commander of Desert Storm General Norman Schwartzcopf.

1st Battalion, 52d Infantry

The battalion was not sullied by the notoriety of its parent and sister units but sustained some unfortunate outcomes.

Even before I left the country, larger than usual groups of enemy were seen moving in the 1/52 area of operation. Between 20 and 50 VC or NVA were detected on multiple occasions by direct contact, observation or reports from various Vietnamese. This was a dramatic departure from their pervious preference for moving in much smaller groups. It did not bode well for the battalion.

LTC William C. Stinson Jr., the battalion commander for the entire period that I commanded Company A, was killed on March 3, 1969, after I left Vietnam. He had just landed in his helicopter during a desperate fight to resupply Company A with water and ammunition and was lifting off with wounded soldiers when he was hit by a high-caliber machine gun round; he was the only casualty on the aircraft.

I know of no other combat commander who was so well respected by his troops as LTC Stinson. He was the man everyone hopes to have as a leader and he never failed at his job.

During one 28-month period in Vietnam, six rifle company commanders in the 1/53 were killed in action. Ten were wounded over a 39-month period. There were only four rifle company commanders at any one time in the battalion. Because I was always so immersed in running the Recon platoon, I was unaware of these statistics and some of these casualties occurred after I left the country. This lack of knowledge, therefore, had no bearing on my declining LTC Stinson's request for me to extend my tour and retain command of Company A.

Company A and Recon

Overshadowing the great responsibility of leading these outstanding men was the thrill that automatically accrued to a ground commander in combat. It was stronger than any fear of becoming a casualty. I can best describe it as follows: Every day I had to judge how long we could move in the oppressive heat with heavy rucksacks before fatigue would dull our responses. I would then call a halt and everyone would flop down while still maintaining all-around security. When the break was over and it was time to go back to work, the platoon leaders had to be notified to saddle up. To do this I would catch the eye of the radio operator with the company radio and nod slightly in the direction of the line of march. At that nod, 120 of the most heavily armed men in the world would struggle to their feet, shoulder their rucksacks and resume their tasks in the tropical heat. If there is a more satisfying job than that, it must be a rare and exquisite experience.

In early February 1969, while on LZ Professional, I relinquished command of Company A to my replacement, a captain, and returned to the U.S. The company then began a successful operation with enemy kills and captures of munitions and provisions. But soon a string of bad luck would overtake them. Beginning on February 13, the men of Company A were wounded in ones and twos. Then, during the five days beginning on March 3, six were killed and 48 more were wounded. This is the period in which the battalion commander, LTC Stinson, was killed. Over a three month period, Company A suffered 20 killed and 96 wounded, a combined number equivalent to the most soldiers I had ever lead in the field at one time. Naturally, some of the wounded were treated and returned to duty and replacements filled the ranks to maintain a viable fighting unit. One of the last fatalities during this time was the captain who replaced me as company commander.

Prior to my departure, the guys from the First Platoon presented me with a touching going-away card. Since we never had access to a PX to buy such an item, this one had obviously been repurposed because the original message had been taped over. There were 30 signatures on the card but a close inspection revealed that number 25 was Mrs. Phu. Thirteen of these soldiers were wounded in the April-May 1969 period—two of them twice—and two others were killed.

It was heartbreaking to read the log entries and accounts of survivors that described the desperate situations that Company A endured. It's a hollow and inadequate analogy, but it was like watching your favorite football team being trounced on television and twisting and turning your body on each play to help the players avoid the inevitable tackles.

In mid May, the 2d NVA Division began a major offensive in the Americal area of operation and did not spare 1/52. These attacks were so overwhelming that the division declared unprecedented tactical emergency. On May 15, the 1st Brigade of the 101st

Airborne Division was deployed to assist the outnumbered and beleaguered Americal.

I had two conflicting thoughts when I learned about these tragic events. First, I had to wonder what impact I would have had during these disasters if I had extended my tour as LTC Stinson had requested. Company A had suffered no casualties—killed or wounded--while I was with them in the field. It would be absurd to expect that such fortunate circumstances would continue under the NVA onslaught, but….

My second thought was about how I would have fared personally in this desperate situation. It is not without possibility that I would have joined those company commanders in the battalion who died in the line of duty.

A final note on Company A deals with one of the platoon leaders. When I had been in my post-Vietnam assignment for about three months, I received a notice from the Americal that I was required to complete an officer evaluation report that had been overlooked during my departure. I completed the two-page form and returned it. In it, I noted that the young officer being rated was aggressive and possessed commendable initiative. However, as I had personally admonished him as his commander, he tended to position himself too far forward in his platoon, even to the extent of walking on point. Thus, he would be unable to control and maneuver his unit if pinned down during an enemy contact.

Two weeks after I sent the completed report back to Vietnam, I read in the "Army Times" newspaper that the lieutenant in question had been killed. Apparently he had extended his tour and was on his eighteenth month in country.

I discovered nearly a half century later that this officer, prior to joining the 1/52, was a platoon leader in the infamous My Lai affair but remained virtually unknown. Investigations revealed that his platoon participated in the crimes but to a lesser extent than Calley's. Only his death in combat in July 1969, prior to the completion of the official investigation, prevented his notoriety.

I had never seen, and certainly would never have tolerated, any kind of remotely similar behavior in Company A.

My opinion of the cowardly actions at My Lai is that inept, misguided and weak leadership was the root cause.

An Unfortunate Coincidence

I have not previously mentioned the Army's officer rating system using the form called an Officer Evaluation Report (OER). OER's were generated when an officer changed jobs, had served in a job for one year or his immediate commander (the rater) changed jobs. The rater's commander (the endorser) also had an equal amount of input into the OER as a sort of balance. Both the rater and endorser had to have exposure to the rated officer for a minimum of 30 days. OERs were very important factors in promotion, assignment and school selection.

As I have mentioned, while in Recon I was assigned to Company E for administrative purposes but was actually supervised by the battalion commander and the S-3 officer. When I moved from Recon to Company A at the end of September, I was due an OER due to job change and was surprised to find that the Company E commander was my rater, not the battalion commander. This should not have been a serious problem except that the battalion commander for whom I had worked for my entire time in Recon had left Vietnam several weeks before my OER was due and could not be my endorser. This also meant that the new battalion commander had less than 30 days as my boss and therefore was also ineligible to be my endorser.

The result of these circumstances was that I would be rated for my entire time in Recon, during which I and others felt I had performed in a very superior manner, by the Company E commander. This was despite the fact that I had never been under his operational command. There would be no endorser to balance any negative rating.

So on my second OER in Vietnam, in the section of 24 ratable personal qualities, I received 14 level 2s on a 1 (top)-to-5 (bottom) scale and one 3 from the Company E commander. CPT Goldman, for my less-than-stellar performance in Company B, had given me seven 2s. In the comments section, the Company E commander used less than half of the available space, apparently unable to find many complimentary things to say about me. He wrote: "He ... willingly accepts and acts on suggestions and constructive criticism." And, "He maintains excellent rapport with his superiors...." This was irony at its best because I had defied him at LZ Chippewa by insisting that he call the TOC for permission to return early from a patrol when he opposed that move.

Without any explicit criticism, he had damned me with faint praise and, while I felt cheated, I had no recourse.

When LTC Stinson completed my OER for my performance in Company A at the completion of my tour, I received 1s in every rating category except for a 2 in "Appearance." To be fair, I receive a 2 in Appearance in all three OERs during the first tour due to my large, unkempt mustache shown in Figure 3.

The Enemy

To this day, some former soldiers and their families who had suffered due to the war and seen their friends maimed or killed, retain a hatred for the VC and NVA and sometimes for the Vietnamese in general. However, I believe most have come to grips with their past and over time have put such animosity aside.

For me, by volunteering for Infantry OCS, I was solely responsible for my presence in that war, unlike some of the soldiers with whom I served. As an officer I considered myself a professional. Active hatred of the enemy was distracting and, if displayed on my part, could have engendered undesirable and/or illegal behaviors in the few unstable men who were unavoidably in the ranks.

Looking back, I can make a loose analogy between the Vietnamese at that time and Americans during the Revolutionary War period. There were two political sides in a homogeneous population whose differences were so severe that they fought each other. There was the presence of foreign troops fighting on one side. Despite setbacks, the side with the strongest belief in its political foundation was the winner.

So, were the VC and NVA anything but patriots? Did the peasants in their ranks have anything to gain except to destroy the caste system in the south and rid their country of the foreigners?

On Fate and Leadership

I had initially titled this memoir "War and Peace" although I knew that title had already been taken. In the second epilog to his novel, Leo Tolstoy discussed a theme that ran throughout his tangled, interlocking stories: the great man theory, with Napoleon, Czar Alexander II and the Russian general Kutsukov as examples. His thesis was that great men don't shape events, but events shape themselves and the major players who inhabit them.

This idea, in my opinion, is moot. However, I like to think that in my very small world in Vietnam I was able to influence events to a degree that I can claim that—mostly—things went my way.

Skill and luck?

Not much has been studied or written about the relative influences between luck and skill in warfare and what is available is exclusively strong personal opinion. I believe that success in combat requires both skill and luck but not in the same proportions at the same times. A leader must enhance his luck by always following proven tactical procedures and fill in the gaps with skill when luck is scarce. As one's skills improve, it is imperative never to lose sight of the basics due to overconfidence. Even a tactical master can be overwhelmed by a coincidental encounter with a vastly superior force. One the other hand, the luckiest poor leader will never ultimately succeed. I think I had a great deal of luck and sufficient skill, despite some significant mistakes, to lead Recon and Company A in a way that absolutely minimized casualties.

In terms of the outstanding soldiers with whom I served in those units, I'm not sure if they can be counted in the good luck column for me or in the highly skilled column in their own right.

The Power of a Commander

The idea of a combat commander having the omnipotent power to send his men to certain or possible death must be examined. For me personally, I never felt that I had the power to send a subordinate to his death. I had the power to put someone in a position that, depending on a myriad of circumstances, could result in death or injury. In the same way I strove to protect the men of Recon and Company A, I was potentially a factor in making them casualties.

There is a shocking example of a commander wasting troops in order to achieve a questionable military objective. It involved the 3d Brigade of the 101st Airborne Division and Hamburger Hill during May 5-20, 1969, in the A Shau Valley near Laos. The enemy had heavily fortified Hill 937 and the decision was made to assault the position after extensive artillery and aerial bombardment. The hill was taken at the cost of 46 Americans dead, 400 wounded and 630 enemy known dead. The abandonment of the hill in June set off a firestorm of criticism in the U.S.

Although the commanders justified their actions on the grounds that the mission was to find and destroy the enemy, the shocking results further discredited the strategy of attrition.

My Way

It is clear that as the mortar platoon leader with Company B under CPT Goldman, I had no operational freedom of action; this is as it should have been.

However, as Romeo, I was always given a mission and expected to accomplish it in the best possible fashion without micromanagement. The battalion commander and S-3 officer had a great deal of other, larger assets to control and didn't spend time fretting over five or ten Recon guys running around in the jungle as long as we generated more successes than problems. To me, this was the operating environment that I had only dreamed of.

There was an ironic postscript to this arrangement. The late LTC Elbert Fuller, commander of the 1/52 during my tenure as Romeo, wrote to me during my interbellum period at Fort Knox asking for help. It seemed that his superior at the 198th Infantry Brigade had given him an officer evaluation report (OER as described above) that found his supervision of subordinates below par and that was blocking his promotion to colonel. Although he hesitated to do so, he had been advised to ask his former subordinate officers to supply rebuttals to this evaluation.

Naturally, my most cherished memory of LTC Fuller was his selection of me to lead Recon and his wisdom in allowing me to perform Recon's missions "my way" after receiving his general instructions. I responded with a statement that the colonel had been an excellent leader especially because his allowed his subordinates to perform without micromanagement. This was probably not the best evidence to prove that he had been an attentive supervisor but it reflected my sincere respect for his leadership. My predecessor as commander of Company A sent him a long and eloquent letter attesting to his outstanding qualities as a leader but in the end it was all of no avail.

PART FOUR

INTERBELLUM

CHAPTER 19

Fort Knox, Fort Benning and Fort Bragg

★ ★ ★

Upon return to the U.S., my new assignment was at the U.S. Army Training Center, Armor, (USATCA) at Fort Knox, Kentucky. USATCA, typical of the Army, was an acronym and pronounced: you-SAHT-kah. This was my third assignment at that post. I had been to Fort Knox for basic training, non-commissioned officer academy and a post-OCS maintenance school. As the name "armor" denotes, the center's primary purpose was to train tankers, both officer and enlisted, in skills at various stages in their careers.

My new job was on the USATCA headquarters staff. This level was comparable in organization to an Army division in that there were brigades, battalions and companies as subordinate units and it was commanded by a two-star general. All of the other officers on the staff were from the armor branch, as would be expected. As an Infantry officer, I was assigned to a branch immaterial position: Assistance Plans and Operations Officer in the G-3 (operations) section. Additionally, I was the range officer, secret document control officer and a few other titles.

One of my less enchanting duties was to task the subordinate units for officers and NCOs to perform recurring duties, such as Commander of Troops and color guard at the graduation ceremonies for the enlisted courses. Despite the abundance of new lieutenants at Infantry training centers such as I had experienced at Fort Lewis, the smaller armor branch produced fewer officers and USATCA was under-strength in cadre. The brigades and lower units always felt that I was placing demands on their manpower that detracted from their primary mission of training. I agreed but had no choice but to fulfill the requirements dictated by my boss. My sympathy, however, did not prevent them from constant foot dragging.

Not only was I a red-headed step child as an Infantry officer, I was a Reserve Officer instead of the more prestigious Regular Army (RA) Officer. A Regular Officer was typically any West Point graduate or the top graduates from OCS and ROTC; I was none of these. During times of war such as we were in then, the Army would increase OCS output and grant most graduates reserve commissions. Reserve officers were easier to discharge involuntarily than Regulars, so that when the war was over and the need for officers diminished, it was easy to eliminate reservists. It was also a good time to eliminate a few RA officers who were substandard. Of course, there was no discrimination in assignments generally, but everyone knew that some plum jobs were tacitly reserved for RA officers. I'll comment more on this later.

The attitude of some RA officers toward reservists was brought home to me one day in the small office I shared with my boss, a decent RA armor major. He was discussing the upcoming change in Army service numbers with a contemporary. At the time reserve officers had their service number start with the letter "O" and RAs had theirs begin with "RA." Soon everyone's service number would change to their social security account number so that the service numbers would no longer reflect the officer's component. After a time, the visitor remarked, "Well, if they go through with this change, how will we know the good officers from the…." and his voice trailed off as they both glanced away from my desk.

I was promoted to captain on time on July 3, 1969. However, I began to surcomb to feelings of unease. Although almost everyone assigned to the staff had been in Vietnam, I got a vibe that, due to the limited assignments for armor officers there, not all of these men would return to southeast Asia. I knew that this would not apply to me as an Infantry officer, for whom combat vacancies always existed. This was exemplified when I had been assigned to a captain's slot as a new first lieutenant back in the Americal. I also had a less charitable thought: I had successfully commanded up to 120 men in combat at one rank lower than authorized and I doubted that many of those men would ever experience a comparable achievement in their long careers. This may have been unfair, unkind or worse, but those were my feelings.

It may have also been the generally relaxed and stress-free atmosphere in the G-3 section that also upset me. After an entire year in the pressure cooker of leadership responsibility in Vietnam, it was difficult to completely unwind, especially since I knew I was going back to more of the same. In short, I was bored.

One day, visiting the rural birthplace of Abraham Lincoln at Hodgenville near Fort Knox with my family, I realized that I was compulsively examining the terrain and tree lines for possible ambush sites.

I remembered an occasion back in Vietnam when Company A was on a firebase and the colonel asked me to fly to a Special Forces camp at Tien Phouc for a liaison visit. I had never worked with the "Green Berets" before so it would be interesting and I was not disappointed. Their camp was much more fortified that our LZs. One of the best features was a command bunker that was sunken into the ground with a low profile and constructed from reinforced concrete. This was considerably different from my under-the-stars experiences in the field or in sand-bagged bunkers on a firebase.

Another very compelling aspect was that a generator powered not only lights but two full-sized refrigerators standing on top of the command bunker—one for sodas and one for beer. I hadn't seen a cold beer in months and these guys had cases within reach every day, all day.

That experience came back to me as I fretted over my circumstances at Fort Knox. I thought that if I was going back to the war—and I definitely was—why not enjoy some luxuries while I was there. However shallow that reasoning may have been, I soon applied for Special Forces training and its prerequisite, parachute school.

Of course, I was to learn later that the Special Forces soldiers in Vietnam, in many cases, were placed in even more perilous situations than I had experienced in the Americal. And much later I was to learn that the Tien Phouc camp, my model for Special Forces comfort and amenities, had been overrun in a desperate battle. Maybe those refrigerators weren't so extravagant after all.

I received orders for my return to Vietnam on March 30, 1970, with a reporting date of October 10, about 20 months from when I had ended my first tour. As I had requested, I would start airborne (parachute) training on June 5 and complete Special Forces qualification on September 26. Upon returning to Vietnam, I would not be a new, inexperienced second lieutenant like last time, but a combat-experienced, Special Forces captain. I sent a letter to the 5th Special Forces Group in Vietnam extolling my virtues and requesting an assignment in that unit instead of pot luck like the last time.

The three weeks of airborne training at Fort Benning involved a great deal of running, rote instruction in parachuting procedures and a few other more frightening activities. Although we eventually made our five qualifying parachute jumps from the massive USAF C-5 jet aircraft instead of the usual propeller-driven C-130s, these were not our most thrilling experiences. At one end of the same parade field upon which I had shed so much sweat during OCS stood the ominous 200-foot towers. They looked like giant high-voltage power line pylons except they had four evenly spaced arms extending from the top. Each arm was connected to a large upside-down cup by a long cable controlled by a winch.

Prior to our first actual parachute jump from an aircraft, we would endure the much more nerve-rattling pleasures of the 200-foot towers. First, a cup would be lowered near the ground so a fully deployed parachute canopy could be attached to it in some manner that I didn't understand. The canopy, as part of a functional parachute, was connected to a harness by suspension lines and risers. Then a lucky airborne school student would be strapped into the harness and winched to the top of the tower.

Although a standard military parachute jump is made at an altitude of 1,250 feet, very few jumpers are aware of the actual distance to the ground before or after exiting an aircraft. This is due to the highly ritualized procedure inside the aircraft prior to the jump and the many details that must be attended to during descent. No such distractions were available while being slowly winched up the 200 feet to the top of the towers.

Once at the top, the student would dangle there for some unspecified period of time. Looking down between his legs, the student could get a true feeling for the height of the tower. A frightening thought that occurred to me while being helplessly suspended there was that the harness or other component of the parachute might malfunction. In nearly one hundred subsequent actual parachute jumps, that idea never came into my mind.

Finally, the parachute would be released from the cup and the student would begin his descent under a fully deployed canopy and enjoy the ride to the ground. The biggest admonition we received prior to this exercise was to slip away from the tower immediately. "Slipping" was accomplished by grabbing the suspension lines on one side and pulling down so that the canopy tipped, allowing escaping air to push the parachute away from the tower. Hitting the tower would result in an unthinkable disaster and everyone was diligent in slipping.

Because I had done some sky diving at Fort Knox immediately after OCS, the actual parachute jumps from aircraft were not particularly intimidating.

During Special Forces training at Fort Bragg I listened to every war story and there were plenty. One theme kept bubbling to the surface: the secret "projects" were where the real excitement was to be found. Of course there was plenty of action everywhere in Vietnam, but these assignments had an air of mystery, thrills and exclusivity. Because the projects' modus operandi was to operate in small, five-man teams sometimes in neighboring countries of Vietnam, they seemed like Recon on steroids and gradually began to displace my preference for concrete bunkers and beer-filled refrigerators.

After eight weeks at Fort Bragg, I graduated from the Special Forces Officer Course and was authorized to wear the coveted green beret. I have a certificate to prove it.

Although it had been far from a sure thing, upon my return to Vietnam I was assigned to the 5th Special Forces Group (Airborne). I reported to the headquarters at Nha Trang and was able to bypass the combat orientation course due to my previous experience. During my interview with the assistant adjutant, Major Glenn Lane, I expressed my preference for one of the legendary projects. He explained that most of those slots were for NCOs and that Vietnamization would soon be eliminating them as well as my secondary choices such as the camps like the one at Tien Phouc. However, he said that there was a new secret mission being planned that would have greater longevity and would be a natural for me. I wasn't enthusiastic but he was adamant. So off I went to Long Hai (long high) and Detachment B-36, thinking that my chances for another "my way" tour in Vietnam were slipping away.

Interestingly, when looking through my official papers from this period I came across the orders assigning me to Detachment B-36. On the same orders, three other Special Forces officers who had arrived in Vietnam with me were assigned to the theoretically inaccessible projects.

PART FIVE

VIETNAM ACT 2

CHAPTER 20

Welcome to Long Hai

★ ★ ★

I arrived at the seaside village of Long Hai, south of Saigon, on October 14, 1970. I had a memorable flight from Bien Hoa in a huey helicopter, flying above small-arms range at a speed of about 80 knots. I had logged numerous helicopter flight hours in the Americal but this one was special because of the very unusual cloud formations. They were in the shape of irregular, puffy cubes with about 100-meter sides, all at the same altitude and evenly spaced about one mile apart. The huey glided in slow, easy turns to maneuver around them.

The clouds' shapes and relationships to each other cast their shadows on the ground like the black squares on a giant checkerboard. Since the terrain was flat and composed entirely of lush, green, geometrically shaped rice paddies, the overall effect was unique and unforgettable.

Long Hai was, and is today, a small resort village on the coast of the South China Sea. See Figure 1, Map of Vietnam. My new assignment was at a permanent Special Forces camp amid a huge expanse of unused rice paddies north of the town. It was called a camp because it consisted of buildings in contrast to the LZ bunkers from my time in the Americal.

The stubby, V-shaped Long Hai peninsula was dominated by a large, jungle-covered mountain ridge that occupied its eastern two-thirds. A narrow valley separated the mountain from another smaller ridge located to the northwest and closer to a two-lane highway that ran along the western side of the peninsula and provided access to the camp and village from the north. Unlike the massive and pervasive ranges of my first tour, these two mountains were isolated like orphan icebergs in a vast sea of rice paddies. A narrow road led from the highway to the camp.

On the western side of the highway were salt flats where the sea water was allowed to flow into shallow pools with flat, smooth bottoms. When the sea water had been evaporated by the sun, workers would sweep up the residual salt as a harvest from the sea.

Across an unnamed bay, 17 kilometers (10.7 miles) to the west, was the town of Vung Tau at the tip of a long, narrow peninsula. Its port was the home of the logistics arm of the 1st Australian Task Force, about which more later. A U.S. in-country R&R center was also located there because of the beautiful beaches and favorable security conditions. The peninsula was called Cap St. Jacques by the French and the lights of the town were visible at night from Long Hai.

The camp consisted of two, 100-meter-square compounds, designated north and south, connected by a thirty-meter-long narrow road. The interval between the compounds and the entire perimeter were protected by a mass of barbed wire and land mines. All of the buildings had three-foot-high sandbag barriers to protect them from anything but direct hits from mortars. The buildings were laid out in neat rows and each had a concrete foundation, five-foot-high wooden sides and a corrugated metal roof. The space between the top of the wooden sides and the roof was screened for ventilation but shutters were available to keep out the rain. When a torrential rainstorm pelted the metal roofs, the interior of a building was like being inside a snare drum. The sun and rain had changed the color and texture of the unpainted wood so that the camp had the appearance of an Old West frontier town. An aerial photo of the camp is at Figure 4.

The enemy situation was dramatically different from my first tour in I Corps. Long Hai had very little rice production and no major population centers to make it a valuable target for the VC and NVA. An under-strength local force VC battalion (D445) was thought to be assigned to our general area but mostly kept to itself in the mountains, which were riddled with caves deep enough to withstand B-52 bombings. In my research for this book, I discovered that the VC referred to the mountains as the Minh Dam Secret Zone with occupancy dating back to the resistance against the French.

Despite their focus on South Vietnamese government forces elsewhere in Phouc Tuy province, the VC would periodically emerge to cause us varying degrees of trouble as will be described later. It was rumored that individual VC soldiers would sometimes come down to enjoy the beautiful beaches for which Long Hai was famous.

I was assigned as Team Leader of Special Forces Operational Detachment A-361. This was a classic 12-man A Team, the basic building block of Special Forces units. Detachment A-361 and the three other A Teams at Long Hai were controlled and supported by Detachment B-36. The camp was sometimes referred to by its location (Long Hai) or it highest headquarters (B-36). Since we were located in III Corps, all Special Forces unit numbers in the corps began with a "3." The next higher headquarters was a C Team located in Bien Hoa (ben wha) near Saigon. As might be expected it was designated C-3. All C Teams in Vietnam reported to the 5th Special Forces Group headquarters in Nha Trang, far to the north.

Most of the A Teams in Vietnam were located in remote camps like the one I had visited in Tien Phouc during my first tour. Their mission was to recruit, train, equip, pay and lead local militia-style units for missions ranging from village self defense to aggressive combat operations. These units were called Civilian Irregular Defense Groups or CIDG (pronounced "sidge"). Their ethnic components included montagnards (mountain people), ethnic Chinese, Cambodians and Vietnamese who were indigenous to the camp areas and were therefore referred to as "indige." They were mercenaries and exempt from being drafted into the Vietnamese armed forces. Ethnic groups were not mingled. Overall, 249 such camps and related facilities had been built in Vietnam. Due to Vietnamization, in early 1970, most of the CIDG camps were closing or converting to Vietnamese Army facilities, and the associated U.S. A Team members were redistributed to on-going organizations such as B-36 and missions like the secret projects I had yearned to join.

The CIDG program was considered a force multiplier in that the skills and leadership of a few U.S. soldiers could be amplified many times by recruiting, organizing, paying and leading locally available manpower. An excellent classic description of this concept from World War II can be found in Tom T. Chamales' novel "Never So Few."

For simplicity, I'll refer to the indigenous mercenaries who continued to serve in the Long Hai security companies as "CIDG."

Of the two companies, one was comprised of Vietnamese and the other was ethnic Chinese who resided in Vietnam.

In addition to the other B Teams in their area, each of the four corps C Teams was assigned one B Team with three-to-four 512-man battalions called Mobile Strike Forces or Mike Forces. The Mike Forces would serve as a corps-wide reaction force and also performed independent missions. Indigenous troops were recruited for the Mike Forces and a Special Forces A Team was assigned to each battalion. Since an A Team consisted of two officers and ten NCOs, one officer would become the battalion commander and the NCOs would effectively become company commanders. Thus, a captain would be commanding an indigenous battalion at two rank levels below that authorized in American battalions. Since NCOs never commanded American companies, such an assignment was a heady experience for most sergeants.

B-36 had been the III Corps Mike Force for a short but memorable period during which it had performed near-legendary service employing the mercenary services of ethnic Cambodians who lived in Vietnam.

When Marshal Lon Nol had ousted Prince Sihanouk as Head of State of Cambodia in March 1970, the Cambodian Army began military actions against the NVA in their country. To support the somewhat weak Cambodian military, know in French as Forces Armees Nationales Khmeres or FANK, the indigenous troops from the III Corps Mike Force at Long Hai, battle-hardened ethnic Cambodians, were shipped to Cambodia to bolster FANK. A prime mover in this action was Dr. Son Ngoc Thanh.

Dr. Thanh was one of the most enduring figures of the anti-colonial struggle against the French in Indochina. Few could match his credentials as a guerilla fighter, revolutionary organizer and statesman. He accepted the premiership after the surrendering Japanese relinquished control of Cambodia in 1945. When the French reestablished control of the region, he was exiled to France where he earned a law degree and, in the French tradition, was awarded the title of "Doctor." When he returned to Cambodia he became the leader of the Khmer Serei (Free Cambodia) movement. His anti-monarchial position along with his massive influence with the ethnic Cambodian population in Vietnam contributed directly to their recruitment into the III Corps Mike Force and their eventual movement to Cambodia after the Lon Nol coup.

With the departure of its ethnic Cambodian troops, B-36 no longer had the ability or requirement to perform as a Mike Force. However, it still retained its four Special Forces A Teams (who were forbidden to follow their former soldiers to Cambodia), two local mercenary security companies and an infrastructure capable of supporting four battalions. These unused assets at Long Hai were a perfect fit for a new, secret mission beginning in the Spring of 1970.

On my first night at Long Hai, I was walking to my room when I saw the silhouettes of two figures. One was very tall and somewhat bulky and the other small and slight. They seemed quiet, only speaking infrequently. They were holding hands.

I had previously been stationed in the Far East for nearly four years and I knew that it was not uncommon for Asian men who were close friends to hold hands. No one's masculinity was ever questioned when Americans engaged in this fraternal local practice. Eventually, I would follow this custom as well.

I soon learned that the large man was a holdover from the Mike Force, an American captain. His companion was an interpreter with whom he had shared extensive and brutal combat experiences. The captain's tour was over and he was leaving the next day. This officer, I was told, had been awarded the Distinguished Service Cross, second only to the Medal of Honor. He was a hero who was going home but the diminutive interpreter would stay behind to an uncertain fate.

Personally, I was no longer an "LT" as I had been during my first Vietnam tour. I had been promoted between tours and would henceforth be referred to as "Dai Uy" (die wee), the Vietnamese term for captain, by locals and Americans alike. This term allowed for the enlisted men to address officers with familiarity but not cross any Army lines such as using one's first name. Another method to express familiarity but remain within bounds was to use the officer's self-assigned radio call sign. Mine, at that time, was Spider. Everyone was comfortable with this arrangement. The custom persisted long after the war when I would still be called Dai Uy by NCOs who had never served in Vietnam.

A typical evening at the all-ranks club would find some of the NCOs playing cards and drinking beer. There were a few selections of hard liquor but beer was the preferred beverage. On my first night at the club I was greeted by the NCOs in proper Special Forces manner. This involved one large sergeant rushing up, clasping me in a bear hug and giving me a tongue kiss in the ear, a variation of the wet willie. No one thought twice about this and certainly no one thought that the sergeant was vague in his masculinity. It was just a charming, fraternal custom, and, while I never resisted the gesture, I never warmed to it.

A dart board was hanging two feet to the right of the club door, which made entering a challenge. Camp lore told us that a former Mike Force commander, Major Ola Mize, had established a rule that the club would close when the clock behind the bar struck midnight and not one minute later. From time to time, the major would feel that another hour would not be harmful but he refused to change his rule. To solve this dilemma, he would take out his pistol and shoot the clock at 11:59pm. Later it was discovered that the compressed propane gas tank for the mess hall stoves was directly behind the clock.

The custom at the club on weekends was that the first drink cost five dollars and the rest were free. The club used chit books to provide some sort of accountability for the money handled by the CIDG bartenders. This was a slippery slope because there was a temptation to make your five dollars back by drinking at least that amount of alcohol and perhaps more. The club's cost for supplies was low and the profits were applied to enhancing the rations in the mess hall.

As the new team leader of A-361, I had arrived in the middle of the training cycle for a Cambodian Army (FANK) battalion. This was the secret mission underway at Long Hai: training FANK infantry. My team, mostly comprised of young, eager NCOs, was fulfilling the last phase of an agreement made earlier in the year between FANK and the 5th Special Forces Group to train eight infantry battalions. It seemed that to interject myself in midstream into the training process would be counterproductive and even arrogant.

That particular FANK battalion consisting of Cambodian nationals seemed to have a cohesive structure and gave the impression of having strong, even harsh discipline. They were not enthusiastic about the training and seemed tactically competent and quietly disdainful of the basics we tried to teach them. The officers were scruffy and uncouth in contrast with the class-conscious leaders I had observed in regular Asian armies. I had the feeling that these were most likely border bandits who had "enlisted" in FANK simply to receive arms and materials and would melt away into their mountain habitat at their first opportunity upon returning to Cambodia.

This group may have been members of a larger political group than the Khmer Serei called the Khmer Kampuchia Krom or KKK. The KKK were ethnic Cambodians endemic to the Mekong delta region of southern Vietnam and neighboring Cambodia. They strove for independence from Vietnamese authority which they considered racially oppressive. The Khmer Serei, on the other hand, were aligned with U.S. Special Forces and were effectively working with the Vietnamese government to defeat the VC and NVA.

Various FANK battalions formed from the Khmer Serei and KKK would be trained at Long Hai but I was unaware of such a differentiation at the time.

One afternoon at the end of their training period, I was invited to their officers' quarters in the south compound. They had a feast laid out with a large quantity of alcohol, which was forbidden for troops in training. I don't know how they got it but I felt that some type of intimidation was involved. The commander was a short, older man and I hadn't had much interaction with him in the short time I had been at the camp. On the surface, he seemed very jolly but was unable to mask a deep streak of ruthlessness.

We were drinking beer and some potent homemade concoctions when suddenly he grinned up at me and poured a glass of beer on my head. No amount of training or war stories had prepared me for that moment. I went with my instincts and poured my beer over his head and grinned back. He seemed to take this in good humor.

Before the night was over we were alternatively dumping mustard, catsup and other less-well-know condiments in each other's hair and laughing like long-lost blood brothers. His officers were smiling at the spectacle but appeared somewhat edgy.

We parted late in the night after pledging eternal friendship and dedication to the cause of Cambodian freedom. Sticky and smelly, I made my way back to the American section of the north compound to clean up for the following day. I wondered how I would have fared if these events had occurred in his remote mountain fiefdom.

Our uniforms were unique. We wore the same tiger-stripe black-green-brown shirt and pants that had been issued to the indigenous Mike Force soldiers. They were made of thin cotton and not nearly as rugged as the standard U.S. jungle fatigue uniform that I had worn in the Americal. Over the right shirt pocket was sewn our name tag but the obligatory "US ARMY" cloth tape was missing from above the left pocket. I doubt that the lack of such a label would have fooled anyone about our country of origin and I knew it was certainly a clear violation of the Geneva Convention. No unit patch was worn on the left sleeve or rank insignia on the collar. Instead, an arc or scroll with the words "3d Mobile Strike Force Command" embroidered on it was sewn in place of a left shoulder patch. The arc had two wings on the ends; one wing had three lightning bolts (land, sea and air) emblematic of Special Forces and the other had the Khmer Serei sun symbol. Therefore, we had no explicit affiliation with the U.S. Armed Forces but instead were identified by a token of a foreign political organization. The words on the arc would differ over time as we were assigned to various headquarters but the symbols remained unchanged. See Figure 5 for a typical example of the scroll. Floppy jungle hats were worn instead of berets. It was not surprising that conservative, conventional senior Army officers were frequently displeased with our attire.

Selection of B-36 to train FANK battalions was a natural choice. First there was the four-battalion infrastructure standing empty in a relatively quiet area. Then there was a fully staffed B Team with four subordinate A Teams manned by qualified Special Forces soldiers with no significant employment since the departure of the Mike Force CIDG to Cambodia. While many Americans think of Special Forces as men with camouflage faces engaged on commando raids, that is a small portion of the overall assigned mission. Training indigenous personnel in insurgency and counter-insurgency is, by a large measure, the predominant focus. The major doctrinal difference in this instance was that the U.S. trainers were not allowed to lead/advise their students when their training was complete. I'll discuss how we tinkered with Special Forces doctrine to maximize training effectiveness later.

This was a time of large and important changes for B-36 and its personnel but I did not know what was being planned and only saw events unfold without any prior knowledge of the next phase of the FANK program. Like my previous experiences during my first tour in the Americal, I was focused on the day-to-day activities

The original commitment for the 5th Special Forces Group to train FANK battalions originated in the Spring of 1970, with an agreement for eight battalions. Although I have no solid evidence on this matter, I believe that some of these were actually recruited from the Khmer Serei and KKK in Vietnam and had been "enrolled" in FANK.

Then, about this time, two major events were being scheduled for implemented. First, the 5th Special Forces Group, as part of the Vietnamization process, would be returned to the U.S. on March 4, 1971, and B-36 and its mission would be reassigned to a newly formed headquarters under the U.S. Army Vietnam (USARV) Training Directorate. Second, the USARV Training Directorate was tasked to train an additional 30 FANK battalions. These battalions would be exclusively formed in Cambodia by combining newly drafted recruits and existing members of FANK, but, as we found, in uneven and random ratios. In addition to Long Hai, two additional, existing Special Forces units would be retained to help fulfill this commitment, each with a three battalion capacity: Detachments B-51 at Dong BA Thin and B-43 at Chi Lang.

In late 1970, without knowing the details about our eventual status after the anticipated departure of the 5th Special Forces Group, we at Long Hai continued to perform our mission as it unfolded in fits and starts. One significant development was that we received a formal, structured, 12-week program of instruction. Previously, the FANK battalions had been trained mostly by individual A Teams for eight weeks in the manner of the CIDG troops in the remove Special Forces camps.

It was at this point that the secret nature of the program was emphasized to us by higher headquarters

The first FANK battalion to arrive in Vietnam under the new, 30-battalion agreement and the new training program was assigned to A-361 at Long Hai. It consisted of a few experienced officers and NCOs but mostly recruits that we categorized as slick city boys and mud-between-their-toes farmers. Without any solid evidence, I can only estimate that this battalion began training in late November 1970.

As we began to implement the new program of instruction for this unit, an issue arose that we had not anticipated. Having been formed as a FANK unit back in Cambodia using a French organizational model, the battalion was originally much larger than the training agreement specified. Therefore, to meet our 512-man training limit, it had somehow been truncated in a way that reduced the riflemen while retaining the non-combat support personnel. As I studied its tables of organization and equipment as written in French (no small task), I realized that it was not a "light" Infantry battalion in the sense we had anticipated.

To correct this imbalance between the designated fighters and support personnel, an important action was taken of which I was not a part. The FANK battalions would henceforth be organized under the 512-man Mike Force structure. This was a much leaner organization than the bloated French model and there was a scramble to implement this change. I believe that the reason for the change to the Mike Force structure was that everyone involved in the decision-making process had been a part of the old Mike Force program and it was only natural to select a solution that was familiar and had proven personally successful.

The fallacy in this organizational change was that the FANK battalions were not comparable in leadership, equipment, enlisted qualification and external support to the American-led, battle-hardened Khmer Serei in the Mike Force. The best way to correct this deficiency was to return to basics by implementing yet another organizational change. This process became imperative as serious events unfolded during the early weeks of training .

CHAPTER 21

Training Begins

★ ★ ★

Although the FANK training program was initially treated as a secret project, we could not conceal over 2,000 non-Vietnamese-speaking soldiers moving between our camp and the open, adjacent training areas and firing ranges which abutted the main north-south road. We fended off curious reporters until the program became public knowledge.

By then we had traded our floppy hats and CIDG tiger-striped uniforms for the standard Green Beret and U.S. jungle fatigues with a camouflage pattern. It was thought that this combination would somehow inspire greater confidence in us from the new trainees. In place of the standard beret flash, or Group emblem, we wore a representation of the Khmer flag which further delighted the FANK soldiers. See Figure 5.

The first few training days were occupied with issuing a full set of clothing and equipment and conducting basic weapons instruction. We moved on to simple tactical unit movement and some maneuver techniques. In the third week a field training exercise (FTX) was scheduled in a large swath of uninhabited territory at Xuyen Moc (Swen Mock), about 40 kilometers (24.8 miles) to thc northeast and accessible by secondary roads. Back at Fort Benning, GA, FTXs did not feature an armed, hostile enemy intent on inflicting casualties on the trainees.

When the Monday came and we were boarding trucks for the training area, I had a distinct feeling of unease about the FTX. The mix of experienced and new FANK officers and NCOs was having difficulty controlling their troops and the battalion commander seemed disengaged. A-361 had to be more proactive in controlling the men than we expected or desired. At least we had a helicopter to help with convoy security on the road to Xuyen Moc and to standby at Long Hai for emergencies during the FTX. Major Crismon, the B-36 commander, had decided to accompany us to get a first-hand feeling for how the battalion would perform in the field.

When we arrived at the drop-off point near Xuyen Moc, one of my worst fears was realized. In the field with the Americal I had constantly emphasized dispersion and spaces between troops. The Cambodians, a very social group, tenaciously clung together and made excellent sniper and automatic weapons targets. Working through interpreters, it was nearly impossible to separate them by using reason, logic or threats. It was a struggle to get them into a decent tactical formation and move to our planned night location. To be fair, they had had only two weeks of military training.

After we reached our first objective, the NCOs of A-361 worked very hard to organize the troops into a decent defensive perimeter for the night. The mortars were set up in the center along with the recon platoon and the battalion headquarters. Master Sergeant "Long John" Silver, Major Crismon, the A Team medics and I set up beside the Cambodian battalion headquarters section. As we began to dig our foxholes I noticed for the first time that the FANK battalion commander had a batman, or servant, preparing his evening meal and soldiers from the rifle companies were digging the FANK headquarters' foxholes. With the many other deficiencies to address, I decided to ignore this practice.

The area was virtually uninhabited and not known to be under active VC control, but our NCOs correctly insisted that the FANK rifle companies, whom they were "advising," send listening posts outside the perimeter to provide early warning of impending attacks. Despite a questionable start, all now seemed right in the world and the American headquarters group settled into the rhythm of the night.

Although it had been nearly two years since I had been in the field in Vietnam, I had not lost the keen sensitivity for minor disturbances in the nighttime tranquility. So when dim, distant firing occurred outside the perimeter I was awake and on my feet with all senses alert, seeking actionable information. I didn't have long to wait for an avalanche of audible and visual input.

Like a fast-burning fuse, the smattering of external firing quickly ignited a similar response on the perimeter itself. It began to spread in both directions around the circular perimeter so that within seconds, one quarter of the men on the perimeter were firing their weapons. In the moonlight, I could see the mortar crews preparing their rounds to join in the festivities.

The situation was crystal clear to me: soon every man on the perimeter in blind panic would be firing as fast and as many rounds as possible until the battalion's entire basic load of ammunition was spent and no one, not the ineffective Cambodian officers or the NCOs of A-361, could make them stop.

In an American Infantry unit in Vietnam, we would periodically select a random time at night when everyone on the perimeter would fire one complete magazine of rounds into the darkness. This would be a nasty surprise for an enemy who was stealthily approaching our location. It was called a Mad Minute. However, this situation was another form of madness that would last more than one minute and spend more than one magazine of ammunition per soldier.

I picked up the radio hand set and called the radio relay station we had set up at the Vietnamese Army local garrison in Xuyen Moc village; we were too far away for direct communications with Long Hai. I told the sleepy radio operator to instruct Long Hai to awaken the helicopter crew and begin ferrying an entire battalion's basic load of ammunition to us.

The relay operator could hear the cacophony of explosions and rifle fire in the background as I spoke and I heard him notify Long Hai that we were in heavy enemy contact. I had difficulty persuading him that this was not the case but we still needed the ammunition. It was very confusing for everyone, especially those at Long Hai who were only indirectly in the communications loop.

By now, everyone on the perimeter was firing blindly into the night. The recon platoon in the center of the perimeter wisely refrained from firing their rifles into the backs of their comrades but the M-79 gunners felt that they could influence the action by firing over the heads of those on the perimeter. Those rounds mostly exploded harmlessly outside the perimeter, except for a few that impacted in trees and showered their comrades with shrapnel.

At some point in the proceedings, Major Crismon awoke near where I was standing. I could see his expression clearly in the flashes of exploding munitions and there was something of awe in it. He later told me that before he was fully awake, he saw me standing fully upright, backlit by explosions, speaking calmly on the radio. It was easy to interpret that image as someone directing supporting fires to repel an attacking enemy with complete disregard for his own safety. It was an action worthy of a Silver Star. The reality, of course, was much more mundane and totally lacking in heroism.

The helicopter began shuttling the ammunition resupply from Long Hai and returning with those Cambodians suffering minor wounds for treatment. There were more candidates for the trip back to Long Hai than there were actual injuries, so the two A Team medics had to apply stringent screening procedures.

When everything was more or less under control, we began to unravel the events that caused the unfortunate debacle. One of the listening posts had been placed on a trail and, against all odds, several local Vietnamese had inadvertently stumbled onto them in the dark. No one could verify that they had weapons or that they were VC. The three listening post troopers had opened fire and then run madly back toward the safety of the perimeter. One of the lads tripped before he could reach his comrades, and almost immediately the entire perimeter was ablaze with every weapon firing at its maximum rate. Either good judgment or paralysis kept him prone for the duration and only a miracle kept him unscathed.

When everything was quiet again, the hapless soldier staggered into the perimeter nearly senseless with fear. A very busy A Team medic examined him and quickly pronounced him qualified for evacuation on the next chopper sortie. I asked the medic what was wrong with the man and the reply was "shock;" he had shined a flashlight into one eye and there was no response or constriction. The man was duly flown back to Long Hai.

This episode was a huge embarrassment but not for A-361. It was abundantly clear that two weeks of training was woefully insufficient to prepare these newly recruited troops for a field exercise. Despite the requirements of the training curriculum, we, or more correctly I, should have recognized this glaring deficiency and acted accordingly before exposing the under-trained Cambodians to this totally avoidable disaster. Radical surgery was required for the training program and we could not wait for some superior authority to do it for us. It was not in Special Forces DNA to rely on higher headquarters to solve a problem and this was just the opportunity I had been waiting for.

As for the unlucky listening post trooper, who had now been shot at more than anyone else in his battalion, the story lived on. It seemed that he had one glass eye into which our medic had shown his flashlight. The medic had a difficult time living that down. Personally, I would have put the poor guy on that helicopter, glass eye or not.

Events were moving quickly. The second, third and fourth battalions were arriving as planned at one-week intervals and the next FTX was scheduled for the following week. If we had kept to the established plan of instruction, much more serious casualties could have resulted and the program itself could have suffered a loss of confidence. In my mind, the battalions' organization, along with the training plan, had to be modified to conform to their raw-recruit status, available equipment and the missions they could expect back in Cambodia. The first step, however, was to postpone the FTXs for all other battalions and then radically revise the program. Major Crismon had the courage to unilaterally implement this action.

I felt that I had nearly perfect qualifications to address the critical problems that confronted the FANK training program. I was mature at nearly 30 years of age and had had almost six years of enlisted experience. I had experienced basic and advanced training, NCO Academy, OCS, Airborne School and specialized officer training. I had been a training officer at the Infantry training center at Fort Lewis and on the staff at the armor training center at Fort Knox. I had successful leadership experience in combat units whose missions were identical to those that the FANK battalions would face. Finally, here was a perfect opportunity to exercise my initiative in order to improve my unit's performance and--do it my way.

To revise the training program, I proposed that it would reflect the U.S. Army's programs of instruction for Infantry training from boot camp up through battalion-level tactics, but scaled down proportionally to fit into the 12 weeks that we were allocated. Some common sense adjustments were required, particularly in the initial phases, but generally this plan was sound. The most important change was to move the first FTX into week seven during which the focus would be on each infantry company operating individually. A second FTX was scheduled in week eleven in which the battalion would operate as a unit.

When we began to address the battalion's organizational structure, some of the old Special Forces hands began to push for retaining the Mike Force model. To me this was unrealistic on several fronts. First the Mike Force had been lead by seasoned Special Forces soldiers and manned by motivated, experienced, paid volunteers. The FANK battalions were lead by inexperienced officers and NCOs and the soldiers were mostly draftees.

Second, the Mike Force battalions and companies had more subordinate units and more complicated weaponry than similar U.S. Infantry units. Such complications would be a challenge even for experienced American officers and especially so for the green Cambodian leaders. The tangible result of this situation was that the company commanders had too many assets to effectively control and the battalion commander had too few to perform his functions.

Several examples illustrate this condition. The companies included a reconnaissance platoon which added to the commander's span of control while the battalion commander did not have such a platoon as in U.S. battalions. The companies' mortar platoons were assigned both 81mm and 60mm mortars which required more complex logistics, training and supervision than with a single type of mortar. At the same time, the battalion commander did not have a mortar platoon with which to influence combat situations.

It seemed obvious that removing the reconnaissance platoons from the companies and adding one of them to the battalion headquarters would simplify the company commander's job and provide the battalion commander with a needed resource. Removing the 81mm mortars from the companies and pooling them under the battalion headquarters would further ease the company commanders' control burden while giving the battalion commander the ability to provide concentrated firepower.

Therefore, by adopting a simpler organization similar to U.S. Infantry battalions, the FANK company officers' and NCOs' spans of control would be reduced and the challenging variety of weapons would be minimized. Simplicity was the key due to the limited time allotted for training. Of course, all of this reorganization had to fit within the 512-man personnel limit per battalion.

Based on my qualification and the strength of my recommendations, I was reassigned as the S-3 (operations) officer of B-36 on January 12, 1971, to implement these changes. It is a credit to Major Crismon that he authorized implementation of these changes even as he pushed them up the chain of command for formal approval. I remember briefing the FANK general in charge of training and mentioning that the new battalion organization would be in effect immediately. He asked for a copy of my organizational chart so he could implement the change for the next battalions to arrive in Vietnam.

One remaining area required improvement: the organization of B-36 itself. Initially, each of the FANK battalions was assigned to one A Team which would provide all of its instruction. Special Forces A Teams consisted of two officers with two NCOs in each of the following specialties: operations and intelligence, communications, engineering, weapons and medical care. Each of them was supposed to be cross trained in at least one other specialty. However, in the hasty buildup for the war, not all NCOs had combat experience and many were not satisfactorily cross trained. Therefore, not all teams were adequately prepared to provide consistent, quality training in every aspect of the FANK program and there was an imbalance of skills among the A Teams at B-36.

Here again, we looked to the successful U.S. Army training center model for a solution rather than attempting to design and test some new concept. We looked at the strengths of each NCO and those most proficient in a particular weapon or skill were assigned to a newly created training committee. The training committee was to be headed by a captain and under my operational control as the S-3 and it would present all formal training. The officers and NCOs remaining on the A Teams would serve as the FANK battalions' cadre and be responsible for administration, compliance with training schedules and conduct of FTXs, similar to the drill sergeants' duties in U.S. training centers. This resulted in six of each A Team's NCOs moving to the training committee, cutting the team in half.

With this new organizational structure we could more effectively control the consistency and quality of instruction due to centralization in the training committee. Any changes to the program were easily disseminated through the training committee chief. Problems and trends among battalions were more quickly detected and reported by the training committee staff because they were exposed to all of the battalions.

For example, one NCO would be assigned to teach subjects during the second week of the program. Since the four battalions arriving at Long Hai began their training at one-week intervals, this would occupy that NCO for four weeks. He could then cover another subject in weeks six and ten for all four battalions without a break and then begin again with week two for the next group of battalions. This would allow an instructor to focus and improved in fewer skill areas than if all instructions were presented by an A Team.

The training committee arrangement also had a beneficial effect on our interpreters, always a weak area. If an A Team had to train a battalion in every subject, then their interpreters had to be proficient and fluent in every subject. This was an unrealistic goal in the time we had available to prepare for the start of the program. However, if a training committee NCO's interpreter had only one subject in weeks two, six and ten of the curriculum to become familiar with, each iteration would yield an improvement. No American in the camp was fluent in the Khmer (Cambodian) language.

In this time of fast-moving problem solving and wide-ranging solutions, some of the old-time Special Forces NCOs were discontented. Some senior NCOs, who had spent time in the remote CIDG camps and were used to carrying responsibilities much in excess of their ranks, felt that they were marginalized and under-employed. They felt that the old Special Forces methods with which they were most familiar were sufficient for the tasks at hand. Some younger NCOs chaffed at the new, more restrictive organization and procedures and they longed for the more free-wheeling atmosphere they had come to expect in Special Forces.

We were also deviating from textbook Special Forces doctrine which dictated that each battalion would be trained exclusively by one A Team. The training committee concept was the polar opposite of that cherished ideal. This deviation was justified because in the classic Special Forces scenario, the A Team would train a battalion and then remain with it to lead/advise as it performed its missions. Since we were limited to training one battalion after another without any subsequent attachment, the concentration of skills in a training committee was a sound decision.

Despite the initial resistance to various aspects of these changes, no one, to my knowledge, failed to perform his duties in the highest traditions of Special Forces.

I felt that because I was personally behind all of these changes, some of the NCOs harbored resentment toward me. After all, this was my first Special Forces assignment and I still wore the basic parachutist badge, the sure sign of a new guy. There were plenty of senior captains with multiple Special Forces tours in Vietnam whom these NCOs would have preferred to make these important decisions, even if the NCOs themselves were not a part of that process.

However, I had something none of them had: recent experience in an American combat unit whose mission matched closely with that of the FANK battalions. I had also served in U.S. Army training centers where American soldiers were successfully trained in skills identical to those we were focused on for the Cambodian units. And I had the will to do it my way.

All of the changes were not implemented simultaneously, but they were in place in time enough for the first four battalions to receive the level of training that was expected from the program. When the first battalion completed its program and was flown back to Phnom Penh, another, fresh battalion was delivered to us on the same U.S. Air Force C-130 aircraft. With this back-to-back rotation, we were never without four battalions or 2,048 FANK soldiers at Long Hai.

CHAPTER 22

Training the Bodes, Segment I

★ ★ ★

Having made the appropriate changes to secure a manageable organizational structure for the Cambodian Infantry battalions, a realistic training program and tailored-for-the-task Special Forces training teams, we proceeded at full speed to fulfill our assigned mission. That is not to say that we had complete control of our environment.

The province in which Long Hai was situated was called Phouc Tuy and it fell under the tactical operational responsibility of the 1st Australian Task Force, headquartered at Nui Dat, 20 kilometers (12.4 miles) to our northeast. Nui Dat was a typical large firebase but also had a helicopter contingent and a unit of tanks and M-113 Armored Personnel Carriers. Various battalions from the Royal Australian Regiment (RAR) rotated into the country to conduct combat operations. We had great respect for these outstanding soldiers.

The Australians frequently provided us with convoy security by road and air when we traveled to our FTX area at Xuyen Moc. We were constantly aware of their unselfish support because we were beyond the reach of most U.S. military assistance. If we had a temporarily assigned U.S. helicopter, it refueled at Nui Dat. Although the Australians used some American equipment such as armored personnel carriers and helicopters, they were justifiably quick to inform us that their country had paid full price for them. I think that these tough soldiers were proud that U.S. Special Forces would ask them for assistance.

As the first FANK battalions approached the end of their training program, Major Crismon thought it would be a morale builder to conduct a graduation ceremony. This would take place on the air strip across from the camp between the bay and the north/south road. For me it was a distraction because I had to insure that the air strip was secure and arrange for a military band to provide inspiring martial music for the ceremony.

After a fairly dismal performance by the motley Vietnamese Army provincial band at our first ceremonies, we again approached the Australians for help. Fortunately, they possessed an excellent pipe band and began to provide us with two bagpipers and a drummer on a regular basis. The last segment of these ceremonies was the pass in review, where the battalions would march in company formation past the highest-ranking Vietnamese, Australian or American reviewing officer we could procure. The pipe band would break into a very stirring marching song—perhaps "Scotland the Brave"—and the pass in review would begin. The troops would have a ragged start but without fail, before reaching the reviewing officer, would fall into a sort of proud, swinging swagger in perfect synchronization with the music. With their M-16s at sling arms, some of the short-statured soldiers' rifle butts barely cleared the ground. It was very satisfying to observe these confident, American-trained Cambodians marching to an Australian band in Vietnam.

The members of the pipe bands seemed to enjoy our camp and usually contrived to stay overnight, although the ceremonies never lasted more than 45 minutes. Over time we learned that their Nui Dat base had a beer ration—not more than two cans per day. Our club had no limits and the CIDG bartender could close only after the last patron had left. This was because we were a 24-hour operation and we made the club available for everyone's use. There were few abuses of this system.

The band members availed themselves of this liberal policy in a hearty manner. If they came to the camp on the day before the ceremony, they were less than spry the following morning but never failed to perform in a splendid manner.

Another group that worked inside the camp was the small detachment of Vietnamese Special Forces, or LLDB (usually called just "LL"), headed by a major. They were the "official" trainers of the Cambodians but rarely left their small office except to go home at night. They also had a large interest in the civilians working in the camp, including the security companies, especially regarding the payroll. Although I had four or five Vietnamese civilians working in my office, their administrative management was handled by another U.S. staff officer so I can't say that any irregularities occurred with regard to the LLDB and the civilian payroll.

Rounding out the camp contingent were two security companies, one Vietnamese and one ethnic Chinese, who were former CIDG or Mike Force members. They were each led by a Special Forces NCO and were mercenaries in the true sense of the word. They performed perimeter security and local ambushes at night, manned the camp mortars and generally maintained the numerous facilities in the camp. We paid them and they were considered extremely loyal.

When the training curriculum and the organizations for both the FANK battalions and the U.S. trainers at Long Hai had been satisfactorily revised, my most significant personal contributions—getting things done my way—were complete. However, the day-to-day operations continued to require creativity and decisiveness.

Our limitations, besides the quantity of Special Forces instructors, were time, firing ranges, maneuver facilities and vehicles.

The biggest challenge was to move four battalions to and from the FTX area at the beginning and end of weeks seven and eleven by truck convoys with a minimum of empty one-way trips. When the first battalion was transported to the FTX area in their eleventh week, we would use the same convoy to return the fourth battalion from their seventh week FTX. We just couldn't sustain the wear and tear on our vehicles by having them go or return empty. To accomplish this, sometimes I had to adjust the FTX schedule so that two battalions were in the field at one time. In addition, we had to schedule 30 kilometer (18.6 mile) round-trip convoys to the Vung Tau airfield to drop off departing battalions and pick up new battalions arriving for training.

To manage the competition for resources, I took a three-month calendar and wrote the dates along a horizontal line on graft paper. Then I drew horizontal lines under the dates that each battalion would be in the field. With this visual aid, I could shift departure and return dates so that the trucks were used with maximum efficiency. I used that same technique to insure that ranges and local maneuver areas were not double booked. Much later I learned that this was a primitive Gantt chart.

In OCS I thought that this much attention spent on troop transportation was boring and strictly a problem in Europe.

When the FANK battalions were in the FTX area, I would send an encrypted message specifying the coordinates for them to reach on the following day. This was exactly like the instructions I had received as the commander of Company A in the Americal and exactly what they could expect when they returned to Cambodia. I can say that putting two Xs on a map and knowing that two battalions totaling 1,024 men would be slogging through the unused rice paddies and interspersed jungle on the next day toward those objectives was a task I took very seriously because I knew firsthand the physical and psychological effort that would be required. So I felt a strong sense of responsibility to make these decisions with as much thoughtful deliberation as I could muster. I had been a captain for less than two years and directing the 2,048 FANK trainees and their U.S. cadre in their field operations was a heady experience for me.

The tall, looming Long Hai mountains were heavily mined. The French had been liberal with mines in this area and the VC had rearranged and supplemented them. Whenever the Australians ventured there, they invariably suffered casualties from mines. We also understood that the VC, knowing what was buried where, had used the mines to make the mountains into a sanctuary.

As far as we and the VC were concerned, Long Hai was a tactical backwater where little could be gained by expending resources against each other. We were focused on training and the VC's attention was on Vietnamese military targets elsewhere in the province. That did not mean that we refrained from prudent security measures including nightly ambushes and harassment and interdiction fire from our mortars. Every night we would fire the mortars into the mountains, hoping that our random rounds might surprise a luckless VC on a trail junction or stream bed. The VC also indulged in periodic action against the camp and its inhabitants.

One of the most devastating attacks by the VC against us involved one of our security companies. Five CIDG were in a medium-sized truck on the edge of the rice paddies gathering wood for the cooking fires in the FANK mess halls. The truck hit a stick that was the activator of a large tilt-rod mine. The truck was shredded and so were the men. The body parts were collected by the U.S. NCOs assigned to the security company. Later in the day, the camp executive officer (XO), a cadre team leader and I drove to the site in a jeep to survey the area.

We were hoping to find a way to avoid a recurrence but the thick brush made such a weapon nearly impossible to detect. Our jeep, normally used for convoy security, had an older .30 caliber machinegun mounted on a pedestal between the two front seats. As we were preparing to return to the camp, I deferred the front passenger seat to the XO and clambered over the rear of the vehicle into the rear seat. In doing so, the top of my bare head struck the pistol grip of the machinegun and opened a nasty gash.

Any head wound produces a lot of blood and an ounce of blood seems like a pint. We drove quickly back to the camp and directly to the dispensary. As we walked toward the door, I had an inspiration: one of the other captains would half carry me into the dispensary in a seeming unconscious state with my head covered with blood. It would be a laugh riot.

The camp's senior medic, a very competent and experienced NCO, was reading a book when we staggered in and he executed a classic double take. He threw his book straight into the air and began shouting orders to the Cambodian student nurses who were another part of our training program. When he realized that he had been the victim of a juvenile prank, he was less than appreciative of the creativity that generated it.

He treated my wound and began to stitch it closed, but I think he used less pain killer than was called for by the four-inch gash. I asked him to proceed in a way that would leave a subtle but visible scar that I could build a credible war story on, but, partly due to revenge and professional pride, he did a masterful job and no scar has resulted.

Special Forces in general had no shortage of colorful characters and Long Hai had its share; my S-3 section was not bereft. For a short period I was assigned an operations sergeant named MSG James T. Craig. He was a through-and-through professional who pried tasks from my unyielding hands and completed them in an exemplary manner. Unfortunately, too soon he had to return to the U.S. on emergency leave due to a sick relative and he never returned. He wrote a fine book about his experiences in Special Forces called "Team Sergeant;" this was the informal title for the most senior A Team NCO. I am obliquely mentioned in his book as the "sympathetic officer who supported the emergency leave."

Another senior NCO was assigned to replace MSG Craig. This individual was much more disengaged and seemed too preoccupied to perform any active work. I was used to running the office alone so this was not an immediate concern, but eventually I felt compelled to discuss this situation with him. He confided in me that he had been personally selected by General Westmoreland, the commanding general of all U.S. forces in Vietnam, to perform a mission so important that he couldn't be distracted by engaging in the mundane activities of the S-3 section. In fact it was so secret that he could not share the nature of this mission with me or the camp commander. This man was very quickly dispatched from the camp, no doubt on another secret mission.

The 5th Special Forces Group had left Vietnam on March 5, 1971, and we were then reassigned to the U.S. Army Vietnam Individual Training Group or USARV ITG (pronounced as an acronym: YOU sar vee followed by the initials eye tee gee). From this point on, I'll refer to the organization by combining an acronym with an abbreviation into a subordinate abbreviation : UITG. This term will be used to reference our higher headquarters from here on.

By this time two other B Teams, B-43 at Chi Lang and B-52 at Dong Ba Thin (sometimes lovingly referred to as Ding Ba Dong), had also been assigned the role of FANK training with three battalions each and joined us in UITG. Although we were apprehensive about our status when the 5th Group left, all of our positions were reaffirmed as Special Forces-qualified slots and we would continue to wear the beret. This last concession was encouraged by the USARV training directorate to add to the prestige of the UITG and to continue inspiring confidence in us from the FANK trainees.

We were no longer called B-36 and the Mike Force had been long gone. Over time, a variety of names were applied to our organization, including Long Hai Training Battalion, Long Hai Training Company, Long Hai Training Detachment, etc. Although we had little interest in these labels in terms of operations, there was an impact on some of the officers. In an American Infantry battalion the commander was a lieutenant colonel's position; so if you were a major commanding the Long Hai Training "Battalion," you were serving in a position authorized at one rank higher that yours. But a major commanding the Long Hai Training "Company," would seem to be performing in a job normally requiring a captain, one rank lower. Without protracted explanation or insight, a busy promotion board could easily misunderstand the level of responsibility in such assignments vis-à-vis the rank of the incumbent.

These inequities had always been a feature of Special Forces in Vietnam. For example, in the Mike Forces and the CIDG programs, each A Team would control a 500-man battalion and the team leader, a captain, would be the commander, normally a lieutenant colonel's slot in our Army. However, his official records would indicate that he was an A Team leader (not commander) in charge of 11 other U.S. soldiers.

For a Special Forces major commanding one of the Mike Forces, there was an even greater disparity. The old Mike Force at Long Hai consisted of four battalions and in conventional American units that was equivalent to a brigade. A U.S. Army brigade commander was always a full colonel or two ranks higher than a major; some brigades were commanded by brigadier generals.

An additional twist in the advancement of Special Forces officers was that their careers, including assignments, schooling and promotions, were controlled by a branch such as Infantry, armor, artillery, etc. There was no Special Forces branch at that time. These branches had "paths" that each officer was expected to follow in order to advance his career. So if an officer, although having gained hard-earned, unique experience in Special Forces assignments, did not revert to his branch's path, he was in danger of missing promotions and possibly being eliminated from the service. As mentioned earlier, some non-Special Forces officers were unsympathetic and uninterested in the unique aspects of Special Forces experiences which occurred outside the branch path. Some senior officers simply resented "elite" units.

For me personally, I was in a particularly vulnerable position since I was a "summer help" reserve officer, now in the Special Forces black sheep channel and had only a two-year college equivalency, the minimum required for OCS. My plan was to continue doing the best job I was capable of and trust that the system would reward me accordingly. In terms of my job assignment, an S-3 officer in the U.S. Army was never authorized below battalion level or less than a major's rank. A cursory glance at my official records would indicate that I was again performing in a position authorized at one level above my rank as I had done in the Americal. I expected this to offset some of my shortcomings on any career checklist.

The FANK training program did not move far beyond its inception without a tragic event. Major Paul Leary, who was the B Team commander when I arrived at Long Hai, had been transferred to Chi Lang near the Cambodian border in IV Corps to convert that Special Forces camp to a FANK training facility. During anFTX, one of the Chi Lang FANK units was attacked by a large NVA force.

In the action, four U.S. personnel and 16 FANK troops were killed. In the confusion of the battle, Major Leary, who had accompanied the battalion, was accidentally killed by a supporting helicopter gunship. Two of the NCOs who died had accompanied Major Leary to Chi Lang from Long Hai. I heard a report of the action at the time and have read several more accounts, but none seem to agree on the specifics. We all knew that Major Leary was a fine officer and a loss for everyone. Eventually the Chi Lang organization and its FANK training mission were moved to a former Vietnamese military training area just south of Long Hai village and renamed Phouc Tuy after the province in which we were located.

CHAPTER 23

Training the Bodes, Segment 2

★ ★ ★

Back in the Americal Division, the battalion S-3 officer was responsible for maintaining the radio logs which became the official records of the unit's activity and I have relied extensively on them to supplement my memory of that first tour. As the S-3 at Long Hai, I was probably responsible for doing the same but I didn't know that and never took a hand in that activity. In any case, I have been unable to locate any records with which to stimulate my memory and provide a timeline for my experiences at Long Hai. The few events to which I can put a date are based on outside accounts. Therefore, I'll relate the events as I remember them but in no particular order.

One of my jobs as the new S-3 officer that I had not anticipated was to conduct briefings for our many visitors. Generals, reporters, congressmen, ambassadors and other dignitaries came to our camp on a regular basis. This was due, I think, to the unique nature of our mission and the diminishing number of competing attractions in Vietnam due to the drawdown during Vietnamization. The late Gloria Emerson of the New York Times and Alan Dawson, old southeast Asia hand and UPI station chief in Saigon, were among the more well-known reporters. I was warned that Ms. Emerson might be overly inquisitive about confidential information. These writers seemed to enjoy pointing out that there were still "Green Berets" in Vietnam although the 5th Special Forces Group had departed. Noted military author Jac Weller also received a briefing and tour of the camp.

I had acquired several cherished emblems of Special Forces during my time at Long Hai: Rolex Submariner watch, star sapphire ring and chunky gold ID bracelet. During briefings, I wore the bracelet on my right wrist and, contrary to what I had learned in OCS, held the pointer in my right hand and reached across my body to point to the charts on my left. I thought this might give the visitors a flavor for Special Forces by providing a contrast to the colorless briefings they had probably received elsewhere.

In one late morning briefing, a visiting official asked me about how the intense training and distance from home had affected the morale of the Cambodian soldiers. Before I could answer, one of the FANK companies, returning from the firing range for lunch, marched past the briefing room singing one of their rousing, patriotic songs. It was perfect. We moved to the windows and watched them striding along, clearly in high spirits. I had to confess that we did not stage this happy coincidence but were tempted to do so in future briefings. I can still recite their refrain.

Without doubt, the most honored celebrity who visited us was the actress Martha Raye, who passed away in 1994. Known affectionately as "Maggie," she was a legend in Special Forces, especially among the old hands. Year after year she had visited Vietnam and brought friendly, down-to-earth cheer to men in the various CIDG camps. Maggie was awarded the extraordinary honor of wearing the

Green Beret with a lieutenant colonel's insignia of rank by President Johnson. Wherever she went, the NCOs would have a bottle of good vodka ready for her. She liked to reminisce with the NCOs she knew from previous visits, so I never intruded on that privacy and never got to know her. She is buried in the post cemetery at Fort Bragg—home of Special Forces.

Helicopters, as I have mentioned before, provided American soldiers in the field with everything from simple amenities to life-saving evacuation. At Long Hai we were extremely fortunate to be allocated a chopper for the two-month period during which our battalions were in the field. We could perform reconnaissance, resupply, convoy escort, medevac and other missions that would have been many factors more difficult without these helicopters.

Although the crews rotated, one of them was with us the most. They were from the 117th Assault Helicopter Company.

My job required that I fly with the helicopter crews on many occasions and some flights were more memorable than others. We were flying to Xuyen Moc one day, and as usual I was wearing an extra flight helmet and I could hear the crew's radio transmissions and their internal communications. We were over a cultivated area and the crew was chatting in the background while I was preoccupied with pending issues. I was vaguely aware that they had reached some sort of agreement among themselves and something was about to occur.

Suddenly I was pressed back into the jump seat and when I looked up, all I could see through the windshield was blue sky—the horizon had disappeared. Then there was the hack-hack-hack of the rotor blades clawing the air. The horizon slipped into and out of view again and only the dark green of the rice paddies was visible ahead;

I felt like I was falling forward and was restrained by the seatbelt. Again the rotors struggled to gain traction and at last the horizon returned to its normal position. We had just experienced the helicopter version of a hammerhead stall in which the craft had been brought into a maximum climb until its lift capability failed and the nose swung downward in an arc to an extreme dive. The trick was to endure that the ship recovered prior to impact with the ground.

During each battalion's FTX, one resupply of food was delivered by chopper. I usually went along to see how the troops were doing and to deliver mail to the cadre. When the FANK battalion's area was in the jungle, the troops had to find the largest clearing for the chopper to land and this sometimes required some felling of smaller trees. On several occasions the clearing was tight but the intrepid crew would try anyway. We would hover, drop down, edge right, slip backwards, slip left and so on until we touched down, unloaded and then repeated the procedure as we lifted generally straight up out of the small landing zone. Inevitably, one day, when executing such a maneuver, there was a slight jink one way or another and the rotor blades struck a substantial tree branch. Ouch. We landed and inspected the rotors blades, which were dented but serviceable enough to make the trip back to Long Hai. New rotors were ordered, delivered and installed. However, the pilot was thereafter referred to as Paul Bunyon.

Not long afterward we were in a similar situation but the pilot decided it was too tight to land and we would kick out the cartons of food and sacks of mail from about 30 feet of altitude. When everything was tossed out and we were lifting up, I noticed a fat newspaper—the Chicago Tribune—that had fallen out of a mail bag. It would be easy to simply pitch it out. Bit instead of just dropping it out of the door, I gave it an underhanded toss and up it went, up and WHACK—right into the spinning rotors blades—again.

Most of the newspaper dropped like a stone but a shower of white confetti was sent swirling downward by the propwash onto the troops below. I immediately confessed to the pilot because, with his record, he was in no position to chastise me. No damage was caused and both the pilot and I were once again spared from infamy.

Another of the seemingly endless thrills provided by the helicopter crew was initiated by one of the security company NCOs. His main concern was the VC who inhabited the Long Hai mountains and who were the principal threat to our camp. He had a theory about where they were concentrated and developed a plan to attack them in their lair. He took an 81mm mortar round and removed the fuse from its nose; the fuse normally would not detonate until it had been fired and travelled a specified distance. He packed the now-empty fuse well with C4 plastic explosive, leaving just enough room for an M-14 toe-popper mine. When dropped from almost any height, the M-14 would explode the C-4 which would explode the mortar round. It was a homemade bomb.

In a weak moment, the Huey crew and I agreed to conduct a visual reconnaissance over the suspected VC location. The sergeant brought four of his bombs along. We were cruising back and forth over the mountains with no clear results when we heard automatic weapons fire. In my usual seat in the cargo compartment, I could see both pilots. In unison, they turned their heads to the right and asked the crew chief if he had fired; negative; both turned left and asked the door gunner the same question; negative. That left only one possibility: we had received ground fire.

The sergeant, having no headset and therefore could immediately hear when the ground fire had begun, had jettisoned his bombs, no doubt surprising the bold VC with his automatic weapon. I had discussed with him the fact that the skids of the helicopter extended beyond the edges of the deck and that unless he pitched the rounds beyond them, he would effective shoot us down.

The pilots began pushing buttons and turning knobs and speaking in aviator abbreviations and acronyms. Apparently the VC had been lucky and scored one or more hits on the aircraft and we were going to make an emergency landing. Unfortunately, we were flying toward the other side of the Long Hai mountains from our camp and a 180-degree turn was not possible under the circumstances. The only thing I knew about that far side was that I didn't want to land there.

We descended quickly onto a dry rice paddy and shut down. The two door gunners stayed in place manning their machineguns and covering both sides of the craft. I gave my .45 pistol to the security sergeant's assistant and told him to cover the front which was a dead spot for the door gunners. The pilots examined the craft and found only one hole—in the rotor blade. They determined that we could safely fly back to the camp by skirting the mountain at the end of the peninsula. They would then order another rotor blade and another chapter was added to the legend of Paul Bunyon.

In the meantime, the Australians at Nui Dat had heard our initial radio distress call and the brigadier, call sign Blackjack, scrambled two helicopter gunships. Since the "bombs" had ignited a smoky fire, they used it as an aiming point for the gunships. With more experience in the mountains and probably more wisdom, the

Aussie gunships fired their rockets and miniguns at the target without actually flying over the mountains.

I was not on another flight to Xuyen Moc that observed a sampan moving in a restricted area along the coast; it was suspected of landing supplies for the VC. The helicopter crew buzzed the boat and its occupants beached the craft and fled into the wood line. The door gunners shot it up but it was so far onto the sand that it didn't sink. I thought we should destroy it completely to prevent its repair and further use by the VC.

I procured a white phosphorous grenade from the ammunition bunker at Long Hai and we began the flight to the derelict craft. White phosphorous is a very hot-burning substance sometimes used to create a smoke screen to mask movement. I planned to throw it into the boat which would then burst into flames.

Although I had used fragmentation hand grenades, white phosphorous grenades were new to me. I was especially not sure about the delay time after the pin was pulled and about the bursting radius. These thoughts were running through my head when the chopper touched down on the deserted beach near the boat. We had agreed that the craft would take off after I exited and orbit over the ocean until the grenade had exploded in the boat. In the meantime I would be on the beach alone, a situation that I had not completely thought through.

I have already described the instances in the Americal when I had been out of sight or touch with my comrades but this was something new. Armed only with my .45 pistol, I was virtually defenseless. The exact delay on the fuse and the bursting radius of the grenade were preying on my mind and I was reluctant to endure a shower of burning sulphur and phosphorous if I miscalculated.

In the end I used an underhand pitch at about 30 feet from the boat and then ran down the beach. Of course the heavy grenade fell short and only a few flaming fragments arced into the boat but at least I remained unscathed. I waved to the chopped to return, hoping that they would not have a little fun with me by "missing" my signal. After they picked me up, the door gunners machine-gunned the craft for a while and we returned to the camp hoping the tide would correct my botched effort.

We were hard hit when, during a period between FTXs, this crew was killed in a tragic accident on March 16, 1971. They were flying what was probably a milk run from one of the rear area bases near Saigon. After they lifted off from the Red Carpet Pad, the transmission froze at about 100 feet altitude. If a helicopter's engine stops in flight, it can usually be maneuvered safely to a bumpy landing by a procedure called autorotation. When the transmission seizes, it drops like a rock.

With all we had been through together, the crew had become a part of our camp and everyone felt an attachment to them. I will not list their names here but they are remembered on the 117th Assault Helicopter Company's web site.

Having flown with them so often, I can vividly remember the unauthorized decal on the back of one pilot's flight helmet: WARNING—CONTENTS UNDER PRESSURE. DO NOT PUNCTURE, CRUSH OR INCINERATE.

CHAPTER 24

Training the Bodes, Segment 3

★ ★ ★

While the training generally was proceeding smoothly, peripheral matters were always demanding our attention. The two security companies were the responsibility of the camp's S-2 (intelligence) officer, but I would designate the general area each night for the CIDG ambush teams. It was brought to my attention that the ethnic Chinese ambush teams would radio their actual positions back to the camp in the clear without encryption. Although this would only be a problem if the VC spoke Chinese, nevertheless I was tasked to address this issue.

I spoke with the Chinese interpreter who was the liaison with the Chinese security company and explained the problem. I showed him several simple but effective methods of encoding numbers so that coordinates could be securely transmitted by radio. He assured me that he understood and that the changes would go into effect the next day.

Two evenings later I encountered the interpreter at the time the ambushes were moving into place and asked him the status of our plan. He said that everything had been put into place and the squads were now encrypting their locations. I suggested that we go to the communications bunker and listen as the ambush locations were being reported.

As the squads called in, the interpreter would listen to the Chinese numbers, think for a few seconds, count on his fingers and then write the six-digit map coordinates on a pad, apparently having just decoded the numbers. We plotted them on a map to verify that they were in the correct position. Everything seemed to be working as I had directed.

I asked the interpreter to accompany me outside. When we were alone, I gave him my best crazy, angry American Infantry/Special Forces officer performance. I informed him that if he ever lied to me again, I would fire him from his comfy, safe job and march him over to the LLDB office to have him drafted into the Vietnamese army. This was always an attention-getter among the security company personnel who were exempt from conscription. I told him I knew unquestionably that the coordinates called in were not encrypted but were in plain Chinese. He knew I was correct about the non-encryption and that I was deadly serious about a career for him in the Vietnamese army.

How did I know? The answer was my high-school devotion to Dixieland music. One of the records from my teen-age years that saw a lot of play was a 33 1/3 RPM album by the Dukes of Dixieland. A song on that record was "Chinatown, my Chinatown." One of the Dukes would count off the tempo to start the song, but instead of "one…two…three…four," he would count, appropriately enough, in Chinese. Phonetically, the numbers sounded to me like "yet…yee…san…say." With dozens of repetitions, I could never forget those numbers.

Coincidentally, the map sheet for the Long Hai area had grid lines that contained only the digits one through four which were enough for me to understand. When the ambush team's coordinates were radioed in, I knew the precise English equivalents and that they had not been encrypted.

I never explained to the interpreter that the extent of my Chinese vocabulary was limited to four digits. And henceforth, I never had a problem with the security companies failing to follow my instructions. I also noticed that they stopped speaking in Chinese whenever I was nearby.

Another episode with the security companies was less benevolent. The camp had two 4.2 inch mortars and several 81mm mortars which were used for general defense, support of patrols and harassment and interdiction fires. The mortar pits had five-foot-high concrete walls for protection and a concrete bunkers to store a large number of rounds. The bunkers had an extension so the crew could sleep next to the guns for rapid response. See Figure 7.

Every day I would place four or five X's on a map along with random times throughout the night for the crews to fire into the Long Hai mountains. This was with the hope that we would catch a careless VC in some obvious place and ruin his night. One of the mortar pits was about 30 feet from my room and I would be awakened several times in the night as a result of my own handiwork.

Early one evening, a dreaded event began to unfold. A fire had broken out in a mortar pit in the north compound. Apparently one of the CIDG crew had been smoking in the living space and a blanket had caught fire. Sloppy habits had left some highly flammable propellant charges lying about and they had spread the flames. Next came the dry wooden boxes and cardboard cylinders in which the rounds were shipped and stored. There were hundreds of rounds of all types in the bunker. If those rounds exploded there would be devastation so vast that it was beyond our experience.

The camp commander was in Bien Hoa for a meeting so we took action as best we could. First we moved the two FANK battalions to the relative safety of the south compound. As we pondered our next step in this ugly, unprecedented situation, the supply sergeant, SFC Meredeth Tripp, hitched a jeep to a water trailer, drove it to the blazing bunker and began to pump water onto the flames. It took a few moments for the rest of us Special Forces heroes to rally to the initiative and courage of this veteran NCO.

Soon all of the Americans were crowded around the burning bunker forming a bucket brigade, bringing loads of water from the large tank in the center of the perimeter and trying to drag flammables from the bunker. There was no way to predict that we would be successful in extinguishing the fire or preventing an epic catastrophe. I ordered CPT Bob Marini, the chief of the training committee and my subordinate, to go to the safety of the south compound so if a bunker explosion wiped out the rest of us, a senior American would survive to take charge. Bob outright refused to leave and I knew that no one else would obey such an order. So we toiled on as we hoped for the tide to turn.

Another sergeant, without prompting, brought out our other large water tanker and a gun jeep and began the trip to Vung Tau, 15 kilometer away, to get the additional water we were sure to need. This was a night-time trip over unsecured roads that no one had dared to try before.

The most comforting aspect of this critical situation was that if the bunker exploded, I would not be around to take the blame for allowing the exposure of so many intrepid men to imminent danger, either from the burning bunker or the trip to Vung Tau.

In the end the conflagration was extinguished and the mini-convoy returned safely from Vung Tau. The other good news was that MSG Tripp was awarded the Soldiers Medal for his heroic actions; the medal includes a lifetime stipend to supplement his retirement. I told Bob Marini that he was a jerk for defying me, but no one could blame him for doing the same foolish thing that we were all doing.

The security companies were not alone in producing regrettable outcomes. One such incident occurred when a lieutenant colonel new to the program was driving in a jeep from his headquarters in Bien Hoa on the Long Hai road. He might have been assigned to the Phouc Tuy camp to our south or may have been one of the UITG commanders.

We had a permanent observation post on the high, steep ridge north of the camp manned by the Vietnamese security company. It had an excellent view of our training areas and rifle ranges and also the Long Hai road. In fact, the road was squeezed to a narrow strip of land between the ridge and the marshy salt flats. The observation post not only provided information on a large area of interest to us but it prevented the enemy from occupying the high ground and gaining that knowledge for themselves.

When the colonel burst into the camp, we knew he was one of us by his beret but we didn't know much else. He told us that as he was passing the ridge north of the camp he saw some "VC" on the hill and took them under fire with his M-16 rifle. The "VC" immediately shot back at him causing him to flee to the camp to report the incident and demand some action against the enemy. The camp commander handled this one but I'm sure no one admonished the security company people at the observation post for defending themselves.

Upon his arrival, I noticed that this particular colonel was wearing black, tight, leather gloves in the heat of the day. By now I had been in Vietnam for nearly two years overall and I had never witnessed this phenomenon. It may have been his version of my big red moustache back in the Americal.

There were a number of camp executive officers (XOs) during my time as S-3. Some of them were my friends and all of them had my respect. Technically, they were my rating officer who completed the all-important Officer Evaluation Report (OER). In reality, I did not work for any of them; I worked directly for the camp commander and the XO supervised the other staff officers. Nevertheless, I was occasionally at their mercy.

One of these gentlemen was a senior captain and somewhat headstrong. While he was making out one of my OERs, he told me: "I don't like you. I don't like anything about you. However, you do such a good job that I'm going to give you an excellent OER." I was at a loss for a snappy response.

This particular individual was involved in an event that transpired in the valley between the ridge with the observation post and the main ridge of the Long Hai mountains. Somehow, one of the Special Forces NCOs had been separated from a security company patrol that he had been leading. Something had to be done to find the lost American.

My solution was that the man had experience and he would eventually walk to the small Australian engineer compound located below observation post. The Australians would call us and we would pick him up.

Unfortunately, the camp commander was absent and of course the XO was in charge. He decided to mount a rescue party and, as fate would have it, night was falling. He gathered the young Special Forces NCOs and officers who were itching for some kind of action besides babysitting FANK trainees. As he rallied his forces and mounted the trucks for the short drive, I made sure he had a radio and asked repeatedly if he had made a radio check with the communications bunker. Yes, yes, of course. And off they went.

At that point, I was the senior officer in the camp and I knew that no good would come of this expedition but was powerless to stop it. I had the communications bunker operators try to reach the XO on the radio but, with no surprise to me, they couldn't. I had them call the Australians, through whose compound the expedition would have to pass to access the valley, but we were too late for that, too.

They flopped around in the valley for several hours before they realized that the man had indeed walked into the Australian compound. They drove back into the camp and I thought that the Crusaders returning from the Holy Land with the Grail could not have been more jubilant. I was joyful that they had not been ambushed, shot each other or shot the missing man.

Another painful and not much more inspiring event involved only one NCO. Somehow, an unofficial "Recondo" course had been slipped past me and was in full swing by an enterprising sergeant in the training committee. A small number of trainees were to be trained as a sort of super Recon group. For me, this should have been introduced after the trainees were exceptionally proficient in the basics, something that was yet to be achieved.

This "Recondo" instructor was teaching rappelling, a dubious skill for a regular Cambodian Infantry battalion with no access to helicopters but beloved by some for its showboat value. We had a 34-foot tower similar to those used at Fort Benning for airborne training. The instructor was at the top of the tower going through the rappelling procedures and acting as his own demonstrator. The trainees stood in rapt attention below.

The instructor was at the point where he was to lean back from the tower into empty space, push off and ease his decent by the friction of the rope on a snap link. Unfortunately, he had left out one step in the demonstration: he had only passed the rope through the snap link once instead of the required two wraps. This oversight provided the rope with no friction for breaking and he fell the 34 feet to land with his entire weight on a bent left leg.

He now had a nasty fracture of his left femur. The Special Forces medics are the best non-M.D. emergency medical personnel in the world and there were always several in the camp. Two of them were on site immediately and some of the others went to alert the helicopter crew for a medevac. It soon became clear that the NCO had also severed his femoral artery, a very serious internal bleeding condition.

As the medics were treating him and preparing to move him to the chopper, the trainees were standing around in mild shock and probably reevaluating their choice of volunteering for Recondo. With sweat running profusely from his forehead, and overcoming the pain of the break and the splint, the sergeant, in the best Special Forces tradition, continued his lecture, calmly explaining his mistake and how to correct it, even as he was being carried away. I was there, hovering, and saw no reason to intervene in the orderly and professional process managed by the medics.

One day an older master sergeant showed up at the camp but didn't seem to have any orders assigning him there. Everyone seemed to know him and, as with some such senior men, he was called "Pappy." He spent a lot of time in the club and was a melancholy, solitary drunk. Although this was not my jurisdiction, I got the impression that he was about to leave Vietnam and had some deep sorrow about his experiences there.

One night I was in the club and I got a call from the inner security gate from a Vietnamese security man. Pappy was there and causing some big problems. The Vietnamese security company people were good at handling outsiders trying to get into the camp, but were reluctant to try to control a Special Forces NCO trying to get out.

I quickly arrived at the security gate and Pappy was there giving the guard a hard time. In the dim security light I could see that he was bare foot and had a wooden box on one shoulder. I got closer and saw that the box was marked "hand grenades." Pappy was trying to get out of the camp at 9:30pm with a box of hand grenades

I accosted him and tried to reason with him. He said he wanted to get even with the VC for killing his buddies. I tried to reason with him again. He was drunk and determined to charge out the gate and up to the VC-dominated mountains to avenge his fallen comrades. I started to lose my temper because he wouldn't listen to reason and because being drunk in our camp just wasn't a professional type of behavior.

He turned away from me and started toward the gate again, so I spun him around, knocked the box off of his shoulder and pushed him over backwards. I sat on his abdomen and pinned his arms to the ground. Then I gave him a full dose of my crazy Special Forces captain persona who should not be crossed. I told him he was a disgrace, that he was disgracing his dead buddies, that he was a disgrace to his living buddies, and that he was a disgrace to people like me who respected him for all of his well-known accomplishments. I told him a lot more things that I don't remember because I was not just pretending to be incensed.

Eventually, I calmed down and helped him up and we went to sit on the sandbagged wall of a barracks building of a FANK battalion that was absent in the field. He apologized and told me why he was behaving so badly. I apologized and told him that it drove me crazy to see a respected NCO, whom the younger men looked up to, behave in such a destructive manner. Eventually we shook hands and started to walk back to the inner compound, me to the club for a drink and him to his room to prepare to leave in the morning. As we walked he said, "You know, you're a good officer. You seem to care about people. Thanks." With that he displayed a large, wicked-looking knife that I hadn't noticed but could have had only one purpose.

Some antics were generated by people who came to join our unit but weren't what they seemed. One such individual was a lieutenant who inexplicably had a jeep for his personal use and drove it from Bien Hoa down to Long Hai alone. The sergeant major brought him into the camp commander's office for his initial interview. The lieutenant handed the old man his orders, saluted and reported in the specified manner: "Sir, Lieutenant So-and-so reporting for duty." The major glanced at the orders and informed him that he had stated a different name from that on the paperwork. Crushed, the man nearly broke down.

It seemed that he was in the CIA on yet another secret mission at Long Hai and he had reported with his real name instead of the false name on the orders. Somehow he convinced the major that he was legitimate, if that's the correct word, and to allow him to stay at the camp. He was given some innocuous duties but he had to make frequent, unspecified trips back to Saigon in his personal jeep.

On one return trip, as he was passing through Long Dien, the district headquarters and the first town north of Long Hai, he managed to flip the jeep. Luckily he was wearing a seat belt, something no one else ever did because it hindered an exit from the vehicle during an ambush. As he was dangling upside down in the overturned vehicle, his CIA credentials fell onto the pavement and were snapped up by a quick-thinking Vietnamese boy.

Before the war, and since, Long Hai was a resort town with wonderful beaches. At the time in question they were quite nice and we used them periodically. This "lieutenant" went to the beach some time later and left his uniform on the sand while he went for a quick swim. If you didn't see this coming, it's true that someone again stole his replacement credentials as they laid unattended on the beach.

CHAPTER 25

Training the Bodes, Segment 4

★ ★ ★

When Major Crismon's tour as camp commander was complete, his replacement arrived and I was scheduled to present a more detailed briefing than the visiting firemen received. Who was his replacement? It was none other than Major Glenn A. Lane, the 5th Special Forces Group assistant adjutant, who had been so adamant that I should be assigned to Long Hai. Whatever his motives might have been, Major Lane and I worked very well together. He obviously knew my background and capabilities and treated me like a competent staff officer. I would prepare suggestions and plans to address problems and missions and he would carefully consider them and make necessary corrections according to his view of the big picture.

When we had settled into a rhythm of interaction, from time-to-time I applied a technique I had developed from studying his methods. If I had a really good idea and didn't want him to tinker with it, I would submit it with an easily detectable but minor flaw. That would allow him to have his input but not spend too much time examining the key elements. Otherwise, I valued his guidance and sometimes very bold, even reckless, decisiveness.

One example of Major Lane's heart-attack-inducing ideas occurred when we were honored with the presence of two ambassadors, one from the U.S. to New Zealand and one from New Zealand to Vietnam, as I recall. New Zealand had a contingent of trainers in the other two FANK training camps. After I had briefed the gentlemen, Major Lane announced that we would all visit a FANK battalion in the field near Xuyen Moc. I was astonished and appalled. To me this was a huge physical risk for the ambassadors and certain death for our careers if even a minor incident occurred. The ambassadors and Major Lane seemed blithely oblivious to any potential catastrophe, so off we went to the field.

In retired Colonel Charles M. Simpson III's book, "Inside the Green Berets," he refers only indirectly to the FANK training program in one sentence. However, photograph 23 in his book is captioned "5th SFG in VN training;" it was taken in the field near where the ambassadors were chatting with FANK officers. In the foreground, alert-looking Cambodian soldiers stare vigilantly into the jungle undergrowth under the watchful eye of an officer from their assigned A Team cadre. I am in the background; my look of impending doom is clearly discernible. Happily, no disaster ensued and, happier yet, no more ambassadors visited Long Hai.

Another fallout from the ambassadors' visit to Long Hai was the exposure of major deficiencies at the camp. It seems that during a post-briefing coffee and cookie social gathering, an ambassador's paper cup sprang a leak—so frightfully gauche. In addition, the paper plates were deemed unstable as well as a few other inelegant shortcomings. The general accompanying the ambassadors thought we could do better. I was certain that this situation had not been addressed in the Officer's Special Forces Qualification Course at Fort Bragg.

Nevertheless, Major Lane not only rose to the occasion, he soared above it. At the next reception after a VIP briefing, china cups and plates on linen table cloths awaited our guests along with a greater variety of food and beverages. I don't know how he did it but I was glad that it was not in my area of responsibility.

This was a time when my luck at Long Hai was at its peak. Major Lane, as camp commander, had extensive responsibilities that extended well beyond training the Cambodians. These included political interaction with the local Vietnamese authorities and the FANK hierarchy. Logistics, in the form of equipping, feeding and transporting over 2,000 FANK troops was a major task. I was gratified that after he had approved my plan for a particular operational activity, he allowed me to execute it without any micromanagement.

There were many events at Long Hai that just can't be logically related together. One such occasion was when Major Lane and I were invited to Vung Tau for dinner with two American officials. It was implied that since the dinner was scheduled so late in the day that we would stay overnight; no one in their right mind would drive from Vung Tau to Long Hai after dark. It was unusual for both of us to be gone from the camp at the same time but this opportunity seemed intriguing.

When we arrived at a house that was something just short of a villa, we were met by two gentlemen in very nice suits. They wore their jackets throughout the time we were there so I assume they had air conditioning. We had drinks and chatted about our experiences in the military. The two gentlemen said they were advisors to the Vietnamese national police which even I could translate to mean CIA.

We sat down to dinner at a neat table with nice place settings and two attractive young ladies served the dinner. When the ladies withdrew the gentlemen came around to the point of our visit. It seemed that along the route that our helicopters were flying to Xuyen Moc, we had been firing a good deal of artillery, mortars, machine-guns, naval gunfire and anything else we could muster. They politely asked us why.

The simple answer was that we had intelligence that the VC in that area had some Stinger-type surface-to-air missiles that would be detrimental to our choppers. We politely asked why this was a concern for them.

They shared with us that they had an important agent in that area whom we, in our understandable zeal, had nearly killed on several occasions. They also assured us that their agent had confirmed that no Stingers were now or ever had been available for use against U.S. aircraft along that route. If we could refocus our firepower into some other area, they would be very appreciative and would keep us informed of any change in the Stinger status.

This seemed to be a small price to pay for a very nice dinner and drinks with two such amiable gentlemen. We stayed the night in comfortable rooms and drove back to Long Hai in the morning. On the drive back, I thought of my first-tour visit to the Tien Phouc Special Forces camp and the two refrigerators. That chance encounter had ultimately led to my very favorable assignment as S-3 at Long Hai. Would this meeting, complete with even more amenities, sway me toward another career path?

One day a message came down from the "highest level of command" stating that in view of the ongoing withdrawal of American forces, no new construction would take place on U.S. installations. Major Lane had been planning an addition to the somewhat shabby all-ranks club that we had mostly outgrown. He wanted a stage, short order window and a few other niceties. Not long after the message arrived, construction began on the new club annex. When the annex was complete, a movie theater was begun. The logic was that if we showed movies outside instead of in an enclosed theater, the VC in the mountains could use the light as an aiming point for their mortars. I don't know where the lumber and concrete came from.

Another amenity available at Long Hai was the Hotel de la Piscine, located about 500 meters south of the camp on the edge of the village. If I have remembered the name correctly, "piscine" is French for swimming pool, and the hotel did indeed have such a pool. The water was the color, and probably the consistency, of lime Kool-aid. Periodically, a Vietnamese rock-and-roll band entertained in the bar on the top floor. A Chinese noodle shop was on the grounds and was a popular weekend hangout. Since the hotel was regularly frequented by our troops, we posted a security company guard there during operating hours.

The hotel was owned by two businessmen, one American and one Chinese. The American was married to an attractive Vietnamese singer. I didn't have much interaction with them but always wondered what their plans were when the war reached its inevitable conclusion. Despite the resort status of the town, business from Vietnamese civilians was not booming at the hotel during the war.

At the time of this particular incident, a Vietnamese militia unit called Regional Force/Popular Force or RF/PF, lovingly referred to as Ruff Puffs, occupied a compound south of Long Hai. The Chi Lang FANK training center would eventually relocate there. The RF/PFs had American advisors from the Military Assistance Command Vietnam or MACV. One weekend the hotel was busier than usual with Special Forces personnel, MACV and even some Vietnamese. I was just outside the main door talking to the CIDG guard when someone came out and said that one of the MACV sergeants had gone crazy and was threatening people with an M-16.

I didn't always carry my issued .45 pistol because I had a Walther PP pistol in a shoulder holster under my uniform shirt. The PP (for Polizei Pistole or police pistol) was Walther's intermediate pistol and was small enough to be easily concealed yet fired a 9mm round. If it jammed, it was still heavy enough to make a dent if you smacked someone with it. I pulled out the PP, chambered a round and put it in my shirt's side cargo pocket. The guard offered to "take care of" the out-of-control sergeant but I waved him off and walked into the foyer.

The MACV sergeant was standing on the stairs overlooking the lobby, brandishing the M-16 and raving. About fifteen people were standing in the foyer, afraid to move. If he started shooting, I figured he'd start with the people closest to him and that would give me time to grab my pistol and fire. If he'd been from our camp, I would have tried to talk him down, but he was an unknown entity to me.

The standoff went on for about 10 minutes before a MACV officer finally arrived and began a dialog with the deranged man. Eventually, the situation was defused and the man was escorted off the premises by the officer. As I left I thought the CIDG guard seemed somewhat disappointed.

The hotel provided a backdrop for other, more relaxing occasions. In one case, Major Lane decided that since our camp was providing so much business for the hotel, the two owners should show their appreciation by hosting an evening of free food and drinks for us. He specified that everything must be top shelf, including the delicacies from the nearby sea. The owners agreed.

Coincidentally, on the day before the big event, a major from our USARV headquarters was coming for a two-day visit. "Visit" was code for informal inspection. I gave him to Bob Marini to escort to the various training venues and to dazzle him with our brilliant performance. That evening, Bob and I were discussing the progress of the visit/inspection and we devised an amusing plan.

The following day at about 5pm, Bob and the major came into my office to discuss a few minor matters. When we had finished, I asked Bob, "Well, should we take the major to the hotel tonight?" Bob replied, "I don't know. It's always the same there, night after night." "Yeah," I said, "it's kind of boring. Maybe we'll just stay at the camp tonight." The major was intrigued by the idea of a hotel at a beach resort and "suggested" that we should go. We reluctantly agreed.

When we got to the upstairs bar, rows of tables lined the dance floor and they were overflowing with the bounty of land and sea as well as a generous variety of spirits. Bob suddenly stopped and exclaimed, "Oh no, not more free lobster again! That's it, I'm leaving." He stormed out.

The major readily forgave our little joke and heartily partook of the feast. However, he decided to stay an extra night and insisted that we visit the hotel again. I think he was making sure that the miracle was really not a nightly affair and that he was not missing out on the best assignment in Vietnam.

Other social events became routine at the hotel. After the first few battalions had completed their training cycles, the new battalions began to host welcome and going away parties at the hotel. These were like the hail and farewell affairs that were conducted in American officers' clubs worldwide.

Since the battalions' arrivals and departures were staggered at one-week intervals, these festivities would be spread over seven weeks, sometimes with two per week. Although the parties were not sumptuous, they were generously catered and we appreciated them.

During these events, the FANK officers would approach us and ask to dance. Naturally, this was disconcerting to the masculine self image of the rough-and-tumble young Special Forces officers, not excluding me. Luckily we soon discovered that this was not the cheek-to-cheek style of dancing but the individual, stylized form usually depicted on travel posters for Cambodia and Thailand.

The dancers would form an "OK" sign with each hand and move them gracefully up and down in front of the body while executing a simple one-two, one-two step. Eventually, I felt that I had become quite proficient in this form of Cambodian dancing. It was always amusing to inform clueless newly assigned officers that they would have to dance with their Cambodian counterparts.

Some events at Long Hai were not always simply quirky, they sometimes had elements of the bizarrely coincidental. On one such occasion, I had been called to Bien Hoa to our higher headquarters for a meeting with my counterpart, the S-3. It was a strange situation wherein an Air Force liaison officer had somehow become the operations officer instead of a Special Forces officer. I saw his name tag—McCormick--and something about it rang a bell. I noticed that he seemed interested in my name tag as well.

Finally he asked me if I had a relative in the Air Force. Well, yes, my brother, Gene, was a pilot in KC-135 mid-air refuelers. Surprised, he told me that he had been stationed with my brother at Lockbourne Air Force Base in Ohio and was his neighbor in the nearby town. I had remembered his name from a war story my brother had told me years ago.

Many stories about American units in Vietnam include accounts of adopted pets. I had never seen one in the Americal or for a long time at Long Hai. However, on one occasion the Cambodians had somehow acquired an eaglet during an FTX and had plans to use it to supplement their rations. One of the cadre bought it and brought it back to camp. He nurtured it and it grew quickly to an imposing size. It would perch on the various antennas and efficiently keep the camp free of rodents.

On some mornings after a late night at the club or reading in my room, I would be walking half awake through the fog to the mess hall. The eagle would rattle me by gliding silently from behind only a few feet over my head, suddenly blocking out the meager sun and casting his ominous shadow on the ground ahead.

The story of the eagle and his other personal adventures at Long Hai during this time are recounted in retired LTC George Lanigan's book, "Alone in the Valley." Lanigan successfully writes in the voice of a very junior NCO who is frequently frustrated by officers who don't see situations and problems with the same clarity that he possesses. Several of his anecdotes, including the "bombs" from the helicopter over the Long Hai mountains, vary significantly from my recollections. Coincidentally, then-Sergeant Lanigan and I were awarded the Army Commendation Medal on the same orders.

On another occasion a new UITG commander was assigned and began the obligatory tour of his subordinate units. When he arrived at Long Hai, I recognized him instantly. He was LTC Edward S. Rybat Jr., an armor branch officer. I had known him slightly back in USATCA at Fort Knox when he was a major. Colonel Rybat was an experienced Special Forces officer and apparently a body builder because of his broad shoulders and muscular arms. He was never especially cordial to me during our shared period in Vietnam. He had a big, toothy smile that reminded me of the Big Bad Wolf.

No account of the post-5th Special Forces Group period at Long Hai would be complete without including the contributions of the Australian Army Training Team Vietnam (AATTV). This was the training organization from the Australian Army that previously had focused on the Vietnamese armed forces. When the 1st Australian Task Force left Vietnam, Long Hai and Phouc Tuy training centers were augmented by members of the AATTV.

Our contingent of Aussies was assigned to the training committee because there was some legal restriction about them accompanying FANK troops to the field as cadre. They were almost all senior NCOs known as warrant officers. A major was also in this group. Since the American camp commander was a major, this AATTV major was assigned to the next most logical position—the S-3. Of course as the incumbent, I was not pleased with this arrangement. I had put too much into the program to willingly step aside and allow someone else, Australian or not, to tinker with my handiwork.

As a result, I employed various artifices to keep control of the S-3 section, including never-ending orientations for the new major to "learn the ropes." Eventually, I think he understood the situation and arranged to be assigned elsewhere in a job where he would have responsibility commiserate with his rank. He handled the situation with much more grace than I did. However, looking back, if I had it to do over again, I would have been just as selfish and boorish in order to keep a job that I really loved.

I can't say enough about the contribution of the Australians to the FANK mission and their unwavering professionalism. However, there was always an element of reserve in their attitude toward the mission, the Cambodians and their U.S. comrades, particularly among the officers. It seemed that there was some looming, overshadowing, unexpressed issue that seemed to wall the Australians off from us.

In some ways, I understood the local Vietnamese officials and their motivations better than I did our Australian Army counterparts, even with the many common characteristics we shared. Despite all of this, one of the most cherished accolades from my Long Hai experiences was when one of the Australian warrant officers approached me in private and said, "You're a good 'un." This is the highest expression of respect from the enlisted men in the Australian armed forces (and in British services) to an officer.

An excellent book about FANK training, from the Australian perspective and containing extensive details on the battalions, is "Training the Bodes" by Terry Smith. As with most accounts, it does not address the initial turmoil we experienced in implementing the program.

Early in my tour, I went into our small mess hall at noon and noticed a small Asian man wearing plain green fatigues instead of the tiger stripes normally worn by the security companies. The only free chair was at his table so I joined him and gave a friendly nod as I would to any of the security company CIDG. We didn't have any lunch-time conversation as we were both preoccupied and there was, presumably, a language barrier.

Later I asked the mess sergeant why a CIDG was eating in the American mess hall. He quickly informed that the man was Dr. Thanh, whom I have previously described. He was the chief political liaison between Lon Nol and Cambodian nationals in Vietnam, including FANK trainees at Long Hai.

Dr. Thanh had been prime minister of Cambodia for a short period at the end of World War II and would be so again in March 1972.

We were given cards written in Cambodian and signed by Dr. Thanh, seen at Figure 8. I have never confirmed the clunky English translation but the text seems to have a whiff of political references.

Dr. Thanh would periodically drive to the camp in his older Mercedes sedan to confer with the camp commander and the FANK officers. Sometimes he would show up if there was a problem with the trainees and his arrival would bode no one well. In the U.S. Army, punishment below court martial level can be administered by an immediate commander and is called non-judicial punishment, or Article 15 of the Uniform Code of Military Justice. It was rumored that Dr. Thanh used a .45 pistol to administer justice and maintain discipline. If a Cambodian officer misbehaved and was seen being taken away in Dr. Thanh's Mercedes, we felt certain that he would be receiving a "Dr. Thanh Article 15."

CHAPTER 26

Training the Bodes, Segment 5

★ ★ ★

Some misfortunes befell the FANK troops due to unfortunate accidents and to some of their quirky, unpredictable behavior.

With the exception of the losses due to enemy action at Chi Lang, the most devastating casualties occurred at the Phouc Tuy training center south of Long Hai. The enterprising cadre there decided that it would be beneficial for the FANK units to observe the capabilities of helicopter gunship firing rockets and miniguns despite the fact that no such support would be available to them in Cambodia. One or more gunships were duly arranged and the three battalions were assembled on a firing range to view the demonstration.

For some inexplicable reason, the gunships approached from the rear of the assembly and began firing over their heads. Something went wrong and several rockets landed among the troops, especially within one battalion's command group. I'm not sure of the number of killed or wounded but the tragedy was 100 percent preventable.

Not all of the Cambodians saw the incident as a lamentable blunder. Always leery of their traditional Vietnamese foes, some of the surviving officers suspected a conspiracy and there arose the real possibility of a revolt among the FANK units. Not until Dr. Thanh was called in was the threat of violence quelled.

In any weapons training anywhere, on at least one occasion the trainees are admonished with the phrase: "Whatever you do, don't ever…." Sometimes working through an interpreter can cause the admonition to lose some of its force and sometimes there are people who simply can't follow instructions. I think the latter occurred in the following episode with regard to an M-79 grenade launcher round.

The shotgun-like weapon's standard projectile is 40mm in diameter. If the projectile didn't explode on impact—a dud-- which sometimes happened, it resembled a gold-colored golf ball and remained extremely sensitive to any disturbance. One of our most emphasized "…don't evers…." was physically interacting with an M-79 dud. When these were discovered on our ranges, the Special Forces engineer NCOs would safety detonate them.

On one fine day as a company of FANK trainees was marching to the firing range, one of the soldiers broke ranks, ran over to a shiny M-79 dud and kicked it. It exploded and instantly killed him, as it was designed to do when detonated. No one could explain the anomalous behavior.

Periodically, we encountered other dangerous munitions in the training areas such as the undetonated 500-pound bomb shown in Figure 9. Our expert engineer NCOs would detonate them with plastic explosives.

The Cambodians instigated some other disruptions that we could simply not tolerate. The north compound at Long Hai had an inner perimeter which contained all of the camp support facilities and the living quarters for the U.S. staff, training committee and cadre for two battalions. Two FANK battalions lived in barracks along the perimeter berm in buildings formerly occupied by the Mike Force mercenaries. The access road into the camp separated the two battalions' barracks.

One evening as I was conducting a security check at the hotel, a CIDG guard notified me that there was an alert at the camp. Since I had a role to play in all alerts, I drove back but was stopped at the main gate by the CIDG guards. Their standing orders were to prevent anyone from entering during an alert, but since I had issued that order, logically I could exempt myself. The guards saw the soundness of this reasoning and wisely let me pass.

I drove into the camp and up to the gate of the inner compound, which was closed according to standard procedure during an alert. A dim electric light illuminated the gate and I walked up to it and tried to enter but the gate was locked. At that moment, one of the senior master sergeants, who was not one of my fans, appeared decked out with helmet, flak jacket and M-16. Although I was clearly visible, he pointed the weapon at me and demanded, "What's the password?" I generally had no patience with fools and certainly not when there was some type of emergency afoot.

I not-too-gently reminded him that we had no such passwords and that if we did I would certainly know them. I ordered him to open that gate, something I would have accomplished with another NCO by a simple request. I located the sergeant major, Johnnie Miller, and asked him about the situation.

SGM Miller succinctly described one of the most serious internal problems we had ever faced with the FANK battalions. Every battalion we had previously trained was strictly and unanimously Buddhist. They had given their Americans trainers medallions or pins with Buddha's images on them which they felt would offer protection in combat. I referred to them as "you-can't-kill-me" pins. I always wore mine out of respect for their belief and maybe a little to hedge any bets on my mortality. See Figure 10.

During this particular training cycle, we had been surprised to learn that one battalion in the north compound was exclusively Muslim. They were called Chams and occupied a small, fairly autonomous region in Cambodia. They also harbored mistrust and animosity toward their Buddhist countrymen, who were an overwhelming majority. This hostility had just erupted into a gun fight between the two groups whose barracks faced each other across the camp access road along which I had just driven. However, for the time being, all was quiet.

Somehow, the handling of this situation devolved to me. I located the senior, and politically well-connected, interpreter named "Blue." I had Blue call across the hard-packed dirt ground to the two warring sides, each about 30 and 40 meters away, to secure a cease fire and both agreed. Blue then called to the Buddhists that we were coming to confer with them first. There was a pause and then they agreed.

As Blue and I were leaving the inner compound gate, SGM Miller volunteered to come along. Before we could clear the gate, our Cambodian friends across the clear open area informed us through Blue that as a condition of the conference we did not bring weapons. This gave us pause but in the end we knew that two M-16s and my .45 pistol would be no match for the 100 M-16s in that barracks if worse came to worse. I tried, but failed, to imagine how my 9mm Walther PP pistol, concealed in my shoulder holster, could be used to our advantage.

The three of us walked out of the gate from the inner U.S. compound into the open space toward the "rebel" barracks. There was sufficient illumination from the light at the gate to show that we were unarmed. Blue was about four feet to my left and slightly to the rear and the sergeant major was on the right, level with Blue. Suddenly I had a very strange thought: this is like the climactic scene in the movie "Gunfight at the OK Corral." The low, weathered buildings; strings of barbed wire and hard-packed, sandy soil were too perfect. I turned my head slightly to the sergeant major and murmured, "Clink…clink…clink," as I took each step, but I don't think he was imagining the sound of jingling spurs like I was. If loud, dramatic music in a minor key had suddenly swept over us, I would not have been surprised.

We were escorted into the barracks and there seemed to be a party atmosphere. Some of the younger trainees were laughing and jumping around the building but the officers were edgy. It was as if nothing had happened and if something had, it was not their fault. I invoked Dr. Thanh several times but for some reason that didn't get the desired effect; they seemed remarkably defiant. I had seen other, less serious, times when their pride would overcome their normal friendly, rational behavior and good sense. We all knew that there were 512 Buddhists and the same number of Chams in the north compound but only about 275 Americans and CIDG in the entire camp.

I made it clear that I was not there to negotiate but to demand their compliance with acceptable behavior between allies. I reminded them that they were far from home and that any further aggressive action would bring down massive firepower from American,

Vietnamese and Australian forces and cause them certain and unrelenting devastation.

Finally they saw the wisdom of my argument and we agreed that no more shooting would occur if the Chams would also respect a cease fire. Blue shouted to the Chams that we were coming over and off we went. Clink…clink…clink. They were more dour that the Buddhists but less antagonistic. As a minority, they had issues and sometimes saw slights when none were there. With the Chams, less explicit threats were sufficient to defuse the situation.

I don't remember the fallout from this adventure; it was not my problem anymore. We learned after the war that Cambodians were ruthlessly murdered on a massive scale in the killing fields by their own people, the Khmer Rouge. There was something dark in their character that was completely foreign to the usually likable individuals we knew at Long Hai.

After I had become the operations officer, my duties kept me mostly at the camp. See the cluttered desk in Figure 6. On a few occasions, it was essential to share some of the dangers of field duty.

One particular battalion was scheduled to be moved by truck to the Xuyen Moc FTX area and no senior American was available to lead the convoy, so I assigned myself to that duty. This was not a particularly desirable job because the lead vehicle would most likely detonate any mines in the road. Also the VC would target and disable the lead vehicle in order to immobilize everything behind it during an ambush. Nevertheless, an American would always lead every convoy to demonstrate our willingness to share the dangers of the unavoidable convoys.

The lead jeep in which I would ride was armed with a .50 caliber machine gun on a swivel pedestal. This weapon fires a half-inch diameter round. The long, thin barrel extended a foot beyond the windshield. It was not only a deadly weapon, it looked deadly. Behind the jeep was a column of perhaps 15 2.5 ton trucks with the rifle and machine gun barrels of 512 FANK troops bristling on either side. Smaller trucks carrying 20 security company CIDG were placed intermittently throughout the convoy; M-60 machine guns were mounted on the roofs of those trucks. Somewhere along the road to Xuyen Moc we would meet Vietnamese Army or Australian armored vehicles that would provide additional security for us.

I stood up in the open jeep and looked back on this awesome array of weapons. I don't know how General Patton felt at the head of the Third Army's tanks in Europe during World War II, but I felt a palpable pulse, or throb, of power and I liked it.

The tense, hot, humid trip along muddy roads and past blown-up bridges was memorable but not because of exploding mines and desperate firefights with enemy ambushes. On the road to Xuyen Moc, about 16 kilometers (10 miles) from Long Hai, we passed through the prosperous village of Dat Do. It was the most beautiful Vietnamese town I had ever seen. It appeared exactly circular from the air, and the trees mingling with the red-tile roofs were picture-post-card perfect. Late in the war this was the village about which an American advisor commented: "We had to destroy it in order to save it." It can be seen today on Google Maps Satellite View, apparently fully restored.

As the end of my tour approached, we had made some changes in the way our local security ambush operations were conducted. Instead of the out-at-night and back-in-the-morning operations, the security companies would have their teams spend three consecutive days in the field. This reduced the likelihood of being observed while coming and going to their ambush locations. The second change was to rename the ambush squads as the "Hatchet Force." This, presumably, would strike fear into the hearts of the VC.

It came to pass that one afternoon, a Hatchet Force patrol ran into a group of VC of unknown size who got the better of them. Several of the team were wounded so that the remaining men were unable to carry them to a helicopter landing zone for extraction. We would have to send a patrol to rescue the Hatchet Force.

I looked around the camp for assets to perform this task. In terms of the security companies, the first team was the Hatch Force, which was eliminated by default. The second team was providing security for an FTX convoy and wouldn't return for hours. That left a less-than-desirable third team. And what about those hard-charging, action-hungry young lieutenants? Some were on R&R; others were in the field on an FTX; some were at the Vung Tau airfield receiving a new FANK battalion. The experienced NCOs' status mirrored that of the lieutenants.

I found myself, with only 10 days remaining in country, the only logical choice to lead the cavalry into Indian country.

I rounded up the unenthusiastic third team CIDG and got them organized. Luckily, I found a young American medic and pressed him into service. One newly assigned lieutenant seemed eager to come along. As the saying goes: you go to war with the army you have at the time.

When everything was ready, I returned to my office, put on my never-before-used helmet and flak vest and grabbed my dusty M-16 rifle. These actions were so unusual that my pretty Vietnamese secretary said, "Where you go, Dai Uy?" I had a flashback to my first tour and Company A. Back then, Bogie, one of my radio operators, was a huge movie fan and he liked to use quotes from them. His favorite was a World War II movie called "A Walk in the Sun." He often said if anyone ever asked what he did in Vietnam, he would nonchalantly respond with that phrase. I couldn't resist. I slapped a magazine into the rifle, chambered a round and replied in a way that I thought would make Bogie proud.

I secured two radios and put them on the camp frequency. I took one for myself and gave one to an interpreter; we agreed on call signs and conducted a radio check. We jumped onto the only remaining truck and sped off to the usual drop off point to access the area where the Hatchet Force was immobilized.

I knew where the Hatchet Force was located because I had given them their assignment before they had departed two days before. Unless they had pulled some shenanigans, they would be at the foot of the Long Hai mountains on a low extended ridge.

We didn't drive too far off of the road because the loss of the wood gathering crew to a mine was still vivid in our memories. As we approached the base of the mountains the vegetation became thicker and movement more difficult. Finally we began to climb up the ridge and quickly came across a fairly wide trail with a large bomb crater exactly centered on it. At this point we stopped to orient ourselves and plan the last leg of our move to the Hatchet Force's location.

We set up temporarily around the bomb crater and I sent three men down the trail for security. I admonished them to keep off of the trail because of the prevalence of mines. I sent two others ahead toward where I thought the Hatchet Force was located. Within minutes a large boom was heard in the direction of the security team. Of course they had not stayed off of the trail and had detonated a mine, seriously injuring one of them. The two men looking for the

Hatchet Force returned shortly, saying that had encountered bunkers in what appeared to be a VC base camp about 50 meters ahead, but it seemed deserted.

In the meantime, a medevac helicopter had arrived at the camp and was standing by to extract the wounded Hatchet Force men. Now we had to use it to pick up the third-string CDIG who had detonated the mine. Another helicopter had also arrived at the camp and I later learned that it carried a general somewhere in our chain of command. He heard the commotion on the radio and decided to observe the proceedings and help out if possible.

The medevac hovered just above the bomb crater and we lifted up the wounded man. As it was lifting off, I called the Hatchet Force and had them throw a smoke grenade. The medevac spotted it and gave me an compass azimuth that placed it just beyond the VC base camp. I took two men and checked the base camp. It was abandoned and contained nothing of tactical intelligence value. Leaving a few men to secure the bomb crater/landing zone, we moved past the base camp until we came upon the battered Hatchet Force. There were more CIDG wounded than I had expected but none were critical.

I directed all of the healthy CIDG to carry the wounded back to the bomb crater/landing zone in shifts since there weren't enough people to get all of them back at once. Then the medic confided to me that he thought we were all going to be killed and he didn't want to die. He said he was casting about for ways to get out of this mess, including running back to the camp alone. This was a new experience for me and unheard of in Special Forces. In combat situations, multitasking in a valuable, even critical, skill. I had experienced this on multiple occasions but I had never been handicapped by someone who was so unstable. I sent the medic back to the bomb crater to work on the wounded Hatchet Force men.

Then I got a radio call from the general's helicopter pilot, now overhead, saying they could see non-Americans with weapons running all over in our vicinity. Now I had to inform the chopper pilot about the location of my CIDG who should not be mistaken for VC. Everyone except us three Americans were Vietnamese CIDG and would surely appear like targets to the helicopter crew. Next I used the call sign we had agreed on to call the interpreter who was back at the bomb crater with my other radio. No answer. I tried again with the same result. I grabbed one of the CIDG who was helping a wounded comrade back to the crater and instructed him to tell my radio man to answer. Nothing. I began to use some colorful, explicit language in my futile attempts to communicate with the group back at the crater.

Finally, the last wounded man was being helped back to the crater and I brought up the rear. The medevac returned for this new batch of wounded and the pilot confirmed that there were indeed lots of other people moving about in our area. The remainder of us was extracted by the general's chopper without incident. As soon as we were clear, the camp's mortars began an extended fire mission on the space we had just vacated.

Several footnotes apply to this event. The general had another reason for being in the area. He was looking for officers who had experience with the FANK program and who were nearing the end of their tours. His staff wanted to meet with them to discuss some issues that they were curious about. I had one week left in Vietnam and was a candidate for this meeting. The general had monitored all of the radio traffic in the camp commo bunker. After hearing my salty expletives aimed at the deficient radio operator, he decided that I was not the man he was looking for after all.

When we got back to the camp, many of the energetic lieutenants had returned and were upset that they had missed the action. I recalled that the young lieutenant who accompanied me had been unusually passive throughout the entire operation. I had assumed that he had been reassigned to us from a closed CIDG camp or perhaps one of the projects. When I asked him about this, he replied that his only previous assignment in Vietnam was as a lifeguard at the MACV headquarters swimming pool.

The actions of the wobbly medic were reported to his team leader and the sergeant major. Having left Long Hai less than one week later, I don't know what was done with him.

As my tour was nearing its end, it was clear that the Americans at Long Hai were becoming more and more isolated as the U.S. presence in Vietnam was winding down. In fact in March 1972, only about 95,000 U.S. military personnel remained in the country, down from the peak of 549,000. The bulk of the Australian combat forces, who had had operational control of Phouc Tuy province and who had been our main source of military support, had departed by December 1971.

I left Vietnam for the second time on April 5, 1972, after completing an 18-month tour. The last U.S. combat troops would leave the country in less than one year.

Just over one year after I had said farewell to Long Hai, I would find myself dealing with unresolved issues that had taken place there shortly after my departure.

CHAPTER 27

Reflections on Long Hai

★ ★ ★

Except for a short period of officer career training, I spent the last 10 years of my Army career in Special Forces, serving in command, staff and advisory assignments that began at Long Hai. Along the way I would cross paths with friends, both officers and NCOs, whom I had served with before in the relatively small Special Forces community.

While this account has contained some descriptions of Special Forces NCOs that have not been flattering, I am compelled to expand and clarify my lasting opinion on them as a whole.

I have described the foibles, vanities and other shortcomings of a few of them. However, these descriptions do not reflect the highest regard in which I have always held these outstanding men as the epitome of professional soldiers. I have mainly focused on their less admirable traits because they have them—not in abundance—and they are not supermen. Sometimes, writers fail to present this more accurate human side and their narratives soar off into mythic fantasy.

One general area of disagreement with some NCOs was that they were not able to disengage their prejudices in order to support the decisions that did not conform to their rigidly held opinions. An example of this was when some of them insisted that the Mike Force organizational model would be best for reorganizing the FANK battalions instead of the U.S. Army model. As I have pointed out before, the Mike Force battalions were more complex in subordinate unit structure and weapons, seriously challenging the inexperienced FANK officers. I felt that this was a case of them being "too Special Forces" and not enough U.S. Army.

I have characterized a few of the NCOs as mean-spirited, as indeed they were. Two or three were downright jerks. But, with all this, I can say that not even one of them failed to perform his job loyally and to the fullest extent of his capabilities when all was said and done. I am immensely proud to have served with all of them and, despite our sometime differences, I have the very highest respect for their outstanding professionalism.

Long Hai, as I hope I have made clear, was not in an active combat zone. That was one reason why it was selected for its purpose and why the FANK troops could train virtually unmolested there. It is simplistic for any hard-core Special Forces fire-eater to disparage the Americans who worked there as wimpy, rear-echelon cream puffs, as some have done because of the lack of "action." Nearly everyone who was assigned there had been sent by someone else, and sometimes, as in my case, against their wishes. Some agreed to come there because it was the only game in town for Special Forces after the departure of the 5th Special Forces Group.

Several coincidences regarding Long Hai involved confluences of the past and present. My old commander from Company B in the Americal, CPT Leonard G. Goldman, left the Army sometime after his Vietnam tour. In the early 1980s, as Gary Goldman, he formed an association with retired and highly decorated LTC James "Bo" Gritz in a series of abortive attempts to rescue American POWs suspected of being held in Laos. Their saga is chronicled in "The Heroes Who Fell From Grace" by Charles J. Patterson and G. Lee Tippin. LTC Gritz, as a captain, was assigned to B-36 at Long Hai in 1967. In my opinion, both men, in addition to their stated altruism, were in need of the danger and action which were no longer available to them as former members of the U.S. Army.

In the end, the Cambodian Army—FANK--was soundly defeated in combat by the NVA and Cambodia communists. The result was the well-documented killing fields that decimated the Cambodian population at the hands of the fanatic, home-grown Khmer Rouge.

Where does the fault lie and how much do all those Special Forces trainers—and I—bear guilt in the defeat of FANK? The answer is that we did the best possible job within the restraints we were given. And it is clear that even then, we exceeded those restrains if it seemed in the best interests of our trainees.

The major component in the FANK structure that we could never control was leadership. This deficit existed at all levels and there were many reasons for this that are beyond the scope of this book. Many of the Special Forces NCOs at Long Hai had previously led ethnic Cambodians in the CIDG border camps and Mike Forces with generally successful results. They knew that the FANK leadership was weak and many American NCOs wished to accompany the battalions back to Cambodia to advise--lead--them, but this was explicitly forbidden by U.S. law.

I have not previously mentioned that a three-week leadership training program was eventually instituted for the FANK officers. This took place before their battalions arrived for the standard 12-week program. This was a good first step and I did not have any hand in its design. The efficacy of the program was marginal. Somehow, these new officers were not like the American minutemen. They could not see the danger to their way of life and the urgency of defeating it.

Certainly other factors at higher levels than battalion combat effectiveness were certainly at work in this debacle, but they were not within my purview. One battalion that trained at Long Hai provided a sharp contrast to the others. This was an airborne or parachute battalion. The commander was tall, lean and mean; we called him "The Stick." His battalion sailed through the training with near disdain for the lack of rigor.

They returned home after training and were eventually destroyed after having been put into a series of unwinnable situations.

The U.S. Army has existed since 1776. Its structure, rules, tactics and rites were originally based on the British model with its own centuries of existence. There was no lack of tradition for officers and NCOs, however new and inexperienced, to follow. But the Cambodian Army prior to 1970 was mostly a ceremonial organization because King Sihanouk had provided for his country's security through wily diplomacy. Although French control of the country ended in 1953, a traditional, effective Cambodian standing army simply didn't exist in 1970. We trained the few regular battalions in 1971, and nearly every subsequent battalion was comprised of new recruits, including the NCOs and officers.

Of course, those soldiers that we trained, especially the officers and NCOs who weren't killed in combat, were prime targets for the Khmer Rouge killing machine. It was one thing for our proudest efforts to bear the bitter fruit of failure such as when our battalions were tragically overwhelmed. But it's quite another for people of whom you have grown fond to suffer endlessly when you are totally powerless to come to their rescue.

It is a lesson that has not been learned by American leaders time after time: foreign foot soldiers can be fully trained, but if they are not led by competent officers and NCOs, they are doomed to defeat. And if they do not have some transcending, unifying cause—national, religious, racial, ethnic--to fight for, they will fail.

During my tenure at Long Hai, I was awarded the Republic of Vietnam Staff Service Medal and the Republic of Cambodia National Defense Medal. Immediately after my departure from Vietnam, I applied for authorization to wear these decorations along with my U.S. awards and was approved. So beginning in 1975, I wore ribbons from two republics which no longer existed.

PART SIX

POSTBELUM

CHAPTER 28

Fort Benning, Okinawa and Fort Devens

★ ★ ★

Leaving Vietnam would not separate me from the many connections that I had made during the war. I would experience influences and coincidences involving people, places and events throughout the remainder of my Army career. Even after retiring from the Army I have continued to encounter these inevitable memories and associations. However, some of the most important occurred while I was still on active duty.

When I arrived at San Francisco International Airport in 1972, after leaving Vietnam for the last time, I wore my full Army Green Class A uniform including beret and paratroop boots. I didn't change into civilian clothes or avoid crowded areas. No one jeered, insulted or spat on me. Perhaps I was under the protective aura of the "Green Beret" legend that had been earned by my predecessors at a great cost.

My new assignment was again at Fort Benning and yet another school. This time it was the Infantry Officers' Advanced Course, popularly known as the Career Course. It was supposed to prepare captains for future assignments as majors and above. It lasted six months.

It had been difficult to leave Long Hai, even with its pressures and responsibilities to become just another captain among several hundred other captains at the Career Course. Almost everyone in my class had been to Vietnam at least once and many had accomplished amazing and outstanding feats. Feeling special in such an environment was not an easy task.

Most of the curriculum was focused on conventional, mechanized warfare in Europe. Our involvement in southeast Asia was in its final stages but the Cold War still lived. Those who had served in Infantry units in Germany had experienced severe manpower shortages due to the demands of Vietnam. Personnel managers in the Pentagon appeared to favor these officers because of their tribulations in fending off the evil Soviet empire with so few resources. As one such manager was quoted as saying, “We won’t hold it against you because you served in Vietnam.”

At the completion of the Career Course, I was glad to leave Fort Benning in April 1973, and move to Okinawa and my new unit, the 1st Special Forces Group. My first assignment, as expected, was as an A Team leader. The Group sent teams on temporary duty all over Asia, but my team was occupied with training on the inland.

Although I had been relatively new to “Group,” as Special Forces’ units are collectively known, when I arrived at Long Hai, I was treated fairly, if not warmly, by everyone there. I would eventually serve in two other Special Forces Groups and later advise two companies in a reserve Group. Because I was at Long Hai when it still belonged to the 5th Special Forces Group, I was authorized to wear the Special Forces patch on the right shoulder of my uniform—the position for a combat zone patch. Thereafter, whenever I reported for duty in a new Group wearing the Special Forces patch on my right shoulder, I was never a "new guy" in the sense of being a Special Forces rookie.

The importance of initial acceptance was never clearer than when I first reported to the 1st Special Forces Group on Okinawa. After leaving Long Hai, I stayed in touch with my friend and former boss, Fritz Eickemeyer. Knowing that I would be assigned to the 1st Group, he suggested that I first check in with his friend, CPT Richard J. Meadows, who was the Group's operations officer. Here was another Special Forces officer serving in a position authorized at one rank higher than he held.

I stopped by Dick Meadows' office before formally reporting into the 1st Group and we spent some time getting to know each other and catching up on mutual friends such as Fritz. This was very generous on his part since I knew the pressures of his job. When we parted, he invited me to come that evening to the officers' club, an elegant establishment that overlooked both coasts of the island and was appropriately named "Top of the Rock."

When I arrived that night, Dick Meadows was holding court with about fifteen Special Forces officers in a circle of low chairs in the bar. When I entered, he jumped up and greeted me as an old friend and found a chair for me in the circle. He proceeded to ask about Fritz and others, as if we had not just discussed them earlier that day. Although this was my first real assignment with Special Forces except for Long Hai, Dick's warm welcome that night validated me as an old Special Forces hand and greatly eased my integration into the Group.

Earlier in his career Dick was the assault team leader on the famous Son Tay raid in North Vietnam and after retirement was instrumental in organizing the elite Delta Force. His career and contributions are memorialized at Fort Bragg, the home of Special Forces, by a statue and a namesake parade field, a truly unique honor. Dick died in 1995. To learn more about this remarkable man, read "**The Quiet Professional: Major Richard J. Meadows** of the U.S. Army Special Forces," by Alan Hoe.

A surprise new development soon changed everything: within months of my arrival, it was announced that the Group would be deactivated and all personnel reassigned. Some off-island missions would continue but for the most part, area-specific training would be pointless. To keep the troops occupied in this mission vacuum, the Group commander, COL Sydnor, decided to request a major inspection—the dreaded IG—to occur just before we departed. Everyone was incredulous, even annoyed, but it was a good idea to keep all hands from potentially mischievous idleness.

In order to prepare for the important inspection, I was reassigned as our battalion S-1, or personnel and administration officer. My job was to keep the office running smoothly while preparing for the upcoming inspection. My ability to read and interpret Army regulations would be a major asset in this job. The S-1 section passed with flying colors and we received a commendation for administering the unit fund.

While I was orienting myself to this new job, I found several immediate links to the recent past. Other officers and NCOs whom I had known at Long Hai were already serving in the 1st Group. A Teams from our battalion had been sent on temporary duty to UITG shortly after my departure from Vietnam, including Long Hai, when the mission expanded to included training the remnants of South Vietnamese units mauled by North Vietnam's massive 1972 Easter offensive. I found myself handling lingering personnel actions and problems that had been generated during those missions.

One particularly annoying task was to address the administrative actions with regard to a sergeant who had been killed in a mine incident. It was annoying because the death was lamentably avoidable. It had occurred when one of the deployed captains had decided to clear land mines from an area near the airstrip at Long Hai. Everyone, Vietnamese and U.S. personnel, knew that this twenty-meter square of ground, surrounded by a sturdy barbed wire fence was mined and no one had any need to go into that area. However, this do-gooder decided that U.S. forces needed to clear the mines and another good man was lost due to a well-intentioned, but poor, choice.

During my time on Okinawa, a very controversial policy was implemented by the Army with regard to officer evaluation reports (OER). These detailed reports were the basis for promotions, assignments, schooling and other personnel action by selection boards and committees who had never met the officers they were evaluating. Therefore the OERs were of immense importance to an officer's career. However, over the years, the most-used section of OERs, the final percentage figure, had become so inflated that it was difficult to differentiate among officers in terms of past performance and potential. One cause of this was the inability of some of the rating officers to tell a subordinate that he was not performing at the highest level. The OER was meant as a tool to identify shortcomings and provide guidance in seeking improvement, but some senior officers were too weak to do this. I learned in NCO Academy and OCS that this was a lack of moral courage. It created a situation wherein a good officer who was given an accurate report could fall behind a less-qualified officer who was given an inflated report.

And so the edict was issued by the Department of the Army that major commands would screen all OERs to insure that subordinate units would not rate all officers at 100 percent and give everyone a fair and honest evaluation. The commanding general on Okinawa, being a good soldier, began to enforce this new rule.

As our battalion S-1, one of my jobs was to oversee the preparation of OERs. Normally this would entail ensuring that directions were followed, correct grammar and spelling were employed and that the form itself had no more than two corrected typing errors. However, the new directive added to the work.

It soon became clear that not everyone was following the rules. Feedback was received from personnel managers in the Pentagon that major commands in nearby Korea were not complying with the OER preparation guidelines. For example, second lieutenants there with six month of service were being rated at 100 percent. Meanwhile our senior Special Forces captains with multiple Vietnam tours and extensive combat experience were forced to be rated in the mid-80s.

To his credit, the Commanding General on Okinawa vowed to place a letter in each officer's file explaining why his rating might have been less that his contemporaries in other commands. However, there would be no revisions of OERs already completed.

My most notable experience on Okinawa was being on the last parachute jump by the Group. I was in the last group or stick to jump but the last position was reserved for the warrant officer who was in charge of the parachute riggers. As might be imagined, everyone went out of their way to accommodate him.

On my way to my next assignment, I detoured to Thailand to visit my buddy Fritz Eickemeyer, who had steered me to Dick Meadows when I first arrived on Okinawa. Fritz was working for the Joint Casualty Resolution Center in Nakhon Phanom. The JCRC was created to recover the remains of U.S. personnel missing in southeast Asia and was headed by Brigadier General Stan L. McClellan who had been in charge of the parent organization of UITG when I was at Long Hai.

General McClellan had been tasked with receiving the first U.S. prisoners of war from the Viet Cong at the end of hostilities in February 1973. He was gracious enough to share those experiences with me including some one-of-a-kind photos. He described how he had taken several helicopters to a designated location to receive the prisoners and then waited for several hours for the VC to comply with the turnover. General McClellan recounted his interaction with the recalcitrant VC officer in charge of the transfer and the choice words he had heaped upon his head. The official accounts of this encounter do not include much of the colorful dialog that the General added to the proceedings. McClellan passed away in 1988.

My new, and next to last, assignment was at Fort Devens, Massachusetts, with the 10th Special Forces Group beginning in August 1974. I found that the shadow of Vietnam still had a lingering and powerful influence even at that distance and time. Still a captain, I again became an A Team leader. Due to a recent change in the Special Forces organizational structure, a sixth A Team was being formed in each company (formerly a B Team) and I was to lead the new team in our company. Some of the team members came from other teams in the company and some were newly assigned, like me.

With the exception of three experienced senior NCOs, the team's seven other enlisted men were very junior young sergeants. They had missed Vietnam but were aggressive, fearless, hard-charging teammates who never let us down. Two of these young men later earned commissions, one became a warrant officer helicopter pilot and another reached the rank of sergeant major.

During my time at Fort Devens with the 10th Special Forces Group, two major events occurred which were directly related to my Vietnam service and were critical to my career.

The first was the Reduction in Forces (RIF) that always followed a buildup of the Army in wartime. I had been a part of the expanded OCS program that provided the Army with officers for newly formed units and replacements for existing units in Vietnam. Nearly all of the lieutenants produced by OCS were commissioned in the Army Reserve instead of the Regular Army. This meant that they were easier to release from active duty when the inevitable drawdown would occur after the war. The RIF was not only a noun, it was also a verb: i.e. to be RIFFed.

Each of the Army's commissioned branches (Infantry, Armor, Artillery, etc.) convened RIF boards to review its officers' records, especially OERs, and select enough individuals to satisfy its quota of officers to be discharged. Naturally, these lists mostly consisted of Reserve officers but this situation also presented an opportunity to eliminate a few substandard Regular Army officers. From the results I saw, the Army missed a chance to shed some poor quality leaders.

The rules of the RIF were somewhat arbitrary. For example, if an officer selected for the RIF had over 18 years of service, he was allowed to remain on active duty and retire at 20 years at his current rank. If he had less than 18 years, he had two options. He could take a pay out and be discharged with no possibility of a retirement pension. Or he could revert to his previous enlisted rank, serve out his 20 years and retire at his highest commissioned rank.

We knew this action was in progress, and for those of us who were subject to being RIFFed, the wait was nerve-wracking.

Naturally, this process was devastating to most of those men affected by the RIF who had voluntarily gone to Vietnam and followed a low-paying Army career in hopes of a retirement. They found themselves suddenly without a job and with few skills that easily translated into civilian occupations. Or they could revert to their previous NCO rank with all of the conflicting emotions associated with such a demotion.

While I was never confident about my personal outcome during the RIF, in the end I was spared. I am positive that I survived that trial due to a short entry on my Department of the Army Form 66, Officer Qualification Record. In Part 18, Record of Assignments, appeared the following line:

25Sep68 1542 CO (Cinsgcy) CoA1stBn52dInf198thLIB
USARPAC-Vietnam

This cryptic entry was easily readable by Army personnel managers indicating that I had been an Infantry company commander in Vietnam—the golden key to retention. A quick glance to another part of the form would have indicated the compelling fact that this had been accomplished as a lieutenant. Also in Part 18 were entries describing my assignments as an A Team leader and Operations Officer at Long Hai, but these were Special Forces jobs and not purely Infantry.

It is also true that without excellent Officer Evaluation Reports, I could not have survived the RIF.

However, there was another entry in the DA Form 66 that was not in my favor: Part 16, Civilian Education and Military Schooling. The significant line in that part read:

DA Evaluation 2 yr Col Equiv

While this line, indicating that I held the equivalent of two years of college, had qualified me for OCS, it did not meet the goal of the Army for its post-RIF officers to hold college degrees, especially for promotion. And this had an impact on the second major event for me at Fort Devens.

After the war, of course there were fewer Army positions into which promotions were possible but, nevertheless, as each officer reached a certain anniversary of his promotion to any rank, he was considered for advancement to the next. After failing to be promoted twice, the officer was dismissed from the service; this was the "Up or Out" policy.

I was faced with my lack of a four-year degree as an impediment for promotion to major.

As so often happened to me in my Army career, an unsolicited opportunity arose to solve a problem with career advancement. My A Team and I were in Key West at the Army's SCUBA school assisting the instructor cadre with a course. Since I was never really a good swimmer, I didn't have much to do there. One day a clerk told me I had a call on hold from the Pentagon. At first I did not have a good feeling about what it might be about but my fears were soon dispelled.

The personnel manager from the Pentagon was calling to tell me that I would be allowed six months of on-duty time to complete my bachelors degree. Six months was cutting it close but I had steadily accumulated college courses whenever possible and portions of my military education would be allowed by some institutions as acceptable credits.

I can only assume that one simple line on my DA Form 66 had again come to my aid and facilitated my advancement.

After my promotion to major, I became commander of Company A, 2d Battalion of the 10th Special Forces Group at Fort Devens.

About 20 years after I left 10th Special Forces Group and been long since retired, a hard cover book was published titled "The Company They Keep, Life Inside the U.S. Army Special Forces." It was a study by a psychologist about the interaction and relationships among the officers, NCOs and wives within Special Forces. I came across it by accident while browsing through books about Vietnam in the library. What caught my eye was the photograph on the front of the dust jacket: it was me and four members of my company at Fort Devens, resplendent in our camouflage fatigue uniforms and berets. The author was Anna J. Simons, who was a Special Forces wife. I later acquired a copy of the book in paperback with the same cover photo but the author's name was now A. J. Simons. I think the publisher felt that "A. J." might be more appealing than the clearly feminine "Anna" as the author of a book about Special Forces.

My last assignment was with the Army's Readiness Group, Los Angeles (RGLA). This unit advised the Army reserves and National Guard in southern California and Arizona. I was the Branch Assistance Team leader for Special Forces, psychological operations and intelligence units. This was the end-of-career assignment for nearly everyone in the unit. The concept was that after gaining experience in 20 or more years, this would be the best place for us to pass on our knowledge to the reserve components in our area.

In actual fact, most of the units were manned and led by experienced and competent individuals, most of whom had been on active duty. We mostly played a game of pretending to advise the units and they pretended to be advised. Occasionally, we were able to conduct some training on new Army concepts that seemed valuable.

Although I called on my experiences in Vietnam on some occasions to assist the Reserve Component units, the last major application of lessons learned in the war was at Fort Devens.

CONCLUSION

★ ★ ★

Upon completion of my second tour in Vietnam, I had no doubt that I would soon be back there for another assignment in about one year despite the ongoing Vietnamization. The peace talks had been interminable and ineffective. Without much deep or critical thinking, I expected to be back and forth to the war throughout the remainder of my career. Since I had had such good luck so far, I didn't expect any changes and looked forward to whatever was next.

Although my Army career ended with retirement at the end of 1981, it can be no surprise that transformative experiences such as those I had had in Vietnam would continue to influence me long after I had left them behind. How could it be otherwise? And I know that, more or less, everyone who served there will always feel compelling emotions returning to them from time to time.

While I bear no physical scars from that conflict, there are some small, positive influences on my daily life directly resulting from living in the field with the Americal Division. I take pleasure in entering a dark room and filling it with light with the flick of a switch. I am conscious of the comfort in sleeping between cool, clean sheets under a warm blanket. Plentiful, clean, hot and cold water flowing instantly from a faucet never fails to give me a small boost of happiness.

This means that Vietnam no longer looms large for me--but it still casts a distinct shadow.

Some of my social and writing activities relate directly to Vietnam. As a member of the American Legion, I interact with other veterans who shared common experiences and even the same unit. The Military Writers Society of America has provided me with a means of sharing stories in its yearly anthology. I've had anecdotes published in the Military Officers Association of America's magazine.

Looking back, it is difficult to provide a simple, unifying description of my Vietnam experiences except for the luck I enjoyed. The successes were something like a linear progression, with each phase steadily improving…improving…improving. And when I try to consider the discrete impact that any of these individual events made on my life, it seems impossible. It is like discovering a mistake in Sudoku and trying to backtrack.

In terms of my decisions before, during and after Vietnam, sometimes, my options were limited, as if coming to a simple intersection where the side roads were blocked and the only choice was to proceed forward. In others, it was like coming into a large town square with many intersecting streets to choose from, not to mention returning by the way one had come. I feel that, for the most part, I chose correctly.

One overall truth has persisted. Since leaving Vietnam, I have never—and will never—achieve the level of trust and authority that I was afforded there. It was an alignment of the planets, apparently, that allowed me to contribute at the level of responsibility that I was given.

This is why, despite the monumental grief and sorrow that the war caused to others, I loved every minute of my time there.

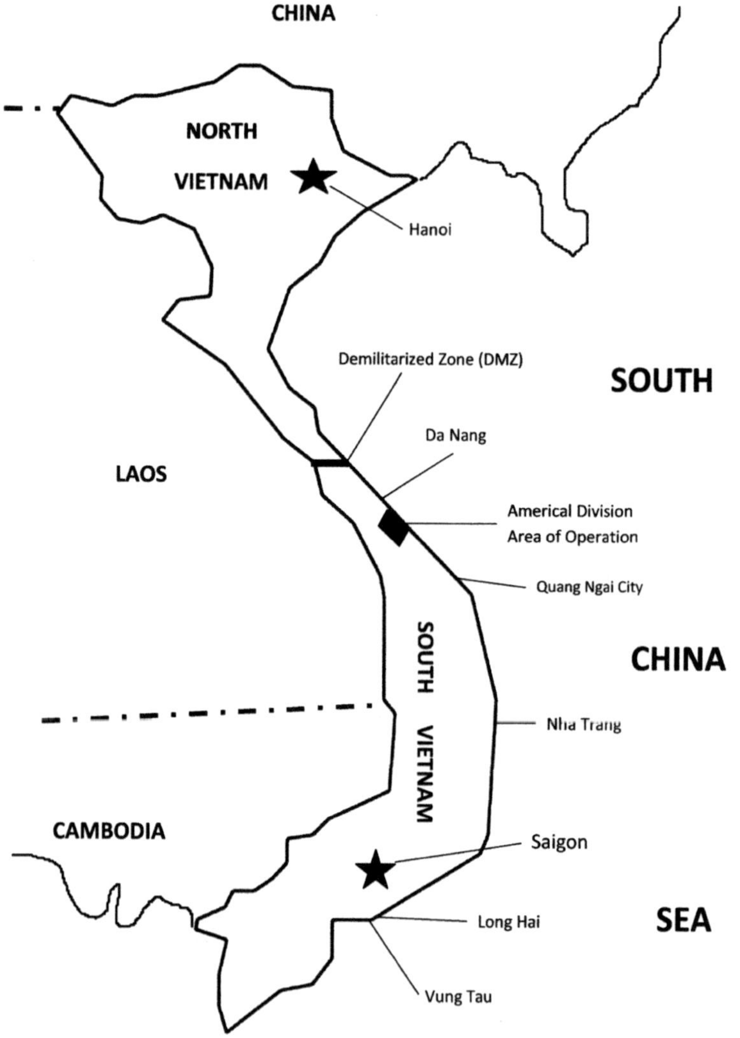

Figure 1. Map of Vietnam

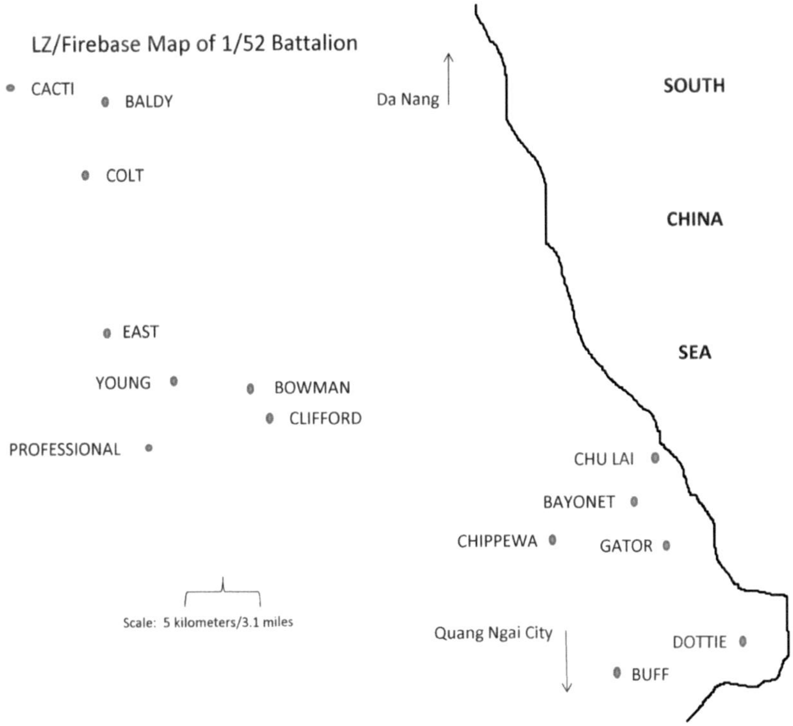

Figure 2. Landing Zones Used by 1/52 Infantry

Figure 3. R&R Passport Photo

Figure 4. Long Hai Camp

The Long Hai mountains loom in the distance. The north compound is at left center and the south compound is at the lower right. The training area and ranges are situated between the camp and mountains. The north/south road runs along the bottom with the camp access road appearing at the bottom left. Image courtesy of Australian War Memorial. Item CUN/72/0017B/VN.

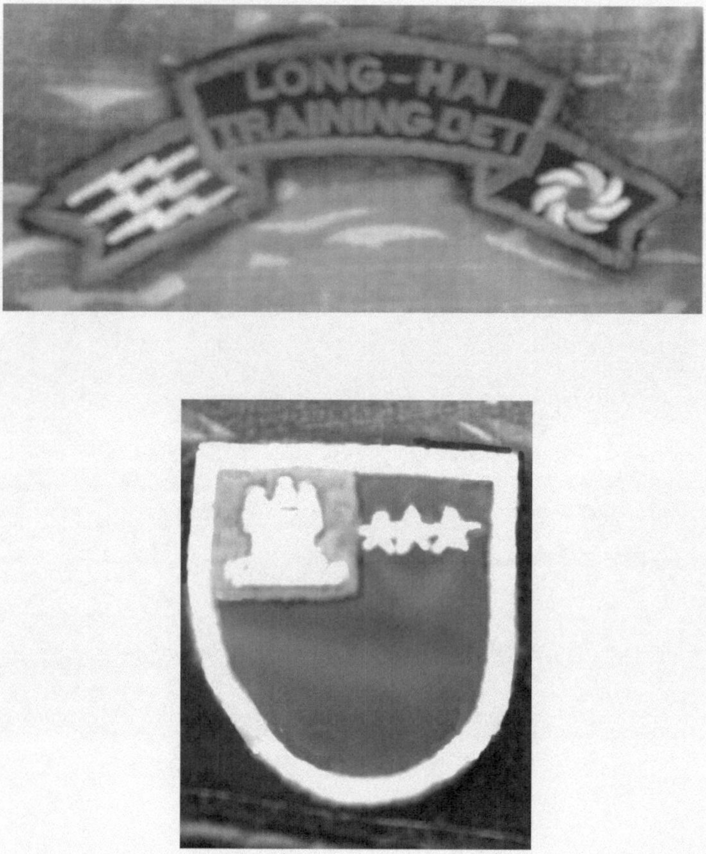

Figure 5. Top: Long Hai Shoulder Scroll

Note the Khmer Serei sun symbol. Bottom: UITG Beret Flash. depicting the Khmer flag. A representation of Angkor Wat is in the red canton (upper left) and the three white stars representing the nation, religion and republic are in the blue field.

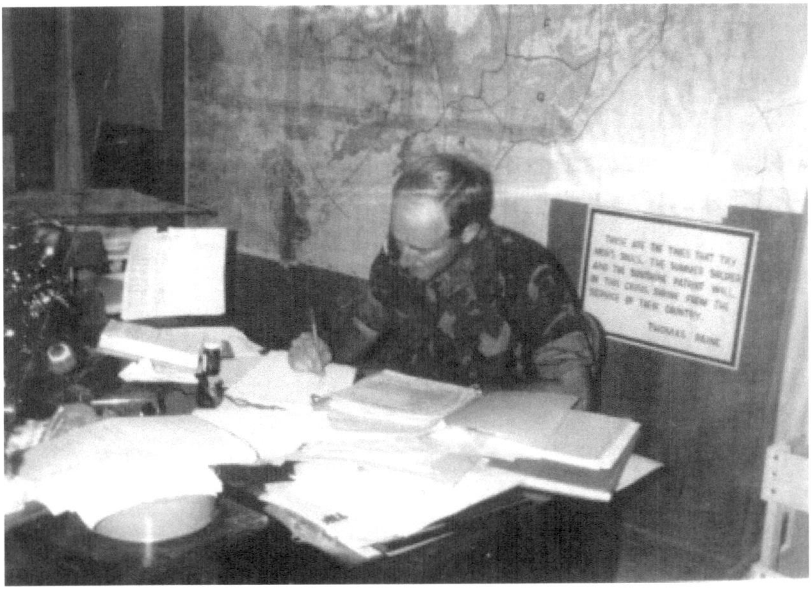

Figure 6. Piles of Paperwork in the S-3 Office

The large wall map shows the sectors of the Xuyen Moc FTX area. The sign behind my left shoulder reads: "These are the times that try men's souls. The summer soldier and the sunshine patriot will, in this crisis, shrink from the service of their country. –Thomas Paine"

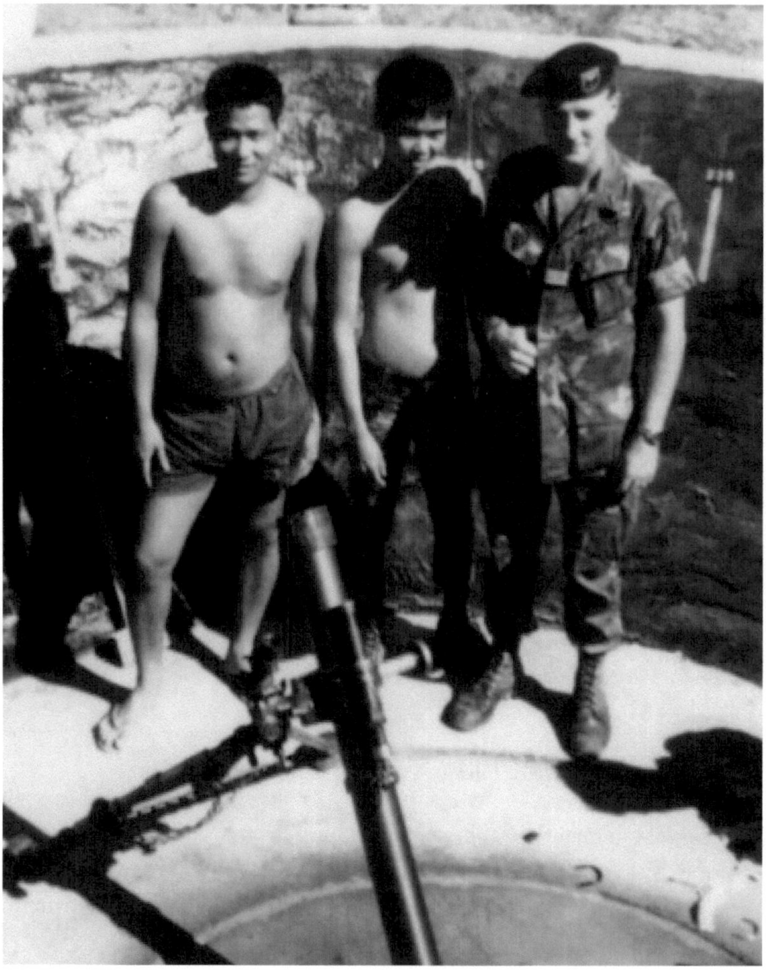

Figure 7. Typical Long Hai 81mm Mortar Pit and Crew

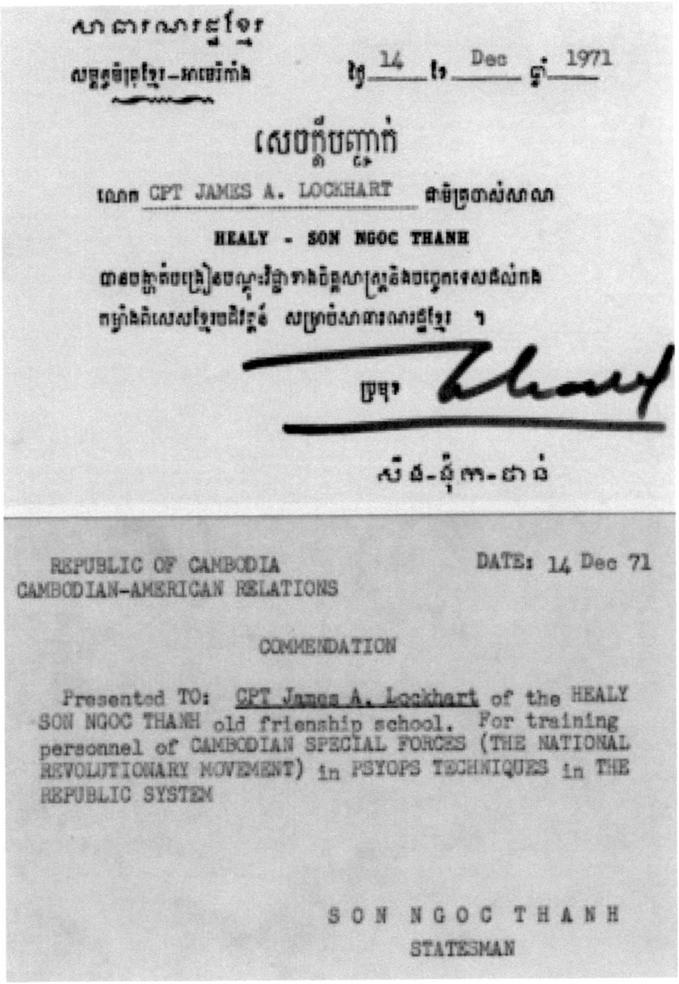
14 Dec 1971

CPT JAMES A. LOCKHART

HEALY - SON NGOC THANH

REPUBLIC OF CAMBODIA
CAMBODIAN-AMERICAN RELATIONS

DATE: 14 Dec 71

COMMENDATION

Presented TO: CPT James A. Lockhart of the HEALY SON NGOC THANH old frienship school. For training personnel of CAMBODIAN SPECIAL FORCES (THE NATIONAL REVOLUTIONARY MOVEMENT) in PSYOPS TECHNIQUES in THE REPUBLIC SYSTEM

S O N N G O C T H A N H
STATESMAN

Figure 8. Dr. Thanh "Get Out of Jail Free" Card.

The card is dated December 1971, and mentions COL Michael Healy, who actually left Vietnam with the 5th Special Forces Group in March 1971, as described earlier. If we ever got to Cambodia, we felt that the card would be good for a lot more than a free drink at a bar.

Figure 9. Unexploded 500-pound Bomb

It was discovered not far from the camp in the training area. Note the CIDG dressed in tiger fatigues and carrying an AK-47 rifle.

Figure 10. A Present from a FANK Soldier

This brass pin with the image of Buddha was known by U.S. Special Forces as a "you-can't-kill-me" badge.